Theologic

Werner G. Jeanrond

Theological Hermeneutics

Development and Significance

SCM PRESS LTD

0 334 01624 X

First published 1991
by the Macmillan Press Ltd
this paperback edition published 1994
by SCM Press Ltd
9–17 St Albans Place, London N1 0NX

Third impression 2002

Printed in Great Britain by William Clowes Ltd,
Beccles, Suffolk

For
Betty

Contents

Preface to the Paperback Edition

The interest in hermeneutical questions is still increasing, not only in theology, but throughout the humanities. A good illustration for this trend is provided by the many hermeneutics readers which have been published recently. Although most of them offer very valuable introductions to the texts by individual hermeneuts, these brief introductory essays cannot satisfy the need for a more coherent discussion of the development and scope of hermeneutical theory. Moreover, all of those collections which have come to my attention limit themselves to the development of hermeneutics since the Enlightenment. This limitation may be understandable in view of the generally held conviction that only post-Enlightenment hermeneutics can be considered to offer 'critical' reflection, whereas pre-Enlightenment theories of text-interpretation are overshadowed by ecclesial and other 'external' influences on interpretation theory. Moreover, it is frequently stressed that only since the Enlightenment has hermeneutical reflection been able to free itself from the predominance of theological concerns.

In this book I shall try to overcome this exclusive emphasis on modern hermeneutics by attempting to discuss the development of hermeneutics since the Greek beginnings of the discipline. I wish to demonstrate that in spite of its belonging to a supposedly 'pre-critical age' the hermeneutical reflection before the Enlightenment has still a lot to teach us today. But my main concern in this book is to discuss the hermeneutical foundations of a critical theology. This discussion follows a predominantly historical path but is motivated by contemporary systematic concerns.

This book offers a discussion of the development of hermeneutics, but not a history of biblical exegesis. The fact that every exeget acts on hermeneutical foundations, whether he or she is aware of it or not, points to the intimate relationship between exegetical praxis and interpretation theory. Both the concrete praxis of interpreting the Bible and the theological interest in such acts of interpretation demand the explicit study of hermeneutics in theology, and, as we are going to see, there is a great heritage of such reflection available for our own hermeneutical consideration today.

Naturally, the effort to discuss the development of theological hermeneutics is in itself a hermeneutical enterprise. I try to 'understand' the development and significance of theological hermeneutics. Any good hermeneut must seek to be aware of his or her limitations. There are many limitations imposed on such an enterprise: the ambition to discuss the hermeneutical tradition in a single though still readable volume, and the conscious focus on the overall development of hermeneutics to the detriment of a more detailed discussion of individual authors or periods. But there is also the limitation of my own competence. I cannot claim to master all the different aspects of any epoch of hermeneutical development. Nevertheless I hope that my effort to highlight the important dimensions of individual hermeneuts and their contexts as well as their impact on the overall development of hermeneutical thinking may be considered worthwhile by the users of this book.

This book has been written primarily for students of theological hermeneutics and for anybody interested in this discipline. But I have tried to present the material in such a way that the book can also serve as an introduction to hermeneutics in general. Thus, readers interested in literary theory and philosophy may find it helpful for their own methodological discussions.

I am very pleased that SCM Press has decided to issue this book in paperback and thus to make it more readily available to the audience for which it was originally written. I wish to thank Dr. John Bowden, Managing Director of SCM Press, for his interest in this book and for his support and encouragement of my theological work.

I have corrected some typographical errors for this new edition. I am grateful to readers and reviewers of this book who drew my attention to these errors.

Werner G. Jeanrond
Dublin, 1 January 1994

1

The Purpose of Hermeneutics

1.1 THE NEED FOR HERMENEUTICS

By 'hermeneutics' we mean *the theory of interpretation*. The word contains a reference to Hermes, the messenger of the Gods in Greek mythology. Hermes' task was to explain to humans the decisions and plans of their Gods. Thus, he bridged the gap between the divine and the human realm. Similarly, hermeneutics is concerned with examining the relationship bewteen two realms, the realms of a text or a work of art on the one hand, and the people who wish to understand it on the other. Yet why is such an examination necessary? Do we not always understand the texts or works of art in front of us? Where is the problem which hermeneutics wishes to solve?

The hermeneutical problem may become clearer to us when we recall the odd experience of reading a book for a second time. Such a re-reading often opens up a new reception of the text. We may discover something new, something different in the text, and we may say now that we see the book with different eyes. Yet it is apparently the same book we see, and it is through our own eyes that we see it. So what is different? What has changed? Our perspective has changed; that is the way in which we look at a text or a work of art. In our case, the way we look at our book has changed since our initial reading. It may not have changed radically, yet nonetheless we now see the text differently. This experience teaches us that understanding is in fact not an automatic and unproblematic exercise of deciphering a set of consistently identical signs on paper in front of us. Rather text-understanding always demands our active participation in recreating the text in question. It demands that we lend of our reality to the text so that it can become real for us.

Understanding then comes about when these two realities meet: the reality of the reader and the reality of the text.

The experience of re-reading a text also shows us that we never read a text 'objectively' or 'neutrally'. It is always we who read and that means that it is through the application of our very particular perspectives that we allow a text to become real for us. Yet we all know that our perspectives are limited. No human reader has an unlimited perspective; and since Hermes is not at our disposal to explain to us the ultimate and authoritative meaning of a text we need to reflect ourselves upon how we understand, how much we can understand, and which factors condition our understanding. This reflection is the business of hermeneutics.

I have defined hermeneutics as the theory of interpretation. For most people understanding and interpretation are one and the same thing. In this book, however, I would like to propose that 'interpretation' be used as the umbrella concept which includes understanding as one of its dimensions.[1] Thus, hermeneutics, the theory of interpretation, is more than a theory of understanding. This distinction will be explained below in more detail, but I wish to alert the reader to it from the outset.

Most people do, of course, interpret texts without ever bothering about the implications, dimensions and conditions of their interpretative activity. Some reading situations do not even leave us time or space for hermeneutical inquiries. If, for example, you are faced with an emergency during a boat journey and reach out to grasp the life-jacket you are not likely to engage in any deeper reflection upon the implications of your act of reading the instructions which are attached to this life-saving device. Rather you expect these instructions to guide you immediately and unambiguously to the correct application of this utensil; time for a second reading may not even be available. Similarly we should not need a theory of interpretation in order to understand the meaning of a traffic sign which informs us about the one-way system in operation. Certain acts of human communication require total clarity, and any ambiguity in communicating their message to the reader might lead to catastrophic results.

Yet other forms of human communication are more ambiguous by nature. Some even create ambiguity productively, such as, for instance, the literary forms of human discourse. While traffic signs and other instructive messages function only when all people respond to them by establishing the same reality in their minds, other texts function precisely by challenging the very procedure of understanding our human reality. A reader who engages in reading a poem allows himself or herself to be led by the text towards a possibly new understanding of reality, to a change in perspective, to a different attitude towards life and the universe. In principle all forms of human communication could become the object of hermeneutical reflection. However, traditionally such reflection has concentrated especially on the interpretation of more complex human expressions, i.e. particular kinds of written texts and works of art. The aim of hermeneutical reflection is not to replace the actual act of reading a text or of looking at a work of art, rather it wishes to help improve such acts by considering the possibilities and limitations of human understanding. Which are the areas of human communication which require hermeneutical reflection most urgently?

1.2 THE INTERDISCIPLINARY NATURE OF HERMENEUTICS

All human expressions which are more complex than sets of straightforward instructive messages may require equally complex acts of interpretation. This is particularly the case with genres of literary texts. They often suggest alternative modes of being in the world and may enagage the reader in a clash of worldviews. But not only in the extreme case of a conflict between reader and text, the question arises whether a given reader really strives to understand the text or tries to impose his or her own prejudices and perspectives on the text in order to do away with the challenges represented by it. On an even more general level, how do we know that the reader 'understands' the text in front of him or her? How do we detect simple or not so simple misunderstandings of certain aspects of the text? Since every reader can understand a text only through applying his or her individual perspectives to the text and since therefore any search for *the* understanding of a text is fruitless, we may at least wish to know what constitutes criteria for an adequate understanding of a text.

Similar questions arise when we reflect upon the act of understanding a work of art such as a picture (photograph, painting etc.), a sculpture or a piece of music. Every work of art calls for interpretation, and every interpretation calls for an assessment of its conditions, which include our perspectives and our interpretative possibilities and limitations. These interpretative abilities are themselves again conditioned on the one hand by our individual biographies and all the factors which have been constituting them, and on the other hand by the contemporary situation in which we live and act.

Christian theology too needs to engage in hermeneutical reflection because it is concerned (among other things) with the interpretation of the biblical texts and of other religious texts, such as creeds, liturgies, theological writings and spiritual expressions. Thus, theology too must try to assess the conditions for interpretation today and ask to what extent these conditions of the Christian interpreter have changed over the centuries and what such changes mean for our ability to understand the meaning of ancient texts today. Even more so than in most interpretations of literary texts, the theological interpretation of the texts of the Christian church has immediate social consequences, namely for the self-understanding of the Christian church, since these texts are seen to provide a major foundation of the church. Thus, the continuous reinterpretation of these texts must affect our understanding of the identity of the church in some way. We shall return to this question in Chapter 7.

The interpretation of the law, that is of legal texts, in a society also affects the self-understanding of that society. No act of law-giving can anticipate all concrete cases which might arise in the future of a constantly changing society. Therefore, the interpretation of those written texts which try to capture the spirit of a society's constitution is a necessary part of the legal identity of a society. Thus, legal experts in society need to reflect upon this process of appropriating legal expressions lest they become victims of uncritical illusions about the function of these legal texts in the society's life.

While the study of literature and art, and the theological and legal interpretation of texts are primarily concerned with the interpretation of a specific body of works, philosophy is more interested in hermeneutical principles as such. Philosophers investigate how we can understand any aspect of reality. They are engaged in what I call 'macro-hermeneutics', i.e. the interpretation of the universe. One could say that their 'text' is the universe and its history, while the other hermeneutically orientated disciplines are usually more concerned with what I call 'micro-hermeneutics', i.e. the interpretation of individual expressions of a linguistic or artistic nature. Yet both hermeneutical concerns are interwoven. Macro-hermeneutics is only possible on the basis of detailed micro-hermeneutical achievements.

In other words, the interpretation of the overall sense of our universe depends on the interpretation of the many textual or artistic approaches to reality, including the approach to the interpreter's own self. Moreover, all of these approaches need to be assessed in terms of their adequacy. Thus, one may wish to speak with Paul Ricœur of the necessarily long and detoured journey of interpretations which may eventually lead to a better, though still fragmentary interpretation of the interpreter's self and of the whole of reality.[2]

But even when we participate in efforts of macro-hermeneutics, in that process of interpreting the sense of the universe, we ought to recall that we never start such an interpretative journey from a totally fresh or neutral point. All of our efforts at interpreting the universe and the meaning of our life in it are already informed and guided by some of the many existing and often conflicting interpretations of reality. Every interpreter is conditioned by such inherited modes of interpreting, which again are responsible for the formation of our perspectives through which we begin to understand the signs of this universe. Moreover, we do not normally begin to read a novel or a poem without any idea of what awaits us. Something, some expectation or information mediated through our already existing hermeneutical traditions directs our choice of particular works to be studied, just as it shapes the initial perspectives through which we approach such a study.

1.3 THE HERMENEUTICAL CIRCLE

In order to understand a text we are already bringing a whole set of pre-understandings to the text. Out of this network of perspectives we shape our questions with the help of which we guide our reading. Of course, we are not always aware of this complex nature of our act of reading. But the task of hermeneutics is precisely to draw our attention to these complexities so that we begin to understand how we are actually understanding a text when we read it.

Our understanding displays then a circular or spiral nature: we need some form of prior understanding in order to begin our engagement with a text or work of art. We need some questions to which the text or work of art can give answers. Naturally, these questions may be refined or even altered in the act of understanding itself. But without any question we are unable to structure our own acts of reading or seeing. This phenomenon is generally referred to as one dimension of *'the hermeneutical circle'*. A second dimension of this circle consists in the fact that we can never understand a whole without understanding all of its parts; nor can we adequately understand the parts without seeing them functioning in the overall composition to which they contribute.

Various degrees of pre-understandings may be distinguished: first of all a reader of a text must be familiar at least to some extent with the linguistic *code*, that is the actual language in which the text is composed, and be able to decipher the linguistic *signs*, that means the words. But a mere knowledge of signs does not yet disclose the world of a text. The process of such a disclosure can only start once the reader has some kind of existential connection with what the text speaks about. But here the hermeneutical problem really begins. What happens to our pre-understanding in the act of reading? Do we allow our pre-understanding to be challenged in the act of reading or do we impose it uncritically and violently on the text?

The unwillingless of having one's perspectives challenged at all may point to 'ideological' behaviour. An ideology may be understood as a rigid attitude over against any object of understanding. Due to personal or social reasons, ideological interpreters defend their particular 'readings' at all cost and remain hostile to all calls for a change of attitude, perspective or world-view. Ideological attitudes may be deliberately or unconsciously adopted. In any case, it is essential for any reader who is keen to proceed to a more adequate understanding of a text to become aware of the possibility of distortions in the act of reading. Thus, hermeneutics and the critique of ideology are very closely related. The precise nature of this relationship will be addressed in Chapter 3 (cf. 3.4.2).

1.4 TEXTS AND READINGS

We have already become aware of the circular, or rather, spiral, nature of all interpretation. We always approach the act of reading a text with a particular set of pre-understandings which are then challenged or confirmed during the reading process itself. This interaction between reader and text receives its energy from the continuous 'provocation' of the reader by the text. That a text can provoke a reader is, however, possible only because of the prior consent by the reader to engage in such an interaction with it. Obviously, not all texts provoke the same reader in the same way; and not every reader is provoked by the same text with equal force. Some texts simply bore us, and therefore lose our attention very quickly, while other texts manage to attract our attention again and again. Normally boring texts and apathetic readers bring the interaction between text and reader to a halt.

Some hermeneuts liken the interaction between reader and text to the conversation between two persons. Yet this image does not capture the full nature of reading.[3] Reading is not a conversation between two equal partners who possess equal ability of acting and reacting. Rather the text is a somewhat weaker partner which, for instance, is unable to defend itself against violations of its integrity by ideological readers. At best the text is empowered by a reader to unfold its meaning during the act of reading.

Hermeneutics does not discuss the detailed requirements which everybody has to fulfill in order to act successfully as a member of a particular linguistic tradition, such as English, Arabic or Cantonese. Such discussion lies within the scope of the different linguistic disciplines. Hermeneutics is more interested in the analysis of the dialectic between reader and text and in the effects of this dialectic for the self-understanding of the individual reader or groups of readers (cf. below 5.1). Thus, hermeneutics reflects upon activities done through language rather than upon the history and grammar of particular historical languages.

We shall presuppose therefore that a reader who, for example, wishes to interpret Shakespeare's texts today must have competence in the particular English language in which Shakespeare wrote, and that a reader who attempts to interpret biblical texts does understand the biblical languages. Without such linguistic competence, or with an only limited competence, the dialectic between reader and text cannot adequately get under way.

1.5 SPECIAL OR GENERAL HERMENEUTICS?

1.5.1 Verbal and Non-verbal Communication

Interpreting a text or a work of art is a linguistic activity. That means it is done through language. Here 'language' is used in the widest sense possible: a sculpture, a painting, a musical score, a ballet, a clown's act with its use of gestures – all these and other artistic expressions are realised in and through some form of language. Thus, 'language' refers to more than merely verbal expressions. Therefore it is useful to distinguish between forms of verbal and of non-verbal communication.

In this book we shall concentrate on the interpretation of verbal expressions, of linguistic texts, because our aim is to clarify the nature and development of text-interpretation as a theological problem. But this concentration on written texts is not to deny the importance of studying the many non-verbal forms of human communication which also occur in a religious context: icons, paintings, sculptures, illustrations, gestures, intonation, dramatic presence and presentation in liturgical settings. The hermeneutical implications of all of these expressions deserve, of course, a full treatment which is, however, beyond our scope here.

1.5.2 Theological and Literary Hermeneutics

Our distinction between macro- and micro-hermeneutics proves to be helpful now when we try to clarify the different natures of literary and theological hermeneutics.[4] *Literary hermeneutics* is concerned with the nature and function of literary interpretation. The interpretation of literature aims (1) at understanding a particular literary work or set of works, (2) at examining the methods and effects of such interpretation, (3) at studying the structure of textual communication, and (4) at reflecting upon the changing conditions of interpretation in our world.

Theological hermeneutics shares, of course, all of these concerns since it too deals with texts and sometimes even with literary texts (cf. *The Song of Songs* and many spiritual writings which are composed in literary genres). Yet while it includes literary interests, its ultimate focus is much wider. It aims at understanding this universe as God's universe. But this macro-hermeneutical goal is achieved only through micro-hermeneutical exercises. In principle, every written text could be interpreted from a theological point of view, that is to say that every text may shed light on our understanding of God's will for and presence in our world. But an all too quick understanding of a text from an exclusively theological perspective raises the question of ideological reading. Not every written text is composed in a specifically theological genre of communication, and therefore must be understood first in its own right, that means in accordance with its own generic place and potential of meaning.

Some texts, however, are composed as theological texts, as we shall see, and these texts require a particular theological interpretation. It is the interpretation of these theological texts *sui generis* (biblical texts, prayers etc.) which stimulates the development of theological reflection and thus prepares the basis for the larger framework which we call theological macro-hermeneutics, that is the interpretation of any kind of text from a theological perspective.

Thus the critical point in any treatment of theological hermeneutics is whether one favours a *theological* hermeneutics or a *hermeneutical* theology. The first claims that all texts have a theological dimension, at least implicitly. The second claims that theology is by its nature a hermeneutical exercise since it deals with a tradition mediated in no small measure by written texts and their interpretation. In this book we shall follow the second path and investigate the hermeneutical nature of theology and its implications for the Christian movement's self-understanding. Only then, on the basis of such a properly examined hermeneutical method, may we be equipped to venture into the related, but much larger question of *theological* hermeneutics.

1.6 THE QUESTION OF METHOD IN INTERPRETATION

Not all hermeneuts are convinced that the theory of interpretation should discuss methodological questions. Hans-Georg Gadamer on the one hand has been fighting a life-long battle against the imposition of method upon the act of understanding. He has emphasised again and again that a text or work of art will disclose its meaning to every competent and good-willed reader who is thus disposed to see what the text has to say. According to Gadamer, the disclosure of a text's sense should be appreciated as an instance of truth manifesting itself, and not as a result of the more or less successful application of sophisticated methods.[5] Paul Ricœur on the other hand is among those hermeneuts who have seen the discussion of methods of adequate understanding as an essential part of the hermeneutical task. He does not wish to describe just what is happening when we understand, as Gadamer intended. Rather he wishes to investigate what may be done to improve human understanding and to protect it especially against possible ideological distortion.[6]

Ricœur's efforts to protect human understanding echo the long tradition of theological hermeneuts who have been trying to establish criteria for a more adequate interpretation of texts. This book wishes both to affirm this tradition and to confront it with modern hermeneutical inquiry outside of this tradition. In a sense the book represents an effort in a mutually critical correlation[7] between theological hermeneutics on the one hand and literary and philosophical hermeneutics on the other.

1.7 BIBLICAL INTERPRETATION AS A THEOLOGICAL PROBLEM

Christian communities have always been faced with the problem of interpreting the Scriptures theologically. Since it is the very nature of the Christian church to reflect upon God's self-disclosure as witnessed by the biblical texts, these texts have always held a prominent and normative status in the Christian community. This status, however, makes the hermeneutical problem even more acute since it points to two related questions, namely the question of adequate criteria for biblical interpretation and the question of who has the competence and authority to validate such criteria as well as any particular act of interpretation in terms of such a set of accepted criteria. In this book I am more concerned with the question of adequate criteria than with the question of authority in biblical interpretation, although I wish to acknowledge that the question of authority is a problem which needs to be dealt with in any discussion of the nature of the Christian church. The question of interpretative competence may be best answered once the question of adequate interpretative criteria has been addressed.

Moreover, in our study I wish to concentrate first and foremost on the development of interpretative criteria in the history of Christian theology and of related disciplines, such as philosophy and literary criticism. Only in the concluding chapter will I offer some critical and constructive reflections on the significance of these developments for the present discussion of Christian self-understanding in this world.

1.8 THE PLAN OF OUR INVESTIGATION

The ongoing debate for or against method in interpretation and the conflict of interpretative methods may be better evaluated in view of the development of hermeneutical thinking in the West. Therefore, Chapters 2 and 3 shall attempt to present an outline of the history of theological and philosophical hermeneutics. Chapters 4 and 5 will examine the dialectic between text and reading. In Chapter 6 we shall return to the more recent discussion of theological hermeneutics. Finally, in Chapter 7 we shall address the implications of hermeneutics for the self-understanding of the Christian movement.

2

The Development of Theological Hermeneutics (I): From the Beginnings to the Enlightenment

2.0 INTRODUCTION

The history of hermeneutics is not identical with the history of the term 'hermeneutics'. Although it is the Greek word *hermeneia* which lies at the root of our modern expression, the activity to which our word hermeneutics refers is as old as the human practice of reflecting upon adequate methods of interpreting linguistic, pictorial and other forms of human expression and therefore is of course not limited to classical Greek culture and its rich heritage. Rather hermeneutical activities can be observed in all cultures wherever people reflect upon their ways of understanding. Nevertheless, in the Western tradition the term 'hermeneutics' cannot be studied without due regard to its Greek origins.

The Greek verb *hermeneuein* originally referred to more general dimensions of linguistic communication, such as expressing and translating language, which are no longer associated with our usage of 'hermeneutics'. Yet it was the interpretative dimension to which the verb also referred which became responsible for the more recent development which led to the now almost universal meaning of 'hermeneutics': the theory of text-interpretation.

The development of hermeneutical activities in Western cultures is linked in a special way to the Jewish and Christian search for models of adequate interpretation of their Scriptures. Both Jewish and Christian traditions have been interested in hermeneutics. They have always needed criteria for the adequate interpretation of biblical texts. These foundational texts of both religious traditions have had to be interpreted in such a way as to safeguard as well as possible the continuing disclosure of God's will which has been believed to be contained in these texts. Thus, the need for hermeneutics in its original theological context arose out of the very practical concerns of these religious communities.

In order to understand the history of Western hermeneutics it may be useful to distinguish between three major periods in its development:

1. The impact of classical Greek literary theory and philosophy;
2. The emergence of Jewish and Christian theories of biblical interpretation, and;
3. The influence of the Enlightenment which led to a broadening of the scope of hermeneutical thinking beyond its so far mainly religious contexts.

The fruits of this new hermeneutical awareness were richly harvested by Friedrich Schleiermacher (1768–1834). His contribution to hermeneutics opened a new era in the development of this discipline. Therefore we shall divide our discussion of the history of hermeneutics into two chapters. In the present chapter we shall study theological hermeneutics up to the period of the Enlightenment. Chapter 3 will trace the development of philosophical hermeneutics from Schleiermacher to the present.

2.1 THE IMPACT OF CLASSICAL GREEK LITERARY THEORY AND PHILOSOPHY ON THE DEVELOPMENT OF WESTERN HERMENEUTICS

Classical Greek culture did not only provide us with the word 'hermeneutics' which since the seventeenth century commonly refers to the 'theory of text-interpretation', but it also gave rise to an important heritage of specific hermeneutical reflection. The context of Greek hermeneutical thinking was the cultural need to determine the meaning, role and function of literary texts in ancient Greek society, especially of Homer's epics. Homeric criticism may be called the cradle of literary theory: it offered a scope, a terminology and a methodological basis for all future literary criticism in the West.

Homeric criticism emerged in response to the need to interpret Homer's works in a society which had accepted the *Iliad* and *Odyssey* as foundational texts for the education of the young and the instruction of the mature.[1] These texts informed the public and private life of classical Greek culture, and their adequate interpretation was thus a matter of public interest – as was the interpretation of the Bible in the Jewish tradition.

The requirements of instructing people in the reading and understanding of these crucial texts led in time to the development and refinement of grammar and text-criticism as well as to deep insights into the process of literary communication in general (cf. Aristotle's *Poetics*). Two distinct though often simultaneously applied methods of critical reading emerged: allegorical interpretation and grammatical interpretation. The legacy of these methods can be traced throughout the history of hermeneutics up to the present and will be the object of our discussion in the following pages. The general features and basic implications of both methods must, however, be clarified first.

Grammatical interpretation of a text tries to reach the text's sense by studying the linguistic devices and connections within it, whereas *allegorical interpretation* looks for the hidden sense of a text with the aid of an interpretative key from outside it.

The crucial question for any ancient reader of Homer's works was: does the text tell stories which need to be understood and appropriated as well as the study of the actual texts allows, or does one have to apply criteria gained from outside the text for a proper evaluation of the events, figures and stories portrayed in it? The allegorical method, on the one hand, confirmed the latter because it could not agree that the text itself would provide the reader with sufficient information and the perspectives required for its appropriate understanding. Therefore this method advocated that the key to the text had to be found elsewhere. Grammatical interpretation, on the other hand, looked for the key to the text's sense in the text itself. It set out to defend the text against readers who subject it to their own arbitrary reading perspectives.

Both methods, however, acknowledged the existence of an initial gap between text and reader, the hermeneutical difference so to speak, and both worked towards establishing ways of bridging this gap. The recognition of this gap is the beginning of all hermeneutics.

Considering what kind of role the Homeric texts played in Greek society we may immediately grasp the possible social and political dimension of text-interpretation. The discussion of adequate ways of interpreting foundational texts in any culture does not happen in an interest-free vacuum. Rather it will always have to wrestle with the presence of various and possibly even conflictual interests operative in society and thus also in hermeneutical reflection.

The development of the allegorical interpretation of Homer's texts was promoted by some later interpreters who read as symbolic those passages in the texts whose literal interpretation would have caused suspicion in a cultural context different from the one in which these texts originally appeared, especially in terms of moral norms and conventions. As long as the Homeric texts were treated as divinely inspired and therefore as being above any substantive critique, such suspicion would have been unacceptable. Hence, the allegorical method proved to be a very useful tool for saving textual integrity and rationality beyond the hermeneutical and cultural gap. This approach to the 'sacred' texts allowed the reader to search for ways of understanding the meaning of these without being forced to dwell on their literal message which may have sounded ridiculous or even obscene to him or her.[2]

These two approaches to the literary text have continued to determine the development of hermeneutics ever since, even though the religious and cultural contexts have changed and new sets of foundational texts have emerged.

2.2 JEWISH-CHRISTIAN THEORIES OF BIBLICAL INTERPRETATION

2.2.1 Jewish Hermeneutics

The Scriptures lie at the foundation of Israel's faith and cultural identity. They contain the divinely given order of life (the *Torah*) and the divinely inspired account of Israel's relationship with Jahweh, its God. Response to the Scriptures is response to God's call. As such, the nature of 'inspiration' of the Hebrew Scriptures differs sharply from the Greek belief in the divine inspiration of their foundational literature. While the Greeks understood human words to be inspired, the Jews have understood the Torah to represent God's own words.[3] Furthermore, the Torah offers the full truth for human life. As a result the ongoing interpretation of its texts has been necessary for everybody interested in translating the meaning of these texts, i.e. the will of God, into the respective situation of God's people. But this task has not always been easy because these texts are not always clear and coherent. The gap between the often difficult text and the readers' own interest in a coherent, comprehensive and intelligible meaning has provided the energy for Jewish hermeneutical reflection.[4] Thus, Jewish hermeneutics responded to the spiritual and cultural requirements of Israel and was never understood in terms of a mere philosophical exercise.

At the time of the emergence of Christianity, Jewish hermeneutics comprised, roughly speaking, four different though overlapping methods: Literalist, Midrashic, Pesher and Allegorical Interpretation.[5]

Literalist Interpretation can be seen as the most basic approach to the texts of the Scriptures. What they say has to be taken at face value by the reader. This approach was applied especially in relation to the interpretation of deuteronomistic legislation. The normative quality of the Torah would, of course, suggest such an approach. Yet such a method of interpretation did not always prove to be totally feasible, nor always desirable. The overall understanding of God's particular relationship with his people overruled at times a literalist interpretation of a passage and thus forced the reader to put the text into a wider perspective.

Such a more general theological perspective is the characteristic element of *Midrashic Interpretation*. This mode of interpretation was usually applied in rabbinic schools. It sought to penetrate the individual text in order to uncover the passage which may transcend the immediately obvious meaning. A set of seven rules attributed to Rabbi Hillel (1st century BC) and subsequently amended informed this method of interpretation. The rules stressed the importance of the context of a passage and the need for a consideration of textual similarities for a more adequate interpretation of the Scriptures. The principal need for such rules arose in view of fears that a spiritual interpretation may be open to misuse. A tradition built on certain foundational texts was seen to require safeguards against intentional and unintentional misunderstandings of these texts.

Pesher Interpretation, characteristic in particular of the Qumran community, claimed a special knowledge of divine mysteries and thus a certain prerogative in the context of an otherwise midrashic interpretation. It set out to apply biblical prophecies to current and even contemporary events.[6]

Allegorical Interpretation of the Scriptures attempted to understand the spiritual meaning of a text with the help of perspectives not derived from the text and usually not even informed by it. Rather the text is understood symbolically: it points beyond itself to a deeper reality. The Jewish thinker Philo of Alexandria (ca. 25 BC–50 AD) used and refined the allegorical method of scriptural interpretation in order to demonstrate to the Graeco-Roman culture surrounding him the rationality, intelligibility and contemporary relevance of the Scriptures and of Jewish thinking as a whole. Accordingly 'he was prepared to interpret allegorically anything that might derogate the dignity of the inspired words of God: anything that is nonsensical in the creation accounts, that is reprehensible in the legal portions, or that is trivial in the historical narratives of the Pentateuch'.[7] Apart from his apologetical and practical concerns, Philo used allegorical interpretation, in line with his theological convictions, in order to safeguard the transcendence of God when biblical passages spoke in an anthropomorphic manner about God.[8] Philo's influence on both Jewish and Christian thinkers was great, though not universal as may be seen from the relative absence of allegorical exegesis in first century Palestine.

Our brief look at ancient Jewish exegetical methods has revealed two related hermeneutical strategies: (1) to go beyond the literal meaning of the text and integrate the interpretation of the Scriptures into a larger theological framework, and (2) to establish a set of rules which instructs and at the same time contains the range of interpretations in the community and thus attempts to protect the community's religious identity and coherence. These and other possible hermeneutical procedures were frequently combined if the overall focus of the interpretative activity so required. For instance, a legal focus would naturally call for a more literalist and possibly a well-defined midrashic strategy; a charismatic self-awareness might direct the interpreter to Pesher Interpretation; and a strongly developed theological interest, particularly in an apologetic context, might have found it necessary to transcend the midrashic approach and allegorize the text.

2.2.2 Early Christian Hermeneutics

The proclamation of the kingdom of God by Jesus of Nazareth can, of course, be adequately understood and appreciated only against the background of the diverse strands of the Jewish tradition of the time. Yet unlike the mainstream of this tradition, Jesus' eschatological preaching in the Gospels is more concerned with the practical response to God's presence and call rather than with a discussion of the most appropriate strategies for scriptural interpretation.[9] However, since Jesus' proclamation and manifestation of God's kingdom have been seen against the background of the sometimes legalistic and authoritarian interpretation of the Torah in pharisaic schools and their particular influence on religious practice, one may be justified in retrieving Jesus' own implicit biblical hermeneutics from his practical response to scriptural texts.

Jesus demanded from his followers a practical and total response to God's call as presented both by his life and preaching which were inspired by his understanding of the Scriptures. He clearly adopted a non-literalist interpretation of the Scriptures according to the testimony of the Gospels (cf. Mt 5: 17ff.; Mt 15: 1–20; Mk 2: 23–28; Lk 13: 10–17; etc.). His hermeneutical position, so to speak, could be located more in the midrashic tradition. The particular focus of his preaching and his critique of the demands of any legalistic exegesis of Torah texts were, however, to become distorted by many of his own later disciples. The proclaimer of God's kingdom, was at times reduced to a topic of a new body of Scriptures which now themselves were in need of adequate interpretation (cf. below 7.4.3).

Hence, the hermeneutical problem for the early Christians was twofold: (1) At first mostly of Jewish background, they now reinterpreted their own Hebrew Scriptures in the light of their experiences of Jesus, of his proclamation, his death and his resurrection; and (2) in time they assembled themselves a second more and more canonical, i.e. normative, corpus of Scriptures, the New Testament, which itself required adequate interpretative strategies.

(1) This reinterpretation of the Hebrew Scriptures was guided now by the perspective that in Jesus God had fullfilled His promises once given to Israel. This, from a Jewish point of view, extra-textual perspective has shaped the Christian interpretation of the 'Old Testament' ever since. The allegorical interpretation of the 'Old Testament' is usually called *typological*.[10] The typological method of

reading the Hebrew Scriptures is based then 'on the presupposition that the whole Old Testament looks beyond itself for its interpretation'.[11] 'Types and prophecies of the coming Christ were sought throughout the Old Testament and, with the life of Christ already known to all, they were readily found.'[12]

The problems of this kind of interpretation were its exclusivist claims and the arbitrariness with which it tended to ignore many of the demands of the texts themselves. Instead of attending to the actual texts of the Hebrew Scriptures and understanding them also against their own communicative intentions, the typological interpreters have forced these texts into the strait-jacket of their own theological presuppositions, so that they then could claim that their interpretation of the Hebrew Scriptures represented the only legitimate approach to these texts. A different religious experience thus led to a radically new appropriation of the texts, and for a long time to come Christians and Jews were to discredit one another's interpretation of the Hebrew Scriptures even though they both applied very similar methods of interpretation, as we shall see now in more detail.

(2) The emergence of the New Testament canon highlighted the hermeneutical question in the Christian communities even more dramatically. Especially in view of the threat to the Christian movement coming from the Gnostics and their particular exegesis, Christian theologians concentrated on the establishment of the canon and of adequate principles for its interpretation. The spectrum of actual interpretative strategies used by Christian thinkers displayed the same options as those applied in Jewish hermeneutics. As in Jewish hermeneutics, the crucial question for Christian interpreters was whether to apply literal or allegorical interpretation. Thus, the increasing rivalry between Christian and Jewish thinkers in no way affected the consideration of hermeneutical *principles*. On the contrary, the two major Christian Schools of biblical interpretation and theology, Alexandria, which was more allegorically inclined, and Antioch, which followed more a grammatical-historical strategy, both owed their respective hermeneutical tendencies to the locally established Jewish tradition of hermeneutics.

As is shown by the struggle of Irenaeus of Lyons (died ca. 202 AD) with gnostic hermeneuts, the demonstration of the 'true' Christian *gnosis* was not possible on purely hermeneutical grounds. Both the 'false *gnosis*' (according to Irenaeus), i.e. Gnosticism, and the 'true *gnosis*', i.e. Christian orthodoxy, employed allegorical methods in their respective approaches to the Scriptures, though, of course, with different results. Therefore, Irenaeus felt the need to complement his hermeneutical demand for adequate interpretation with an ecclesiastical criterion: wherever the good-willed interpreter aligns himself with a local church which itself stands in an uninterrupted apostolic tradition, he can be sure to interpret the text according to the accepted Christian norm. This norm, represented solely by the apostolic tradition in the church, Irenaeus called 'the canon of truth' (*regula veritatis*). Thus, according to Irenaeus, only the legitimate community of Christian interpreters is in a position to provide the framework necessary for authentic Christian interpretation.[13] We shall return to Irenaeus, hermeneutics below in Chapter 7 (cf. 7.3.1)

While Irenaeus was engaged in refuting gnostic exegesis with arguments related to the understanding of the biblical texts themselves, the more radically apologetic thinker Tertullian (ca. 160–after 220) categorically ruled out the validity of any non-Christian exegesis of the Bible. Outside the church there can be no true interpretation at all. Moreover, the Scriptures, he insisted, are the exclusive property of the church. Therefore the Gnostics have no legal right whatsoever to engage in biblical exegesis at the first place.[14] Here the ecclesiastical criterion functioned no longer as a supplement. Rather it had become the basis for the distinction between authentic and inauthentic biblical exegesis.

The most systematic development of Christian hermeneutics took place both in Alexandria and Antioch where Jewish interpretation theory and practice had enjoyed a long and fruitful tradition. In *Alexandria*, the hermeneutical heritage of Philo continued to influence also Christian thinkers. Clement of Alexandria (died ca. 214) suggested that since all Scripture speaks in the mysterious language of symbols, allegorical interpretation was required. But he did not yet offer a systematic reflection on such a method.[15]

This systematic task was first undertaken by Origen (ca. 185–254) in his major theological work *On First Principles*.[16] Significantly Origen treats of hermeneutics in the fourth and last part of this book. Only after having dealt with such important theological topics as God, the cosmos and human salvation, does Origen move on to a discussion of his own hermeneutical method. Thus, his theological thought shaped his interpretative method.

For Origen, Scripture is inspired by God, and the fulfilment of Israel's prophecies in Jesus Christ is for him the obvious proof of biblical inspiration. This starting-point demands then an allegorical method of reading the biblical texts.

Although Origen was thoroughly engaged in textual criticism in order to prepare a critical and reliable edition of the biblical texts which could then be theologically interpreted, the crucial point of his study of the text remained the disclosure of the text's spiritual sense.[17] The Scriptures contain the ultimate mystery which can never be expressed other than in symbols, and symbols can never be properly understood when taken literally. Therefore only an allegorical approach can provide the key which is needed to unlock the mystery hidden in the text.[18] In theory Origen distinguished a threefold structure of textual sense: literal, moral and spiritual. In practice, however, he distinguished only between 'letter' and 'spirit'. Like Irenaeus, Origen too acknowledged the need for the interpreter to be guided by the church's rule of faith.[19]

In *Antioch,* Christian thinkers, following the local Jewish exegetical tradition, advanced a theory of biblical interpretation which was primarily concerned with literal interpretation, and therefore emphasised textual and grammatical investigation of the Scriptures. Antiochene theologians such as Theodore of Mopsuestia (ca. 350–428) saw the dangers of Origen's hermeneutics in the Alexandrian denial of the biblical stories' actual reality. The Antiochenes therefore insisted 'on the historical reality of the biblical revelation. They were unwilling to lose it in a world of symbols and shadows. They were more Aristotelian than Platonist. Where the Alexandrians use the word *theory* as equivalent to allegorical interpretation, the Antiochene exegetes use it for a sense of scripture higher or deeper than the literal or historical meaning, but firmly based on the letter'.[20] As opposed to the Alexandrians, the Antiochenes rejected a hidden sense of Scripture. Rather they thought that the meanings of the text refer to actual realities, clear and intelligible for every reader who cares to look. Thus, Israel's prophecies do not contain a symbolic but an actual reference to Christ. The prophet talks in real terms and consciously about the coming Jesus Christ.

On the basis of this literal reading of Scripture the Antiochene theologians re-examined the texts of Scripture one by one in order to check which of the texts was actually divinely inspired and which was not and thus ought to be excluded from the Christian canon of Scripture. A diagnosed absence of any direct prophetic, messianic or christological reference would have provided sufficient reason for excluding the text in question from the true canon of Scriptures.

'Antioch' and 'Alexandria' then stand for two different hermeneutical paradigms: 'Antioch' studied the text's open message and assessed the text's spiritual quality in a literal manner, whereas 'Alexandria' disclosed the text's spiritual sense from the perspective of an overall theological knowledge. Though neither of these paradigms was ever applied purely in the early church, these two hermeneutical positions mark the intellectual poles between which – following Greek and Jewish hermeneutics – Christian interpretation theory was to be developed further in centuries to come.

2.2.3 Augustine's Hermeneutics

Augustine of Hippo (354–430) brought both of these hermeneutical traditions to a new synthesis. Having suffered under Gnostic propaganda against the validity of the Hebrew Scriptures, a propaganda based on literalist interpretation, Augustine experienced the freedom of an allegorical reading method which allowed him to move closer to the church. Yet having been well trained in classical rhetoric, he had sufficient semiotic sensitivity to realise quickly how distorting a free-floating allegorical reading of the biblical texts could be. Thus, he advocated a thorough linguistic analysis of a text in order to control the accompanying spiritual reading of it. In a sense one may be justified in calling Augustine the father of 'semiotics', the theory of signs. The word 'semiotics' is derived from the Greek word for sign: *semeion*.

In his influential book on systematic hermeneutics and on the art of preaching *De Doctrina Christiana* [On Christian Doctrine],[21] Augustine concentrates his attention on examining the communicative functions of a sign. We use a sign in order to refer to a specific reality. Signs are not themselves what they refer to. They function rather as signifiers. This semiotic insight leads Augustine to reject all efforts to identify the Scriptures with what they talk about and point to. Against such confusion Augustine insisted that the Scriptures are human texts which refer to God. They themselves are not to be treated as a god, but instead they need to be used by the Christian reader as guides to the proper attitude towards God, towards him or herself, and towards the reader's fellow human beings.[22] In this context Augustine distinguishes between things which we use and things which we enjoy. Only unchangeable eternal things can be enjoyed, whereas everything changeable serves at best to guide a person towards authentic enjoyment of eternal things. Thus, since only God can be enjoyed, the Scriptures are given to us to be used in and for our faith-praxis. The attitude necessary for us in order to relate properly to God and God's law expressed in the Scriptures is identified and named by Augustine as 'love'.

Augustine's understanding of the hermeneutical task of a Christian reader represents a significant advance upon the Antiochene-Alexandrian debate on adequate interpretation theory. On the one hand, Augustine offers a semiotic framework in which the biblical text like any other human text is seen to function and in which it therefore needs to be interpreted. On the other hand, he provides us with a reading perspective, namely love, which is itself derived from a reading of the biblical texts. The love of God and of our fellow human beings is the proper reading perspective for a Christian believer.[23] This overall focus is no longer taken from outside the biblical text, but, as Augustine claims, it is the only perspective through which the biblical canon itself wishes to be read.

The semiotic dimension of Augustine's interpretation theory frees the reader of biblical texts both from any crude literalism and from the dangers of an arbitrary allegorization; and it encourages the reader to embrace a theological reading perspective which is informed by the biblical texts themselves. As such his proposed reading perspective becomes open for verification by every reader and no longer refers to any extra-textual key.

Moreover, Augustine's hermeneutics may be called a praxis-oriented hermeneutics. The particular theological and communicative orientation of his reading theory follows from his reflection on the praxis of the Christian search for ultimate meaning. Augustine's hermeneutics is thus not the result of pure speculation, but the fruit of systematic and practical consideration.

Due to its clearly defined horizon, Augustine's theory of biblical interpretation rules out what we today would call 'biblicism', that is an attitude of uncritical reverence towards the biblical texts based on the belief in the absolute inerrancy of these works. According to Augustine, the Bible is there for us and for our instruction. Yet it is not essential that the Christian receives the instruction which the Bible can give from his or her personal encounter with the texts themselves. Important is only that the Christian disciple arrives at the same order of salvation to which the biblical texts refer.

> A person who bases his life firmly on faith, hope and love, thus, needs the Scriptures only in order to teach others. Therefore we

> may find many people who live on this basis even without sacred texts.[24]

Having thus clarified his hermeneutical presuppositions, Augustine proceeds to a discussion of the details of the biblical interpreter's task. First he distinguishes between natural signs (for instance smoke coming from a fire and thus pointing back to it as its cause) and given [conventional] signs, the latter being the category to which all linguistic signs belong. Because of the conventional nature of all linguistic signs it is imperative for the biblical reader to be familiar with the particular linguistic conventions in which the biblical texts were produced. Hence, Augustine demands the knowledge of both Hebrew and Greek from any serious interpreter of the Bible.

Usually difficulties and possible misunderstandings which may arise in interpretation are connected with two problematic features in texts: (1) Signs may have a direct reference or they may function figuratively; and (2) signs may be unknown or appear ambiguous to the interpreter. Tackling the latter set of problems, Augustine urges the reader to understand a sign always in its context and to draw on all available knowledge for help in understanding difficult biblical passages. The problem of the sign's possible ambiguity may be solved by seeking the guidance of the church. The rule of faith may shed light on dark passages. However, should it be unable to do so, then the careful reader may decide for himself. Once the reader is moved by love towards God and the neighbour, he cannot totally miss the spiritual sense of the biblical text. Discussing the first set of problems, Augustine offers this clarification:

> With regard to figurative expressions the following rule should be observed: that what one reads should be carefully considered until a reading is established which reaches the kingdom of love. But if the text sounds as if it is used in its proper [literal] sense, then the expression is not to be taken figuratively.[25]

Augustine treats the Scriptures as a unity. Therefore he can advise the reader to understand darker passages through clearer passages.

As far as the Hebrew Scriptures are concerned Augustine remains committed to the traditional typological way of reading. 'The total or nearly the total content of the Old Testament must be understood not only in the literal sense but also in the figurative sense.'[26]

In sum, Augustine's biblical hermeneutics is based on a well-defined general semiotic theory and it offers a coherent theological perspective of reading which is derived from his own interpretation of the New Testament itself. In his hermeneutics, Augustine drew from both traditions of Christian hermeneutics: his semiotics is in line with Antiochene considerations, his insistence on the priority of spiritual praxis as context for interpretation follows Alexandrian concerns. This hermeneutics, then, represents a significant progress over all of its predecessors. The rule of faith, i.e. the living tradition of the community of Christians, is the context for the responsible reading of the Scriptures.[27] Thus, this tradition lives in a dialectical relationship with the process of reading itself: reading the Scriptures instructs the community, and the community which lives according to the Spirit of love, to which the Scriptures refer, provides the necessary perspective for responsible reading. Hence, the Scriptures are eminently useful, but not absolutely necessary for the Christian who is moved by God's Spirit.

> Whatever a person may have learned elsewhere [i.e. outside the Scriptures], if it is harmful, it will be condemned here [i.e. by the Scriptures], but if it is useful, it will be found also here [i.e. in the Scriptures].[28]

Thus, the Scriptures provide nevertheless the ultimate criterion for the determination of true Christian faith.

With Augustine's hermeneutics we have reached a depth of hermeneutical insight which was not known before and which was to influence most theologians and also interpreters of literary texts throughout the Middle Ages and beyond. However, the problem with Augustine's and subsequent hermeneutical reflection in medieval Christianity is that the faith praxis of the church which provided the perspectives for proper reading was itself an interpretative construction with more and more formalised institutional support structures. Particularly the emerging clergy-laity division, the Roman claims of primacy in the church of the West, and the increasing legalization of doctrines often guaranteed by state support for the church, affected the actual praxis of interpretation in the church. While Augustine's *De Doctrina Christiana* was still inspired by the author's concern to instruct every intelligent reader, subsequent hermeneutical reflection aimed exclusively at educating the theological expert. A comprehensive sociology of

Christian knowledge would need to examine this development and its consequences for the church more fully.

2.2.4 Medieval Hermeneutics

Although major parts of Augustine's hermeneutical thought remained influential during the centuries following his death, the careful balance in his interpretation theory between the function of Scripture and the function of tradition was soon distorted in favour of ecclesiastical concerns.

Shortly after Augustine's death, Vincent of Lérins (died before 450) in his *Commonitorium* offered the henceforth prominent definition of an ecclesiastical norm in response to the question of what constituted 'catholic faith':

> In the Catholic Church itself, all possible care must be taken, that we hold that faith which has been believed everywhere, always, by all. For that is truly and in the strictest sense 'Catholic,' which, as the name itself and the reason of the thing declare, comprehends all universally. This rule we shall observe if we follow universality, antiquity, consent.[29]

Vincent's definition documents the increasing shift from Augustine's reading perspective which was based on a reading of the texts themselves and thus could be called 'a material reading perspective' now towards a more institutionally oriented and formalistic concern for the orthodox understanding of Christian identity (cf. below 7.3.1).

A second shift in theological hermeneutics which occurred in post-Augustinian thinking was the increasing separation between biblical interpretation and theological speculation. On the basis of an exegetical discovery of the text's literal sense, theology assumed more and more the task of reflecting systematically upon the theological implications of a particular textual passage. Text and interpretation were being separated from one another, a process which culminated in the works of the great scholastic theologians.

But let us look first at the history of medieval hermeneutics in the period after Augustine and before Thomas Aquinas (1225–1274). Here we observe that hermeneutical thinking followed closely the path marked by Augustine's work. The places where hermeneutics was discussed most were the monasteries and the leading schools of the time, especially the Library of the Victorines in Paris. Here Hugh of St. Victor (died 1141) composed his influential work *Didascalicon* [In didascalicon liber][30] which was heavily inspired by Augustine's *De Doctrina Christiana*. In his hermeneutics, Hugh intended to advance wisdom (*sapientia*) not only in the reader of sacred texts but also in the reader of secular writings.[31] The first part of his study is devoted to a discussion of the system of the *artes*, that is the medieval canon of sciences taught in schools, and the second part deals with the problem of an adequate reading of the sacred Scriptures. Like Augustine in his *De Doctrina Christiana*, Hugh recognised that any adequate approach to the sacred texts requires a decent general education. And like most theologians of his time, Hugh compared the interpretation of the sacred texts with the construction of a building, that is a spiritual building within the human person. The spiritual dimensions of interpretation form the walls and the roof and also contribute to the interior decoration. The basis of this building must be the principles of faith.[32] Accordingly, Hugh demanded from every reader both a spiritual disposition and a willingness to be guided by the leading Christian authorities, the *doctores* [teachers] of the church.

In medieval hermeneutics generally, the spiritual sense of the Scriptures is further distinguished in three subcategories: the allegorical, the moral (or tropological) and the anagogical sense, so that biblical interpretation altogether follows a fourfold path. Nicholas of Lyra (died 1349) eventually summed this up in a verse:

> Littera gesta docet, quid credas allegoria,
> Moralis quid agas, quo tendas anagogia.
>
> [The letter shows us what God and our fathers did;
> The allegory shows us where our faith is hid;
> The moral meaning gives us rules of daily life;
> The anagogy shows us where we end our strife.][33]

These verses characterise well the principles which were to dominate theological hermeneutics, and indeed literary interpretation, for many centuries. According to these verses, the literal sense is the foundation on which the allegorical reading establishes the content of faith, the moral reading deduces rules for Christian behaviour and action in the world, and the anagogical reading illustrates the text's importance for the understanding of the goal of Christian life.

However, actual interpretative practice usually distinguished only between two senses of reading, the literal and the allegorical. Nevertheless, the theory of the fourfold sense of Scripture prepared the way for the more radical separation between theological disciplines, namely by emphasising the need for an independent consideration of the literal nature of the text as distinct from any discussion of its theological implications. These theological implications were approached from three angles: speculative theology based on the allegorical sense, moral theology based on the moral sense, and eschatology (i.e. the teaching of the last things) based on the anagogical sense. Thus, both the split between the various disciplines of theological thinking and the split between theological theory and Christian praxis which in our time have been perceived as fateful for Christian thinking and living, and which many contemporary theologians wish to overcome, have their origin in these medieval distinctions.

Since the rediscovery of Aristotle's philosophy in the twelfth century and the subsequent emergence of Scholastic theology, theologians attended anew to hermeneutical reflection. Interest in the allegorical sense, so far the stimulus for all theology, declined, whereas the literal sense of the text received a measure of attention hitherto unseen. Even though some parallels with the ancient Antiochene tradition of interpretation can be pointed out, the scholastic theologians were motivated chiefly by their own particular interpretation of Aristotle's understanding of nature to which the pre-scholastic symbolism was quite alien. Now the literal sense is the prime subject-matter of biblical interpretation. The truth of the text must be explicated without reference to a deeper or higher meaning.

The greatest medieval theologian, Thomas Aquinas, discussed his hermeneutical approach right at the beginning of his work on systematic theology, his *Summa Theologica*. Although Thomas maintained the principle of a fourfold reading of Scripture, he redefined the scope and importance of the literal sense.

> The author of holy scripture is God, in whose power it is to signify his meaning, not by words only (as man also can do), but by things themselves. So, whereas in every other science things are signified by words, this science [i.e. theology] has the property that the things signified by the words have themselves also a signification. Therefore that first signification whereby

> words signify things belongs to the first sense, the historical or literal. That signification whereby things signified by words have themselves also a signification is called the spiritual sense, which is based on the literal, and presupposes it. . . . Thus in holy scripture no confusion results, for all the senses are founded on one – the literal – from which alone can any argument be drawn, and not from those intended in allegory, as Augustine says. Nevertheless, nothing of holy scripture perishes on account of this, since nothing necessary to faith is contained under the spiritual sense which is not elsewhere put forward by the scripture in its literal sense.[34]

Thus, for Thomas understanding the literal sense is what any theologian should strive for. His devaluation of the allegorical sense is a sign of his determination to provide theology with a scientific basis. All theological thinking was to be organised in a way that would meet the newly formulated scientific standards.

This new concept of theological science had been further influenced by two separate developments. Firstly, in order to guide the reader's interpretation of the biblical text and to provide him with the authoritative exegesis of past generations, the medieval interpreters usually provided glosses, i.e. explanations of text passages, and glosses of former glosses, called *sententiae*. This tradition had led to a highly complex philological exercise which since the twelfth century was more and more considered to hinder rather than to help the appropriation of the sacred texts. Secondly, under Peter Abelard's (died 1142) influence, a new understanding of theology began to emerge. He rejected philological learnedness as useless and demanded the construction of a scientific theology on the basis of philosophical speculation. Logic and dialectic were to become the helpmates of theology. New textbooks of theological thinking were needed, and Thomas Aquinas' *Summa Theologica* was to become the most prominent introduction to this new academic theology.

Thomas' rejection of allegorical interpretation tried to bring theology and the study of the actual biblical texts more closely together. However, his turn towards philosophy made theological thinking again independent from biblical interpretation.

Even though the scholastic interpreters rediscovered the text of the Scriptures and tried to take it seriously in itself, their new interest was predominantly theological – as was the interest of the Church Fathers before them. However, their [scholastic] theology differed significantly from that of their predecessors. Still, theology was to be based on Scripture, but now the preparation of Scripture for theological speculation had become the sole aim of exegesis. Theology proper became *sacra doctrina,* sacred teaching, which claimed to represent adequately the content of *sacra scriptura,* sacred Scripture.[35] But contrary to its claim *sacra scriptura* moved quite independently from the biblical texts. The texts were increasingly reduced to providers of proofs for speculative theological thought ventures. As a result, popular piety took over the concern for spiritual interpretation in late medieval culture while theology followed its own academic agenda. Subsequently, the originally dialectical relationship between Scripture and the living tradition of faith was abandoned in favour of two increasingly independent developments of biblical interpretation. Christian theology used the biblical texts to substantiate its own theological premises, and popular Christian spirituality did the same on its own grounds.

2.2.5 Hermeneutics and the Reform of Christian Theology

The sixteenth-century Protestant Reformation in Europe may well be described as a hermeneutical event. But as we shall see in this section, the Reformation does not so much represent a new departure in philological or hermeneutical theory as the result of a new interpretative praxis. This new praxis of reading Scripture emerged when churchmen, thoroughly educated according to the humanist spirit of their time, reinterpreted the biblical texts, now read in their original languages and no longer in the official Latin edition (the *Vulgata*), and contrasted their interpretations with the ecclesiastical and spiritual realities of the late fifteenth and early sixteenth century.

The most important difference between the emerging humanist interpretation theory and the still influential hermeneutical programme of the Church Fathers, especially of Augustine, does not so much concern the requirements for a skillful act of biblical interpretation, but rather it lies in the radically changed self-understanding of the interpreter himself. For Augustine and his hermeneutical followers, biblical interpretation was ultimately linked to the Christian church, whereas for Luther, Calvin, Zwingli and other Reformers, biblical interpretation became more and more the decisive mode of assessing which aspects of the Christian tradition and of ecclesiastical life corresponded to authentic Christian faith, and which did not and therefore required reform. Thus, while the Reformers could easily continue to read a biblical text according to the methods developed by Jewish and Christian thinkers before them, they differed from many of their theological predecessors in terms of their view of the authority and legitimacy of any particular reading of biblical texts. In this context it is, however, important to appreciate that this reformational breakthrough had been prepared for by a number of critical thinkers in the late medieval period. Theologians like William of Ockham (ca. 1285–1349), John Huss (ca.1372–1415), Wendelin Steinbach (1454–1519) and John Major (ca.1469–1550) had already problematized the relationship and possible conflict between a truthful reading of the Scriptures and an authoritarian understanding of the right of ecclesiastical authorities to determine the ultimate meaning of a biblical text.[36] For the Reformers the exclusive criterion for adequate theological understanding of Christian doctrine and existence became now the Word of God as perceived through their renewed reading of the Scriptures. They no longer sought the additional authentication of their biblical understanding by an ecclesiastical institution, such as the Roman authorities.

The Bible communicated the Word of God. Hence more than a proper understanding of the Word of God was not necessary for the right guidance of Christian faith. Every person who listens carefully to the Word of God in the Bible and uses all his or her ability to read and study the texts of the Bible will find everything he or she searches for. In this sense the Reformers could say that the Bible was self-interpreting. No other norm was required. For them, however, this self-interpretative nature of the Scriptures did not mean that human reason was no longer necessary at all as an instrument for the proper study of the text. An explicit hostility towards human reason in biblical interpretation emerged only in the period of Protestant Orthodoxy (cf. below 2.2.6).

This principle of *sola scriptura* (Scripture alone) must, however, not be confused with the later doctrine of the verbal inspiration of the Bible. Martin Luther (1483–1546), Ulrich Zwingli (1484–1531) and John Calvin (1509–1564) did not hold such a doctrine. All of them, as indeed the mainstream Christian tradition before them, held that the Holy Spirit was the 'author' of the Scriptures, and that therefore God does speak through the texts of the Bible in a way that was clear, coherent and sufficient for human salvation. Accordingly, the apparent inconsistencies and ambiguities in these texts do not invalidate this belief in the clarity of the Scriptures, but rather they present a lasting challenge to the finite and thus very limited interpreter.

Luther, Zwingli and Calvin agreed on the need for a theological reading perspective which would allow the individual reader of the Scriptures to grasp the overarching theological sense of these texts. The reformational breakthrough consisted then both in the development of such a theological reading perspective which tried to understand the biblical texts as a unity, and in the changed consciousness of the reader who, as promoted by humanist thinking, became now individually called to study the texts and also individually responsible for responding to the claims of these texts in his or her Christian existence.[37] However, the same humanism which had impressed this new interpretative freedom from all traditional impositions and institutional boundaries on the Reformers was itself to be challenged by the new theological reading perspective which the thus-freed Reformers now began to develop.

In order to understand these origins of reformational hermeneutics more clearly it might be helpful to look in some detail at the beginnings of Martin Luther's hermeneutics.[38]

Martin Luther was first and foremost a teacher of Sacred Scripture. That means that his primary academic concern was biblical exegesis. Like the scholastic theologians before him, Luther at first accepted the theory of the fourfold sense of Scripture as is evident from his first lecture course on the Psalms (1513–15). However, already in his second series of lectures on the Psalms (1519), his turn to the literal sense of the biblical texts and his enmity towards allegorical interpretation are clearly visible, even though the new hermeneutical programme is not yet always matched by a corresponding interpretative practice.[39] Nevertheless the change in his hermeneutics which occurred between these two sets of lectures on the Psalms and which coincided with his reformational breakthrough on the theology of justification is very clear: Luther had redefined the relationship between 'letter' and 'spirit'.

So far, technical terms referring to the twofold sense of Scripture, 'letter' and 'spirit' are now used by Luther as theological terms. 'Spirit' is everything which is understood *coram deo*, i.e. in the light of God's self-disclosure and concealment in the cross of Jesus Christ. This christological concentration in Luther's theology is now expressed by reference to the 'spiritual sense' of the text. But this spiritual sense becomes a reality only in so far as it is evoked by the literal/historical sense of the biblical texts during the acts of reading or preaching. Thus, the text is not the Word of God, rather it discloses the Word of God to the faithful interpreter or listener.[40] Accordingly the theological understanding of the Scriptures decides whether or not the text becomes *littera* or *spiritus* for the reader. The theological horizon presupposed by Luther's hermeneutics is characterised by two radically different views of human existence: an existence *coram deo* (according to God) and an existence *coram mundo* (according to the world). The meaning of an existence *coram deo* is revealed in the cross of Christ and can be accepted only in faith (*sola fide*). Therefore, adequate interpretation of the Scriptures is only possible once the primary existential decision for or against *spiritus* is made. The spirit of the biblical text can only be understood by an interpreter who has opted already for the spiritual mode of existence beforehand. Yet, the decision for this mode of being is provoked by the reading of the Scriptures itself.

Luther's hermeneutics is circular: the Scriptures provoke first a principal existential decision for or against 'spirit', and secondly, only on the basis of such a principal decision in favour of a spiritual existence can the reader embark on the detailed task of interpreting the Scriptures. Thus, Luther's hermeneutics requires first a macro-hermeneutical decision from the interpreter before the micro-hermeneutical activity, i.e. the detailed theological reading of the Scriptures, can begin.

This macro-hermeneutical demand distinguishes Luther both from his hermeneutical predecessors and also from many of his hermeneutical contemporaries. It means (1) the principal rejection of allegorical exegesis, and (2) the material transcendence of the chiefly philological approaches to the texts undertaken by the leading humanists.

Luther's macro-hermeneutical perspective was essentially christological: in the cross of Jesus Christ a new mode of understanding human existence was revealed by God.[41] This revelation must guide the theological reading of the Bible, and it is this perspective which grants a unity and coherence to the collection of biblical texts. Only when the Old and the New Testament are read together does this difference between an existence under the law and an existence under the spirit become obvious. This is not to imply that the Old Testament does not have 'spiritual' relevance, rather according to Luther the prophetical character of Old Testament texts can only be understood when these texts are interpreted christologically.[42] The christological reading thus helps Luther to distinguish between two literal senses: the ordinary 'literal sense' and the 'prophetic literal sense'. On the basis of the latter, Luther felt free even to interpret allegorically. But his application of allegorical interpretation differs from previous allegorical modes of reading: it is no longer the basis of theological conclusions, but it is the conclusion derived from a new theological (i.e. christological) basis.[43]

Perhaps this difference illustrates best the new departure in theological hermeneutics in the sixteenth century. The reading of the Scriptures is guided by a strong theological belief in the christological coherence of the Scriptures. This belief is itself a product of the new reception of the biblical texts partly facilitated by the humanist programme. However, unlike some Lutherans after Luther, the Reformer himself never treated the Bible as a 'system without contradiction'.[44] He was well aware of the theological differences between individual texts, and he approached all these differences from a particular theological perspective which allowed him both to perceive a unifying focus in this collection and to criticise individual texts for failing to comply with his christological focus, for instance the *Letter of James* which, according to Luther, lacked christological substance.[45]

While all the Reformers of the sixteenth century were inspired by the same humanist rediscovery of hermeneutics, their individual hermeneutical practices often differed significantly from each other. Luther's particular christological interpretation perspective remained quite unique. For Calvin, who was more faithful to humanist principles than Luther, the Bible itself was the ultimate norm of Christian faith rather than a particular theological interpretation of it. On the one hand he was more open to recognise a diversity of exegetical judgement: 'Each may use his own judgment, provided no one tries to force all others to obey his own rules.'[46] Yet on the other hand he put all his trust in the formal authority of the Scriptures for Christian belief. Thus, he promoted, at least implicitly, the growing belief in the Scriptures themselves (rather than in what they talk about) which helped to prepare the ground for the coming 'biblicism'. Although Calvin himself mastered the skills of the rich hermeneutical tradition and felt free to criticise individual passages of the Bible in the light of his research[47], future generations of Calvinists sometimes lost these skills and instead defended uncritically the absolute and literal authority of all the biblical texts.

Impressed by the humanist reconsideration of the human being and his individual ability to interpret classical texts, the Reformers had approached the Scriptures from a new horizon. Luther, Zwingli, Calvin and the Reformers in England all wrestled with the effort of determining the relationship between faith and the Bible, and all the Reformers agreed on the need for a critical interpretation of the Scriptures. The Scriptures provided the only foundation for a continuous systematic reconsideration of the Christian faith, but they were not a quarry to be exploited by people with an intention of organising a lasting doctrinal system. However, this originally Protestant commitment to critical interpretation was soon to be qualified or abandoned altogether.

2.2.6 Hermeneutics in Roman Catholic and Protestant Orthodoxy

In response to the theological programme of the Protestant Reformation the Roman Catholic theologians assembled at the Council of Trent (1545–1563) confirmed the two-source theory according to which both the Bible and the Christian Tradition together provide the sources for authentic Christian faith and theology. Thus, they contradicted the reformational insight that only the Bible provided a clear, coherent and sufficient guide for Christians to understand God's word and will. According to Tridentine theology, the traditions of the Church also form an essential source for authentic Christian faith, and the ecclesiastical authorities remain the ultimate judges whether or not a particular interpretation of a biblical text is 'orthodox', i.e. in line with the officially defended exegetical and dogmatic tradition of the Church.[48]

In the flourishing theological controversies between Roman Catholic and Protestant theologians, the debate about the *sola scriptura* principle occupied a very prominent place. The arguments employed in this debate reveal a particular set of hermeneutical convictions and thus are of importance for our discussion.

On the Protestant side, in the period usually referred to as 'Protestant Orthodoxy', theologians, such as Matthias Flacius Illyricus (1520–1575), Johannes Andreas Quenstedt (1617–1688) and Abraham Calov(ius) (1612–1686) defended the doctrine of verbal inspiration of the entire Bible and accordingly developed the principle of biblical infallibility. The actual text of the Scriptures was said to be infallible, dictated verbatim by the Holy Spirit. And since these theologians identified the Bible with the Word of God, nobody claiming to be a Christian could doubt the truthfulness of any part of the biblical text. For these thinkers, Christian faith meant the intellectual acceptance of a set of dogmatic texts derived from this infallible text. It is interesting to see how both Lutheran and Reformed theologians fought against one another while using the same rationalistic method of deriving at their doctrines from this infallible text, and how each of them then claimed to represent alone *the* orthodox faith.[49]

While attempting to safeguard the authority of the Bible, these theologians betrayed one of the essential aspects of the Protestant Reformation, namely the freedom of every Christian critically to study the biblical texts. For such theologians the Bible had become a principle to be defended against every kind of critique, including the demands of human reason, as we shall see in a moment. Hence the Bible functioned as a principle of formal authority, and biblical interpretation was reduced to dogmatic theory. The Bible as the only principle of Christian faith can never be wrong. Rather it must always be right, otherwise the Christian faith as such ceases to be authentic. This dogmatism is, of course, a form of integralism: either everything is right or everything is wrong. This kind of ideological interpretation theory was very useful for the polemics against the enemies of this kind of Protestantism both from within and outside the Protestant church.

The defenders of this rigid biblicism attacked especially the advances of the natural sciences, which led to doubts about the possibility of an unqualified literalistic reading of the Scriptures, for instance the creation accounts in the Book of Genesis. Lutheran, Reformed and Roman Catholic orthodoxies were thoroughly united in their rejection of the emerging scientific and rational world-view. Kepler's and Galilei's discoveries, as well as the attacks against the traditional form of Christian chronology and the belief that Adam was the father of all humanity, began to upset orthodox theologians of all camps. What was at stake for them was the inherited biblical view of cosmos and time, i.e. the foundation of all thoughts and beliefs since the emergence of Christianity in the context of the Graeco-Roman world. Therefore, this confrontation of Christian faith with the evidence of natural sciences, and even more the systematic claims of philosophers such as Descartes and Spinoza that theologians ought to accept human reason as the only norm of all thinking and believing, caused a terrible uproar in theology. The orthodox theologians feared that the end of the supremacy of theology had come. But instead of wrestling critically, though constructively, with the demands of the new philosophy and the natural sciences, these theologians blocked themselves completely against any claim of human reason and thus developed an attitude of hostility towards any sort of scientific progress. This hostile attitude was to remain the hallmark of theology and at times even of Christianity as a whole for many centuries to come.[50] Instead of a critical dialogue with the promoters of the new world-view, the orthodox theologians, especially in Germany, understood human reason only as the hand-maid of theology. 'The orthodoxy is proud of the rational argumentation through which it thought to safeguard the concerns of the Christian faith, but it does not permit human reason to be critical.'[51]

Outside of Germany, especially in the Netherlands, theologians such as Balthasar Bekker (1634–1698) and Christoph Wittich (1625–1687) developed a moderate Cartesian approach to theology. Their attempt to mediate between the demands of modern reason and the traditional claims of theology was based on four presuppositions. (1) The separation of philosophy and theology. Both modes of recognition are different, dealing and concerned with different subject-matters. (2) In the theological sphere Holy Scripture has absolute authority insofar as it provides clear and unambiguous statements. (3) In the sphere of natural things the philosphical mode of knowing must be accepted as the legitimate method which operates freely and critically. And (4), the statements of both methods must be free of contradiction.[52]

This programme for a division of method and knowledge represented for the first time a well defined theological critique of the Scriptures. The Scriptures can no longer be taken as the only sourcebook for human knowledge. There are spheres about which the Scriptures do not offer secure knowledge at all. The obvious contradiction between scriptural and scientific statements about nature and history was explained with the help of the theory of accommodation, according to which the Holy Spirit through the biblical authors had to speak about nature in a way that was accessible to the 'prejudice' of the people of the time. Although this theory was meant to maintain the general authority of the Bible, it offered at the same time the clue for the further development of critique, namely the problematization and rejection of ancient 'prejudices' in the coming period of the Enlightenment.[53]

However, the defenders of this moderate position towards the new world-view did not succeed in promoting the dialogue between theologians and scientists. On the one hand they were attacked by their Orthodox colleagues for betraying what they saw to be the only legitimate position of Christian theology. On the other hand they were attacked by the new scientists for not going along far enough with the new insights into nature and thinking.[54] But these moderate theologians must at least be credited with having understood the new hermeneutical situation in theology: how can Christians understand their foundational texts in view of the new fundamental critique of the validity and authority of these texts?

Because of their ideological nature, the interpretative approaches to the Scriptures by Orthodox theologians during the seventeenth and eighteenth century did not and could not advance the development of hermeneutics. Rather these approaches may be seen as escapes into the illusion of a rationalist transcendence of the tension between the text as authoritative object and the reader as a thinking and critical subject. But as theologians in the late eighteenth century were to prove, neither the hermeneutical achievements of the humanists and the Reformers, nor the by now systematic critique of both the entire biblical world-view and the universalist claims of traditional theology, could be wiped out completely by such new forms of dogmatism and escapism.

Another form of protest against this formalistic and dogmatist treatment of the Bible emerged from the Pietist movement. Here individual human experience was seen as an essential requirement for Christian faith. The personal experience of the faithful provided the foundation for theological insight and scriptural study. Such a programme, of course, led to a more qualified treatment of the Bible. Instead of being an absolute principle of faith, the Bible could now become again a source for Christian faith.[55] However, the new emphasis which the individual faithful received in Pietism brought along a new set of problems. Does the personal, private experience of faith supersede the biblical communication of God's presence in history? Is Christian faith now found and expressed exclusively in the realm of private faith and no longer the concern of the public *ecclesia*, the church? A balance between private and public use of the Bible in Christian faith, indeed a balance between subjective and communitarian understanding of Christian faith, needed to be worked out. And what role does human reason play in biblical understanding? Is reason the enemy of biblical truth, as the representatives of Protestant Orthodoxy claimed, or is reason a necessary instrument for every act of biblical interpretation, as the defenders of a moderate theological Cartesianism in the seventeenth century and those of an 'enlightened' Christian theology in the eighteenth century demanded? To the latter group we are now turning.

2.2.7 Theological Hermeneutics in the Age of Enlightenment

The University of Halle played a significant part in the propagation of enlightened thinking in the eighteenth century. Here a number of influential philosopers and theologians, such as Christian Wolff (1679–1754), Siegmund Jakob Baumgarten (1706–1757), and Johann Salomo Semler (1725–1791) contributed through their teaching and writing to the reappreciation of human reason and to the growing protest against the manifestations of unreasonable authority. Whereas both Wolff and Baumgarten were concerned to develop better rational criteria for a defense of the traditional Protestant understanding of faith and church, Semler worked for a radically new hermeneutical beginning in theology. In terms of his concern for a rational theology he was, of course, influenced by both Wolff and Baumgarten, but his hermeneutical programme of an historical-critical study both of the Scriptures and of the history of dogma opened a new epoch in Protestant theology. Emanuel Hirsch correctly identified Semler as the first German Protestant theologian who approached the Bible through the eyes of the historian of religion and of the critical explorer of history.[56] However, as we have seen in section 2.2.6 of this chapter, Semler's methodological reflection was prepared to some extent by the questions raised both in the theological attack against the Protestant Orthodoxy and in the theological struggle with Pietism.

Semler did not offer a detailed description of the method of text-interpretation, but he did propose a radical transformation of the foundation of theological hermeneutics. He demanded that biblical interpretation must stop being nothing more than the verification of a particular set of doctrines. In other words, the dogmatic reading of the text must end, and a truly critical reading of the text begin. For Semler hermeneutics had a very wide scope. It included the treatment of questions of grammar, rhetoric, logic, the history of the tradition of the text, translation, the critique of text editions and of exegesis proper.[57] The main task of hermeneutics, however, was to understand the texts as their authors had understood them. Thus, over against the synchronistic text-understanding in the Protestant

Orthodoxy, Semler demanded a diachronic reading of the biblical texts: what counts for the interpreter is the disclosure of the *sensus litteralis historicus* [i.e. the literal-historical sense] of the biblical text.[58]

According to Semler, the following two rules are essential for a critical interpretation theory. (1) The interpreter of the Bible must be aware of the historical distance between him and the texts of the Bible. (2) Biblical hermeneutics must respect the universal rules of text-interpretation, but must also attend to the specific nature and content of these texts. This second demand, however, did not mean that Semler agreed with those theologians who claimed a spiritual prerogative for their text-interpretation. Instead, Semler sharply distinguished between the biblical text and the Word of God. The biblical texts must be interpreted and not destroyed through reading all kinds of pious things into them.[59] But the biblical texts themselves do communicate certain things about God and God's relationship to us, and these things need to be retrieved by the interpreter in a historical-critical manner.

As a result of his historical-critical method of interpretation, Semler's view of the Old Testament differed significantly from that of his hermeneutical predecessors, including Martin Luther. Semler could no longer agree with the typological method of reading the Hebrew Scriptures. He denied that all these texts contained prophecies of Jesus Christ. He went so far as to state that certain Old Testament books contained nothing of the Word of God, such as, for instance, the historical books or *The Song of Songs*.[60]

Although he followed Martin Luther in many ways, especially in accepting the radical freedom of the Christian to re-read the texts of the Bible without dogmatic and authoritarian caveats, Semler went beyond the great Reformer by pointing out that in theology as in all other sciences the rules of logic must apply. Thus, Semler rejected any special status of theology as an inspired discipline. He blamed Luther for having downgraded human reason, and he also rejected the pietist claim that personal revelation could add to the capacity of human reason.[61] Ultimately, Semler did not abandon the reformational scripture principle [i.e. the *sola scriptura*], rather he attempted to free the biblical interpreter from the formal authority of the Scriptures for a new appreciation of the material authority of the biblical texts. In that sense Semler stands firmly in both the Antiochene and the Lutheran hermeneutical tradition.

Finally, we must mention Semler's theory of 'accommodation'

which further illustrates his critical approach to the Bible. Semler was a great admirer of the Roman Catholic scholar Richard Simon (1638–1712). Semler even organised the German translation of Simon's works concerned with the critical understanding of the Scriptures, and he edited and introduced this publication himself. Already a century before Semler, Simon's great insights into the make-up of the biblical texts, for instance his discussion of the multi-authorship of the Pentateuch as well as his critique of the traditional belief in a monistic Patristic tradition, had seriously undermined the orthodox doctrines of the Scriptures. Semler saw himself in this critical tradition, and like Simon, he aimed at fighting all those theologies which tried to silence the biblical texts through imposing their own doctrines on them instead of properly studying the texts themselves.[62]

Now, Semler's own contribution to this kind of critical biblical scholarship was his theory that Jesus and the authors of the biblical texts needed to accommodate their audiences through adopting the language and concepts of the people to which they were talking. According to Semler, this theory of accommodation could not only explain the linguistic differences between various New Testament texts, but also the doctrinal variations in the Bible.

Semler's theory of accommodation must not be confused with two other theories of accommodation which had different intentions. Representatives of the Lutheran Orthodoxy had developed a theory of accommodation according to which the Holy Spirit accommodated himself to the style of the biblical authors when dictating the text of the Bible. This theory, then, was purely apologetic in trying to safeguard the theory of verbal inspiration. Another theory of accommodation was put forward by Semler's teacher Baumgarten who was concerned to explain why there was such a discrepancy between the biblical accounts of natural phenomena and those of modern scientists. Baumgarten therefore claimed that the biblical authors knew very well the true laws of nature, but had to respect the ignorance of their contemporaries. Both of these theories of accommodation are regressive and apologetic by nature, whereas Semler's theory of accommodation tries to advance biblical scholarship by pointing out a genuine diversity within the biblical tradition.[63] Semler's theory, then, is a first result of his genuine effort to read the biblical texts without fear of breaking doctrinal taboos. But Semler's theory of accommodation was, as we have seen, anticipated already by the Dutch theologians Bekker and Wittich.[64]

Semler's contribution to theological hermeneutics was enormous. He exposed the Orthodox dogmatism and biblicism and demonstrated that a truly scientific theology must develop properly academic, i.e. rational and critical, methods of biblical interpretation. He insisted strongly that Christian theology is not a religious exercise, but a rational discourse on Christian religion which operates according to a public and rational methodology. He began to develop the hermeneutical aspects of this methodology. But, as the title of his four volume work on hermeneutics suggested, this work represented only a *Preparation for Theological Hermeneutics* (1760–69).[65] Thus, more work needed to be done in theological hermeneutics in order to achieve a critical clarification of the true challenge to traditional hermeneutics presented by the new philosophical world-view, and hence the achievement of a truly critical theological hermeneutics.

2.3 CONCLUSION

In this chapter we have studied the development of Christian theological hermeneutics from New Testament times until the Enlightenment. Our concentration on *Christian* theological hermeneutics does not mean to suggest that the history of all hermeneutical discourse since Philo was identical with the history of Christian hermeneutics. Rather a more general study of the history of hermeneutics would necessarily need to include a discussion of the development of both Jewish and Muslim hermeneutics. Moreover, it should be noticed that at various points during the development of Christian theological hermeneutics, Jewish and Muslim thoughts have provided essential stimuli to the inner-Christian hermeneutical discussion. A study of these cross-religious hermeneutical encounters is urgently required.[66]

Summing up the authors and movements characterised in our chapter we could say that all hermeneuts in the Christian tradition moved between two poles: they either favoured more the literal-grammatical method initially propagated by the School of Antioch, or they were influenced by stronger doctrinal concerns and therefore found the Alexandrian method with its allegorical tendencies more useful. In a sense, all forms of theological hermeneutics are variations of these two poles. Another way of expressing these hermeneutical leanings would be to point to the fact that all hermeneuts had to decide if they wished to respect the texts themselves as much as possible, or if they preferred to read the texts more according to specific reading traditions. The question of the legitimacy of doctrinal readings of the biblical texts has remained an important point of discussion in theological discourse up to the present day. Related to it is the question of interpretative authority. Is there an authority, such as the church, the local community or the individual readers themselves which ought to decide whether or not a particular biblical reading is authentic? It appears to me that all those hermeneuts who followed the Antiochene tradition were generally more open to new theological discoveries and to theological reform, whereas the more Alexandrian minded hermeneuts tended to defend a certain theological *status quo*. One could say that with Semler theological hermeneutics finally adopted an Antiochene character. But a proper method of theological hermeneutics based on the inductive philosophical principles of Aristotle, the godfather of Antiochene hermeneutics, was not yet accomplished at the end of the eighteenth century.

3

The Development of Philosophical Hermeneutics: From Schleiermacher to Ricœur

3.0 INTRODUCTION

In this chapter I wish to explore the development of philosophical hermeneutics from Friedrich Schleiermacher to Paul Ricœur. We shall see that all the hermeneutical proposals discussed in the following pages are related to one another. Nevertheless each of these proposals is motivated by particular interests and concerns; we shall try to discover these motivations, follow their respective development through the last two centuries, and offer critical comments. In the context of this chapter I cannot, however, treat of all hermeneutical movements and proposals which have emerged since the Enlightenment. Instead I concentrate here on some major figures from the Continental philosophical tradition in Europe which have had a lasting impact on the development of hermeneutical thinking.

3.1 SCHLEIERMACHER'S REFORM OF HERMENEUTICS

Friedrich Schleiermacher (1768–1834) is generally known as 'the father of modern hermeneutics'. He fully deserves this title, because he was the first thinker who appreciated the universal scope of the hermeneutical problem and as a result demanded a *philosophical* theory of understanding. Thus redefining the nature and scope of hermeneutics he also freed theological hermeneutics from the prison of ecclesiastical ideologies into which Roman Catholicism and Protestant Orthodoxy have led it, as we saw in Chapter 2. Some of Schleiermacher's thoughts and lecture notes on hermeneutics have been published only recently so that we are today in a better position to evaluate his contribution both to the development of a philosophical theory of understanding and to theological hermeneutics.[1]

3.1.1 Schleiermacher's Approach to Philosophical Hermeneutics

As described in Chapter 2, the development of hermeneutics had been fuelled by Jewish and Christian theologians who were concerned to find adequate modes of appropriating their ancient Scriptures. As preacher, theologian and also as translator of classical texts Schleiermacher shared, of course, the specific hermeneutical concerns of all text interpreters. Yet he transcended this merely exegetical focus by asking also the universal question: what is human understanding and how does it happen? In response to this philosophical question he redefined 'hermeneutics' in general terms as 'the art of understanding'. He was convinced that only a philosophical treatment of hermeneutics as such could provide the necessary and critical foundation for the more specialised concerns of hermeneutics, such as biblical exegesis. However, since such a philosophical foundation was still lacking, Schleiermacher set out to develop it.

First he pointed out that we cannot assume that understanding was an easy process. Instead we must reckon with the fact that we often misunderstand what has been said or written. However, hermeneutics concerns not only those instances where understanding is difficult to achieve. Rather it concerns all aspects of understanding. Schleiermacher proposed that understanding should be considered as an *art*. But that does not imply a sense of arbitrariness. Rather he insists that the personal or *subjective* dimension in the process of understanding must always be accompanied by a proper regard for the linguistic nature of the object to be understood, i.e. by an *objective* dimension.

Secondly, he considered this linguistic nature of human communication in more detail. All understanding presupposes language; in language we think and through language we communicate. There is no understanding without language, and therefore hermeneutics and rhetoric, however distinct, cannot be separated. Language occurs always as a combination of general patterns of convention (its grammatical or objective aspect) and of individual performance (its technical or subjective aspect). Schleiermacher calls this latter aspect also the 'psychological' aspect of interpretation. Although the terminology remains somewhat unclear, it is important to distinguish between the technical/psychological aspect on the one hand and the grammatical dimension of interpretation on the other hand.

Schleiermacher described the task of the *grammatical* dimension of *interpretation* as 'the art of finding the particular sense of a certain discourse in the language and with the help of the language'.[2] The *psychological/technical interpretation* seeks to grasp the whole or unity of the work and the major features of its composition.[3]

Thirdly, Schleiermacher insisted that these two dimensions of interpretation are of equal importance in every act of text-understanding.[4] As every text-production is the result of a particular or personal application of conventional linguistic rules, every act of text-reception is based on an individual application of conventional modes of understanding texts.

Fourthly, Schleiermacher also paid attention to the nature of texts. He sees a text as an individual universal where a network of individually applied conventions and rules work together in order to create a new and meaningful whole. The particularity of composition forms the 'style' of the text.[5] No purely grammatical consideration could ever produce a concept of a particular style, because the very conceptualisation of the individuality of a text would dissolve this individuality. Accordingly, a text can never be understood totally. Therefore Schleiermacher's theory aims at approximation rather than at the total grasp of a text's sense. Nevertheless, this interpretative approximation towards the sense of a text must be guided by certain rules in order to safeguard the critical and responsible character of the interpretative process.[6]

Fifthly, Schleiermacher defined these rules as follows.

> The rules for the art of interpretation must be developed from a positive formula, and this is: 'the historical and divinatory, objective and subjective reconstruction of a given statement.'[7]

Objectively, these rules, then, are to help the interpreter to acknowledge both the relationship between the text and the linguistic system out of which the text has emerged, and the text's own particular impact on this linguistic system. Subjectively, these rules instruct the interpreter both 'to know how the statement, as a fact in the person's mind [i.e. the author's], has emerged' and 'to sense how the thoughts contained in the statement will exercise further influence on and in the author'.[8] The aim of this process of understanding is 'to understand the text first as well and then better than its author did'.[9] This interpretative goal implies that the interpreter must be perfectly familiar with the author's language, and moreover, he must acquire a knowledge of the author's internal and external life. However, Schleiermacher hastens to add that this knowledge of life and language of the author can only be found through interpreting the author's writings.[10]

A point of enormous misunderstanding in Schleiermacher's programme has been his use of the word 'divination'. For Schleiermacher this term did not mean a secret or mysterious feeling of or entry into the world of the text and its author, rather it described the necessarily courageous risk taken by an interpreter who approaches a text even though he knows that no approach will ever exhaust the individuality of the text. Understanding is a never-ending task and challenge. Schleiermacher's insistence on the dipolar nature of this task, i.e. its psychological and its grammatical dimensions, emphasises on the one hand that divination must not be understood as an individualistic escape from given semantic facts, and on the other hand that no (objective) knowledge of the text's linguistic composition can ever replace the interpreter's obligation to grasp the text's overall sense, although such a grasp will at best lead only to an approximate reconstruction. Because the general and the individual penetrate each other in a text, their combination can be understood ultimately only through divination.[11]

Finally, Schleiermacher has prepared the ground for a renewed reflection upon the various aspects of the hermeneutical circle. He agreed, of course, with the ancient insight that the whole can only be understood from the parts as indeed the parts can only be understood from the whole. But he went beyond this classical knowledge by pointing out that two related moves are essential in order to respond to the circular nature of our understanding: the divinatory and the comparative. These moves are to happen with respect (1) to a particular text's internal structure, i.e. how we appropriate the overall sense from its parts and how we learn about the parts from a comparison of the linguistic devices in the text, and (2) to the text's relationship with the whole of similar linguistic productions, i.e. how we can grasp a text's sense in the light of similar texts. But Schleiermacher also cautioned us against overrating the comparative move.

> [T]he explanation of words and contents is not in itself interpretation but provides only aspects of interpretation, and hermeneutics only begins with the determination of the sense, though with the help of these aspects.[12]

Thus for Schleiermacher, hermeneutics aims at understanding the sense of a text rather than the context which produced it, though knowledge of the circumstances of a text's production may prove to be helpful in order to focus the interpreter's divinatory faculties. But, as we have seen, all divination must be thoroughly accompanied by grammatical interpretation. Therefore, one must never exclude the grammatical dimension from the hermeneutical circle.

Schleiermacher's hermeneutical thinking represented a revolution in the development of hermeneutics. Once a subdiscipline of theological and literary disciplines, hermeneutics was now presented as a philosophical discipline in its own right and of essential importance for everybody who wished to understand the linguistic expression of another person.

> Since the art of speaking and the art of understanding stand in relation to each other, speaking being only the outer side of thinking, hermeneutics is a part of the art of thinking, and is therefore philosophical.[13]

Though Schleiermacher spoke of 'the still chaotic situation of this discipline',[14] he made an impressive effort to provide a proposal for philosophical hermeneutics as an autonomous discipline which in fact eliminated much of this chaos.

Although no subsequent discussion of philosophical hermeneutics could ignore Schleiermacher's proposals, he has often been misunderstood and incorrectly quoted. This has been so partly because his hermeneutical writings and notes suffered for a long time from poor and inadequate editing, partly because his concepts, especially that of divination, were quite simply misunderstood, and partly because his hermeneutics was considered hostile to a particular version of 'orthodox' theology. More recently however, the importance of his hermeneutical thinking has received more adequate recognition so that the view for a really critical discussion of his proposals is less blurred today.[15] However, before we enter into this discussion, we must see how Schleiermacher dealt with theological hermeneutics, now understood as one of a number of special hermeneutics.

3.1.2 Schleiermacher's Discussion of Theological Hermeneutics

Schleiermacher subordinated theological hermeneutics fully to his general hermeneutical principles. The theologian as interpreter of the Scriptures enjoys no special privileges, rather he is bound by the hermeneutical rules like any other text-interpreter. Therefore, Schleiermacher spent considerable energy refuting the claim that the biblical texts, once they are considered to be inspired by the Holy Spirit, deserve a different set of interpretative rules. He insisted that a '*dogmatic* decision about inspiration cannot be expected because this [decison] rests itself on interpretation'.[16] In other words, that the Sacred Books are sacred one only knows through having understood them.[17] Schleiermacher does, of course, agree that the Sacred Books require also a particular hermeneutics, but he adds that 'the particular can only be understood through the universal',[18] which means that any special hermeneutics rests on the grounds of general hermeneutics.

In his hermeneutical writings Schleiermacher often used illustrations from biblical interpretation in order to clarify his general hermeneutical principles. Thus, he gave a number of hints and examples as to the requirements of a special biblical or theological hermeneutics. However, he himself did not systematically develop such a special hermeneutics, though he did make certain proposals towards such an enterprise.[19] That must not surprise us in view of the fact that Schleiermacher first of all tried to convince his theological colleagues of the need to respect the principles of general hermeneutics. Studying his hermeneutical observations which have emerged during his teaching life we can still see today his eagerness to impress on his audience the need both to abandon any special interpretative authority and to take texts seriously as texts instead of isolating certain passages or verses from them.[20]

In his *Brief Outline on the Study of Theology* of 1810, Schleiermacher addressed once again the relationship between general and specific hermeneutics.[21] He stated that protestant theology could not accept any treatment of the biblical canon which would not submit itself to the validity of the principles of general hermeneutics (§ 134). Only on the basis of these general principles can a special hermeneutics of the New Testament now be developed in relation to the particular character of this canon. Here he thought of the need to balance the treatment of one New Testament text with a treatment of the whole collection of the New Testament (§ 136). With regard to the interpretative task itself, he warned, however, not to build uncritically on the knowledge of individual interpreters. Rather he urged the biblical interpreter to use all available sources of help to improve his craftmanship. The academic task of biblical interpretation is defended here as an essential requirement for any dogmatic conclusion of some validity. For Schleiermacher, in accordance with his hermeneutical principles, this academic task included both the philological aspect (cf. grammatical interpretation) and the aspect of art (cf. divination in psychological or technical interpretation) (§ 148).

3.1.3 Schleiermacher's Impact on the Development of Hermeneutics

By submitting biblical/theological hermeneutics to the principles of general hermeneutics, Schleiermacher diversified the study of hermeneutics. From now on a still uninterrupted tradition of philosophical hermeneutics has emerged. On the one hand, this tradition has been viewed with great suspicion by those biblical hermeneuts who refused to agree with Schleiermacher's acceptance of the validity of general philosophical hermeneutics even for biblical exegesis. On the other hand, those interpreters of the Bible who could agree with Schleiermacher have felt very positively influenced by the now emerging tradition of philosophical hermeneutics.

Before we come back to the requirements of a special theological hermeneutics below in Chapters 6 and 7, we must first reflect upon the development of general or philosophical hermeneutics since Schleiermacher. As we shall see, Schleiermacher's influence on modern hermeneutics has been so strong that we shall have many occasions to come back to some of his far-reaching proposals for a critical hermeneutics, partly in order to commend them for today, partly in order to challenge them from a renewed critical perspective.[22]

3.2 HERMENEUTICS AND THE IDENTITY OF THE HUMAN SCIENCES: WILHELM DILTHEY

3.2.1 The Foundational Function of Hermeneutics for the Humanities

The immediate impact of Schleiermacher's hermeneutics was small. Beyond the circle of his students and friends, Schleiermacher's revolutionary concept of theological hermeneutics and his project for a general hermeneutical theory at first did not find much response. It was not until the end of the nineteenth century that his hermeneutical thoughts were retrieved. This constructive retrieval of Schleiermacher's hermeneutical programme was the work of the philosopher Wilhelm Dilthey (1833–1911). Thus, the theologian Schleiermacher's effort to develop a general philosophical hermeneutics was now promoted by a philosopher who was not particularly concerned about theological hermeneutics, but who was interested in philosophical hermeneutics as such. For the purpose of our book Dilthey's hermeneutical thoughts are very important, because they provide the bridge between Schleiermacher and hermeneutical developments in the twentieth century.

Like Schleiermacher, Dilthey was at home in virtually all the branches of the humanities. Yet unlike Schleiermacher, he experienced the humanities as being endangered by the rise and aggressive self-understanding of the natural sciences who claimed that they alone were able to yield objective insights into nature thanks to their superior methodology. However, Dilthey interpreted the relatively low self-esteem which characterised the humanities in the second half of the last century, not only as the result of the expansive course of the natural sciences, but also as a result of the lack of a critical foundational theory on the part of the humanities themselves. Since by now the attribute of authentic 'academic' progress was dependent on a set of 'objective' methodological criteria, it seemed imperative also for the humanities to develop such a theoretical framework which would guarantee their academic credibility and their scientific identity.

Dilthey defined the respective tasks of the natural sciences and of the humanities in this way: natural sciences aim at *explaining* the natural phenomena, whereas the human sciences aim at *understanding* human life and its complex forms of expression. Of course, both types of research, the sciences and the humanities, may indeed deal with the same phenomena, but they do this from different perspectives and with different methods. Thus, *understanding* is the key term which characterises the task of the humanities.

> We explain by means of purely intellectual processes, but we understand by means of the combined activity of all the mental powers in apprehending. And in understanding we begin by presupposing the connectedness of the whole which presents itself to us as a living reality, in order to grasp the individual in this context. Precisely the fact that we are living in the awareness of this connectedness makes it possible for us to understand a particular sentence, a particular gesture or a particular activity.[23]

Since the task of understanding life-expressions characterises all the humanities, hermeneutics, the theory of the understanding of written records, presents itself as the foundational theory for all the humanities which Dilthey was looking for.[24]

Under the heading 'The Task of a Psychological Foundation of the Humanities', Dilthey explained that the natural sciences must first construct a connection between natural phenomena through a set of conclusions, with the help of a relationship between their hypotheses; whereas the human sciences always find the connection of the psychic [i.e. human] life as originally given. 'We explain nature, but the psychic life we understand.'[25] Life is the datum of the human sciences, it calls for understanding. But first the process of understanding must be clearly understood. And this is the task of hermeneutics.

This description of the task of hermeneutics ultimately points to a very large subject-matter, namely to the understanding of life itself. However, as we have seen already, Dilthey qualified this task by proposing that life as a whole can only be understood through an understanding of the various expressions of life. 'What is given always consists of life-expressions.'[26] In particular the written expressions of human life, the 'works', form the objects to be understood. However, all works are the works of human persons. Thus, the task of understanding finally aims at an understanding of persons, though through their works. But as Schleiermacher did before him, Dilthey adds that 'the final goal of the hermeneutic procedure is to understand the author better than he understood himself; a statement which is the necessary conclusion of the doctrine of unconscious creation'.[27]

3.2.2 Dilthey and Schleiermacher on Hermeneutics

Here, as everywhere in his hermeneutical thoughts, we realise the influence of Schleiermacher on Dilthey. In view of Dilthey's lifelong interest in Schleiermacher this must not surprise us. Dilthey wrote an extensive biography of his hermeneutical predecessor, and as long as he lived he never stopped writing about all sorts of aspects of Schleiermacher's life and work. One could say that besides his effort to provide us with a foundational theory for the human sciences, Dilthey's other major occupation was to understand Schleiermacher and his heritage. But Dilthey's keen interest in Schleiermacher must not lead us into an uncritical reading of Schleiermacher through Dilthey's eyes and concerns, nor should we assume Schleiermacher's and Dilthey's concerns with philosophical hermeneutics to be identical. They clearly overlap, but they also differ.

Both hermeneuts share a strong interest in language, in grasping the structure of the individuality of expressions, in a kind of psychological theory, and in developing a philosophical basis of the human sciences. But in spite of these common features, we must not overlook the fact that Dilthey's thought developed at a very different time from Schleiermacher's. Dilthey and his fellow philosophers wrestled with the problem of temporality, i.e. the problem that no phenomenon and no approach to it can be seriously studied without an awareness of the historicality [*Geschichtlichkeit*] of human life and consciousness.[28] Accordingly, Dilthey invested a lot of energy in the project of a 'Critique of Historical Reason'. The title of this project reminds us of Immanuel Kant's *Critique of Pure Reason* in which Kant tried to analyse the conditions of knowing as such. Dilthey did not reject Kant's work, but he limited its significance to the sphere of the natural sciences alone. However, the human sciences according to Dilthey, needed a different theory of knowledge, i.e. a different epistemology.

In his essay 'The Development of Hermeneutics', written in 1900, Dilthey puts the epistemological question for the humanities like this:

> [W]e must ask if it is possible to study individual human beings and particular forms of human existence scientifically and how this can be done.
>
> This is a question of the greatest significance, for our actions

> always presuppose the understanding of other people and a great deal of human happiness springs from empathy with the mental life of others. Indeed, philology and history rest on the assumption that the understanding of the unique can be made objective. . . . While the systematic human studies derive general laws and comprehensive patterns from the objective apprehension of the unique, they still rest on understanding and interpretation. These disciplines, therefore, like history, depend for their certainty on the possibility of giving general validity to the understanding of the unique. So, from the beginning, we are facing a problem which distinguishes the human studies from the physical sciences.[29]

The clarity of this hermeneutical programme, however, is not matched by a comprehensive analysis of a particular process of understanding, such as, for instance, the reading of a written text. Nevertheless, at various places in his writings, Dilthey offers a number of pertinent insights into the task of hermeneutics which were to be picked up by his hermeneutical successors and to be incorporated in their own particular hermeneutical syntheses. With this lasting significance in mind, I now wish to discuss some of Dilthey's hermeneutical insights in more detail and point to major problems present in his proposals.

3.2.3 Problem and Significance of Dilthey's Hermeneutics

All of Dilthey's valuable insights into hermeneutics must first be understood in the context of his life-philosophy [*Lebensphilosophie*] before we can assess them for our use today. For Dilthey, 'life' referred to the whole of realty about which we can think. As such, it provides both the starting-point for philosophical discourse as well as the goal of thinking. Since it is always larger than scientific analysis, no analytical approach will ever be able to grasp it in its complexity. Of course, not even a hermeneutical approach can ever exhaust the meaning of life. But at least it remains aware of the totality of life, it respects the wholeness of life when it interprets the expressions of it.

Dilthey distinguished between three basic classes of life-expressions. The understanding of these expressions differs according to their class: (1) *Concepts, judgments, larger thought-complexes*. Here 'understanding, focusing entirely on the content which remains identical in every context, is more complete than in relation to any other life-expression'.[30] (2) *Actions*. Like the first class of expressions, 'action, too, separates itself from the background of the context of life and, unless accompanied by an explanation of how circumstances, purposes, means and context of life are linked together in it, allows no comprehensive account of the inner life from which it arose'.[31] (3) The *lived experience* [*Erlebnisausdruck*]. Here, 'a particular relation exists between it, the life from which it sprang, and the understanding to which it gives rise'.[32] This third class of life-expressions contains the classic works of art. They stand truthful in themselves – 'fixed, visible and permanent'. Therefore a methodical and certain understanding becomes possible.[33]

This list underlines Dilthey's idealist tendencies: the best expression of 'life' is that which springs from the hand of a genius. Such congenial expressions are above the suspicion of distortion. While Dilthey sees deception at work in everyday expressions of life, the 'classics' are above such daily problems.

> What springs from the life of the day is subject to the power of its interests. The interpretation of the ephemeral is also determined by the moment. It is terrible that in the struggle of practical interests every expression can be deceptive and its interpretation changed with the change in our situation. But in great works, because some mental content separates itself from its creator, the poet, artist or writer, we enter a sphere where deception ends.[34]

These idealist tendencies are manifest also in Dilthey's description of the different forms of understanding. In this context he speaks of the 'objective mind', that is 'the manifold forms in which what individuals hold in common have objectified themselves in the world of the senses'.[35] This 'objective mind' is the source for our personal development, it functions as the medium through which we understand others, in short one could define it as that spirit or soul which connects everything meaningful in the life of our culture. Here, Dilthey comes very close to Hegel's concept of the unifying Spirit. In their respective efforts of either unifying (Hegel) or grounding (Dilthey) the particularities of human life-expressions, both thinkers transcend their own method of induction. Dilthey speaks of 'an induction from individual life-expressions to the whole context of a life. Its presupposition is knowledge of mental life and its relation to environment and circumstances. As the series of available life-expressions is limited and the underlying context uncertain, only probable conclusions are possible.'[36] Thus for him, 'understanding itself . . . has to be considered as induction'.[37]

There can be no doubt that Dilthey is right that we always relate to phenomena by means of analogical thinking. That is to say that we understand any life-expression in analogy with all of our own past experiences. The result of this analogical character of human understanding is that every interpreter *must* understand a given object somewhat differently. This necessarily different understanding in every act of interpretation gives rise to the phenomenon of interpretative pluralism. But as soon as we define this connectedness of all thinking in such a substantive way as 'objective mind' we have left the realm of inductive possibilities and, indeed, of a productive and critical pluralism in understanding.

Schleiermacher saw in language the channel of human understanding, that which links all efforts of communication, whereas Dilthey attributed more material content to his foundational principle of communication, and as such associated himself in this respect with quite a different philosophical stream. This is surprising, particularly in view of Dilthey's general effort to ground all thinking in a concept of 'life'. But perhaps the lack of conceptual clarity of this very concept is responsible for his occasional lapse into idealist territory.

For the purpose of our report on the development of hermeneutical thinking, Dilthey's problems are of enormous concern, because they reveal how even hermeneutics is not independent of philosophical presuppositions. The very concept of 'understanding' is not free from interests. Here, the example of Dilthey may function as a warning to those people who put all their hopes in the development of one foundational theory for the humanities. Dilthey was certainly right in disclosing the potential of hermeneutics as one necessary ingredient of every effort in the humanities to come to terms with their self-understanding. But Dilthey's mistake was to put all his hopes into hermeneutics as a neutral and scientific basis theory. Richard E. Palmer has aptly characterised Dilthey's dilemma:

> Ironically, from the present vantage point, it is possible to see the extent to which scientific conceptions, and even the historicism that Dilthey strove to overcome, do creep into his conception of the human studies, for his quest for 'objectively valid knowledge'

was itself an expression of the scientific ideal of clean, clear data.[38]

Dilthey's proposal to ground the humanities in a theory of understanding, whereas he saw the natural sciences as grounded in a theory of explanation, is in itself idealist. But this proposal was able to shape many future projects for a philosophical hermeneutics. Only more recently, as we shall see below in our critique of Hans-Georg Gadamer, have 'explanation' and 'understanding' both been taken to be necessary moves in every human effort of coming to terms with any aspect of our universe.

In spite of the necessary criticism of Dilthey's hermeneutics, we must acknowledge that it was he who reintroduced hermeneutical thinking into philosophical discourse and thus influenced many future hermeneuts. As we are going to see now, Dilthey's hermeneutical thought prepared the ground for such significant hermeneutical proposals as those by Martin Heidegger, Hans-Georg Gadamer and Paul Ricœur, and, through these thinkers, has influenced the development of theological method in our time.

3.3 FROM PHILOSOPHICAL HERMENEUTICS TO HERMENEUTICAL PHILOSOPHY: MARTIN HEIDEGGER

The theologian Schleiermacher demanded the development of a philosophical hermeneutics in order to provide theological interpretation with a proper foundational theory. The philosopher Dilthey tried to promote hermeneutics as the foundational theory of all humanities. Thus, since Schleiermacher, hermeneutics has received increasing attention in philosophy: once a subdiscipline of theological thinking, it was now treated as a promising candidate for the role of a foundational theory for the human sciences. Although Dilthey's proposal did not win general approval, Dilthey's recovery of the importance of hermeneutical thinking must be seen as one major influence in Martin Heidegger's hermeneutical philosophy. But there are more influences and impulses which Heidegger (1889–1976) used and transformed in his new philosophical departure, most importantly the work of his teacher Edmund Husserl (1859–1938), the founder of the phenomenological movement.

3.3.1 The Phenomenological Movement and Heidegger

Although the beginnings of the philosophical movement referred to as 'phenomenology' were quite independent from the development of philosophical hermeneutics under Dilthey, the impact of phenomenology on the further career of hermeneutics has been enormous. Therefore we must try to understand some basic features of phenomenology in so far as they have been important for the transformation of hermeneutics under Heidegger, and later also under Gadamer and Ricœur.

3.3.1.1 Edmund Husserl's Phenomenological Programme

Against the increasing positivism in the late nineteenth century, but also to some extent in opposition to the return to Kantian ideas in the movement called Neo-Kantianism, Husserl emphasised the need to free philosophical thinking both from the impositions of all kinds of philosophical systems and from speculation and dogmatism. In his numerous writings, and especially in *Logical Investigations* (1900–01)[39] and *Ideas: General Introduction to Pure Phenomenology* (1913)[40], he propagated a return in philosophy to the things themselves. He understood his programme as a reform of philosophical reflection towards a basic orientation to the phenomena, i.e. the things as they appear to the persons who reflect upon their own intentionality in the act of experiencing these things.

> Through reflection, instead of grasping simply the matter straight-out – the values, goals, and instrumentalities – we grasp the corresponding subjective experiences in which we become 'conscious' of them, in which (in the broadest sense) they 'appear.' For this reason, they are called 'phenomena,' and their most general essential character is to exist as the 'consciousness-of' or 'appearance-of' the specific things, thoughts (judged states of affairs, grounds, conclusions), plans, decisions, hopes, and so forth.[41]

Accordingly, Husserl's programme transcended the problem of a subject-object split by recognising that a grasp of the phenomena was only possible in terms of a co-consciousness which allowed the essence of things themselves to appear. This principal openness was propagated towards all phenomena, and thus obligated the philosophical craft anew to all aspects of the universe. But in addition to this descriptive impetus, phenomenology was understood by Husserl 'as a science which is intended to supply the basic instrument (Organon) for a rigorously scientific philosophy and, in its consequent application, to make possible a methodical reform of all sciences'.[42] Thus, as with Dilthey, here we are confronted once again with a philosophical effort of providing a foundational theory, though now not only for the human sciences, but for all sciences. This evaluation was not the result of an intentional hybris, but arose from Husserl's genuine conviction that only a detailed and laborious attention to phenomena established a secure position from which a truly 'honest' science could start again and again. And that means, of course: 'In the way of true science this path is endless.' Husserl continues:

> Accordingly, phenomenology demands that the phenomenologist foreswear the ideal of a philosophic system and yet as a humble worker in community with others, live for a perennial philosophy [*philosophia perennis*].[43]

Husserl developed two rather complex procedures which were supposed to yield the promised grasp of the purified phenomena. The first was called *epoché* (Greek for 'to hold back'), the second the *eidetic reduction*. *Epoché* describes the attitude of the phenomenologist who stands back from all judgements or involvements in the experiences under review. The *eidetic reduction* is that process in which the phenomenologist frees those strands which every experience (and other things), that can be described in that way, must have, i.e. it frees the essence of this experience. Thus, phenomenology 'speaks of apperceptions, judgements, feelings etc. *as such*, i.e. of that which . . . is theirs a priori. . . . Hence, not psychology, but phenomenology is the foundation of the purely logical (as of all those *vernunftkritischen*) explanations [*Aufklärungen*].'[44] The goal of both procedures was then the 'transition from the factual to the essential form, the *eidos*'.[45]

From our hermeneutical perspective today we are critically aware that Husserl's programme was directed exclusively towards grasping essences outside their worldly context. But since this wordliness is the very basis of all these essences, it cannot simply be bracketed or dissociated from them.[46] Thus, while Husserl freed our attention to the phenomena from all kinds of impositions and distortions, he distorted human understanding by excluding the historical, i.e. spatial, temporal and social contexts of the phenomena from the act of understanding.[47]

3.3.1.2 *Heidegger's Hermeneutical Phenomenology*

Martin Heidegger, for a while Husserl's closest associate, now reintroduced these contextual dimensions into phenomenological thinking. As the title of his programmatic book *Sein und Zeit* [*Being and Time*] (1927) already suggests, Heidegger's goal was not to add to Husserl's *Logical Investigations*, but to offer a fundamentally ontological approach to the meanings of human existence (*Dasein* [literally: being there]) in this universe. 'The essence of *Dasein* lies in its existence.'[48]

However, Heidegger's approach was strongly influenced by Husserl's phenomenology:[49] Heidegger too paid close analytical attention to the most basic phenomena of human existence, such as death, world, being, temporality, etc. But unlike his teacher Husserl, Heidegger understood his analysis of these phenomena not purely in terms of freeing their essential nature as it were from their context, but bringing these essences to light in their context, i.e. as a hermeneutical activity. Hence, Heidegger recognised that any phenomenological analysis which is aware of the historical context both of the phenomena and of the analyst can only be understood as 'interpretation'. Accordingly, Heidegger entitled the first part of his analysis in *Being and Time* (there was no second part to follow) 'The Interpretation of Dasein in Terms of Temporality, and the Explication of Time as the Transcendental Horizon for the Question of Being'.[50]

In *Being and Time*, Heidegger did not only present for the first time a Hermeneutical Philosophy as such, but also offered a number of specific hermeneutical reflections which were to have a significant impact on generations of philosophers and theologians and therefore must be discussed in the context of our narrative of the development of philosophical hermeneutics.

3.3.2 Heidegger's Reflections on Hermeneutics

Our narrative does not provide the occasion for a critical discussion of Heidegger's philosophical hermeneutics. Nevertheless it is important for us to appreciate the context of Heidegger's more specific insights into hermeneutics. In the first section of *Being and Time* Heidegger sets out to analyse the existential conditions of Dasein in this world. After treating both of the basic constitution of Dasein as being-in-the-world and of the existential situation of Dasein's being-with-others, Heidegger discusses the dimension of understanding as one of the existential structures of Dasein. 'Understanding' can mean two things: either the fundamental existential structure of Dasein, or one of many possible modes of knowing. 'Understanding' now used in the first meaning, i.e. as the existential structure of Dasein, emphasises the openness of Dasein towards its own possibilities.

> The kind of Being which Dasein has, as potentiality-for-Being, lies existentially in understanding. Dasein is not something present-at-hand which possesses its competence for something by way of an extra; it is primarily Being-possible.[51]

Here, Heidegger is not interested in reviewing all the kinds of possibilities which Dasein could grasp, rather he wishes to distinguish between two principal possibilities, i.e. that Dasein reaches out to grasp its very own possibility of Being, or not.[52] Hence, understanding can be characterised as 'project' and is either authentic or inauthentic.[53]

The concrete forms in which understanding works out its possibilities Heidegger calls *Auslegung* [interpretation]. However, this act of *Auslegung* of something as something is always based on interest [*Vorhabe*], fore-sight [*Vorsicht*], and pre-apprehension [*Vorgriff*]. Thus it is never free of presuppositions.[54] Heidegger illustrates these insights by pointing to the interpretation of texts: 'If . . . one likes to appeal to what "stands there," then one finds that what "stands there" in the first instance is nothing other than the obvious undiscussed assumption of the person who does the interpreting.'[55]

These reflections allow Heidegger now to advance to a definition of *Sinn* [meaning – better: sense]. '*Sinn* is that in which intelligibility of something is found.'[56] But this intelligibility is always already structured by the pre-judgments of the understanding person. Thus, *Sinn* cannot be discovered outside the human context. Rather, *Sinn* as an existential structure belongs only to Dasein which alone can be either *sinnvoll* [meaningful] or *sinnlos* [meaningless].[57]

Given the necessary pre-structure of all understanding, it follows that understanding is always circular: 'Any interpretation which is to contribute understanding, must already have understood what is to be interpreted.'[58] Heidegger warns us that this circle is not to be regretted, but that it contains the very possibility of knowing:

> In the circle is hidden a positive possibility of the most primordial kind of knowing. To be sure, we genuinely take hold of this possibility only when, in our *Auslegung,* we have understood that our first, last, and constant task is never to allow our interest, fore-sight, and pre-apprehension to be presented to us by fancies and popular conceptions, but rather to make the scientific theme secure by working out these fore-structures in terms of the things themselves.[59]

The final phrase 'in terms of the things themselves' is important for it underlines Heidegger's phenomenological interests. He is not saying that every understanding is adequate, but that every understanding has to be measured against the best grasp of the things themselves, although, of course, nobody can grasp the things outside the rule of pre-judgments, i.e. outside an hermeneutical circle. The question arises then: what constitutes a relatively adequate understanding of something?

3.3.3 Heidegger's Turn to Language

There has been some debate among historians of philosophy whether Heidegger's move to language in his later work represented a move away from his existential hermeneutics or a logical extension of his basic approach to philosophy. There is enough evidence to suggest that Heidegger became indeed very preoccupied with reflection on the essence of language. But surely such a reflection imposes itself on every hermeneutically minded thinker as we have already seen in our discussion of Schleiermacher's hermeneutics. Thus, whether one wishes to read Heidegger's work as a whole or in two parts is not as important for our concern as the realisation that some reflection on the nature of language is essential for any theory of text-interpretation. This realisation, however, does not yet imply that Heidegger's particular discussion of the essence of language is wholly adequate.

In a series of lectures and articles published in the 1950s Heidegger wished to correct the traditional understanding of language as a human instrument for the expression both of inner movements or feelings and of the world-views which guide them.[60] He claimed that this widely-held scientific view of language could never reach the essence of language. Over against this understanding of language, he stated that '[t]he language is essentially neither expression, nor an activity of the human being. The language speaks [*Die Sprache spricht*]'.[61] He detected the purest form of language's speaking in poetic language. Here it is not important to know the biography of the author or the conditions of the original emergence of the poetic work. What counts is the fact that in poetic language, language speaks itself, unfolds its true essence. This true essence lies in language's ability to evoke the nature of things, but in such a way that the painful difference [*Unter-Schied*] between thing and world becomes manifest.[62] Thus, for Heidegger the reflection on language represented the refined key to promote anew his original concern with the essence [*Wesen*] of being.

The essence of language needs the human speaking in order to transmit the call of being. The poetic language appeared to Heidegger to be the truly original manifestation of human language, and ordinary language as its poorer derivate.[63] 'Language speaks. The human being speaks insofar as he or she corresponds to language. The corresponding is listening.'[64] According to Heidegger, thoughtful listening to language was the key for the re-establishing of contact with true or authentic being.

However, we may wish to know what strategies could help us to make sure that our listening is true listening and not a distorted or ideological listening. Moreover, we may ask whether the listening to poetic language alone does in fact present an adequate move to disclose the essence of our being and the being of being. To what extent then does Heidegger's existential, hermeneutical and linguistic reflection, i.e. his macro-hermeneutical theory, promote the development of a critical theory of text-interpretation?

3.3.4 The Significance of Heidegger's Hermeneutical Philosophy

Heidegger's insight into the nature of the hermeneutical circle and into the productive role of pre-judgements for understanding has strenghtened further the interest in hermeneutics in this century. His clarification of the conditions for understanding prepared the ground for an explosion in hermeneutical studies. Once it was accepted that 'what is decisive is not to get out of the circle but to come into it in the right way',[65] hermeneutical procedures and phenomenological analysis could merge into a fruitful methodological programme. This productive symbiosis has influenced not only many Continental European and American philosophers, but also a great number of theologians.

As we shall see in greater detail below (cf. 6.2.3 and 6.3), Heidegger's influence in theology was threefold. (1) His philosophical description of the person's existential possibility to decide for or against an authentic life has motivated Rudolf Bultmann and other theologians to develop new theological programmes in response to this existential situation. (2) His reflections on language gave rise to a second Heidegger-reception in theology which became generally known as 'The New Hermeneutic'. And (3) Heidegger's overall insights into the hermeneutical condition of human beings have influenced the continuing theological reflection on the proper method for biblical interpretation.

However, in order to allow the reader to grasp more fully the impact of Heidegger's hermeneutical achievement in both philosophy and theology, it seems appropriate first to continue the report on the development of philosophical hermeneutics before we attend to the parallel development in theological hermeneutics and the interrelatedness of both movements in Chapter 6.

In the remainder of this chapter we shall discuss Hans-Georg Gadamer's and Paul Ricœur's hermeneutical proposals and point to some important aspects of the continuing debate on hermeneutics in contemporary philosophy.

3.4 TRUTH OR METHOD? HANS-GEORG GADAMER'S HERMENEUTICS

Hans-Georg Gadamer's (born 1900) major work *Wahrheit und Methode* [*Truth and Method*] appeared in 1960. Since then it has provided a challenge and a yardstick, both positively and negatively, for the evaluation of all kinds of hermeneutical reflection in the humanities. In addition Gadamer has published a great number of essays on hermeneutical issues, and therefore can be regarded as the chief spokesperson of philosophical hermeneutics in this century. I shall first offer an introduction to his hermeneutical reflection, and then add some critical observations. I shall concentrate here on the essential strands of his argument since I have dealt with Gadamer's hermeneutics elsewhere in more detail.[66]

3.4.1 Understanding as Human Attitude

Following the phenomenological tradition Gadamer understands his own hermeneutics as a reflection on that which always happens when human beings understand, and not as a methodological programme in itself. In fact, his hermeneutics has a definite anti-methodological nature. Gadamer suspects that the combination of hermeneutical insight and interpretative method would lead towards a purely technical concept of hermeneutics and thus lower it to the level of other modern technologies. Instead he wishes to stress the *philosophical* character of hermeneutics: hermeneutics is interested in promoting human understanding and human self-understanding and as such it must be understood as 'practical philosophy'.[67]

Gadamer analyses human understanding by using the example of text-interpretation. Following Heidegger's insight into the role of pre-judgments in the process of understanding, Gadamer emphasises that the process of text-understanding is always fuelled by the reader's pre-understandings and by his or her interest in participating in the meaning [*Sinn*] of the text. According to Gadamer, the ultimate purpose of text-understanding for a reader is the material agreement with the text; and the aim of understanding is described as the fusion of two horizons, i.e. the horizon of the text and the horizon of the reader:

> Understanding is not to be thought of so much as an action of subjectivity, but as the placing of oneself within a process of tradition, in which past and present are constantly fused. This is what must be expressed in hermeneutical theory, which is far too dominated by the idea of a process, a method.[68]

Gadamer likens this process of understanding to the experience of a game. The reader is like a player who subjects himself to the rules of the game and who will ultimately be directed or 'played' by the game. He allows the game to happen. Accordingly, Gadamer understands his hermeneutical reflection as a reflection upon the conditions of this 'game' to which the persons seeking understanding must subject themselves.[69]

Essential for our understanding of these hermeneutical conditions is the insight into the effective-historical consciousness [*wirkungsgeschichtliches Bewußtsein*]: we approach a text always with a certain set of questions. That means that before we actually understand the text we have already been shaped to some extent by the text's potential to disclose meaning for us. It is through this horizon of expectations, right or wrong, that we enter the process of understanding. In that sense we are always conditioned by the historical reality of communication in which we have experienced how texts can exert a certain influence.

> In the process of understanding there takes place a real fusion of horizons, which means that as the historical horizon is projected, it is simultaneously removed. We described the conscious act of this fusion as the task of the effective-historical consciousness.[70]

According to Gadamer, the structure of this effective-historical consciousness is language. 'Language is the middle ground in which understanding and agreement concerning the object take place between two people.'[71] The particular form in which language mediates between two people could be described as 'conversation'. Of course, the text does not relate to the reader in an active or correcting way. Yet still, it makes sense to liken the process of reading to human conversation in order to highlight the to and fro movement between text and reader. This movement is of course initiated by the reader: 'The text brings an object into language, but the fact that it achieves this is ultimately the work of the interpreter. Both have a share in it.'[72]

Language, however, must not be considerd in purely instrumentalist terms. For Gadamer, as for Heidegger, language is more than a medium of communication. According to Gadamer, the true essence of language appears in the process of communication: 'It is the centre of language alone that, related to the totality of beings, mediates the finite, historical nature of man to himself and to the world.' Thus, he can conclude that 'Being that can be understood is language.'[73] That means that language is the primary place for the disclosure of truth. Truth can happen in the process of understanding linguistic forms, and such an event of truth is for Gadamer the ultimate blessing of the hermeneutical experience.

The hermeneutical experience is then not just one among many other human experiences, but represents the singular opportunity for human beings to approach truth. Because of this nature of the hermeneutical experience, Gadamer claims that hermeneutics as the process of becoming conscious of this experience represents a 'universal aspect' of all philosophy and must not be reduced to being merely the methodological basis for the humanities.[74]

Here Gadamer rejects Dilthey's appreciation of hermeneutics as a foundational theory of the humanities, and instead follows Heidegger's existential interpretation of Dasein. For Gadamer, hermeneutics is the reflection on the phenomenon of human understanding and on its implications for an adequate understanding of the human being. It is, as we have indicated already, a practical philosophy.

Gadamer's reflection on the nature of hermeneutics has advanced significantly the development of philolosophical hermeneutics. Especially his description of effective-historical consciousness and his analysis of the productive role of pre-judgments in the process of understanding have concretised Heidegger's insight into the hermeneutical circle. But many problems have arisen and a number of questions remain unanswered. First of all the question of critique. How can the reader protect him or herself against misunderstandings? What role does tradition play in the process of reading? Why does a text have authority and therefore can demand submission to the tradition it represents? Is the fusion of horizons a happy fusion or could it not at least sometimes be thought of also as a conflict between reader and texts? How does truth manifest itself in the interpretation of texts?[75]

3.4.2 Interpretation and the Problem of Ideology: Jürgen Habermas' Critique of Gadamer's Hermeneutics

According to Gadamer, understanding will always be successful as long as understanding persons are willing to submit themselves to the claims of the text and to enter into the tradition which the text represents. Gadamer's insistence that this kind of hermeneutics ought to be seen as a universal aspect of philosophy has provoked sharp criticism. Especially Jürgen Habermas (born 1929) rejected this universal claim and pointed to the limits of understanding. 'Hermeneutical consciousness is incomplete so long as it has not incorporated into itself reflection on the limit of hermeneutical understanding.'[76] Habermas has been particularly concerned to demonstrate that Gadamer's model of understanding cannot work when ordinary communication is systematically distorted.

> The self-conception of hermeneutics can be shaken only if it becomes apparent that systematically distorted patterns of communication also occur in 'normal' – that is to say, in pathologically inconspicuous-speech. That, however, is true in the case of pseudocommunication, in which a disruption of communication is not recognizable by the parties involved. Only a newcomer to the conversation notices that they misunderstand each other.[77]

Habermas has demanded both a depth-hermeneutics and a theory of communicative competence. The first would need to diagnose forms of systematically distorted communication, and the second could analyse the conditions of non-repressed communicative activity and the ways by which a distorted communicative situation could be tackled.[78]

Once more, Habermas does not deny the numerous values in Gadamer's reflection, but firmly calls into question 'the ontological self-conception of hermeneutics which Gadamer explicates, following Heidegger'.[79]

Gadamer has rejected Habermas' critique and pointed out again that he, Gadamer, had intended only to demonstrate how knowledge could be gained in the hermeneutical process. In this process he could not see forces of repression at work. Instead the submission to the authority of the text and its tradition was an act based on the freedom of the interpreter.[80] However, Gadamer has not satisfied Habermas' call for a critique of all kinds of ideological repression in human communication and for a particular analysis of the role of ideological behaviour in interpretation.

Habermas' critique does not invalidate Gadamer's universalist claim as such, as Paul Ricœur has pointed out, since even a critical or depth-hermeneutics remains a hermeneutics. Therefore, it would seem to be most appropriate to incorporate Habermas' concerns into a revised model of interpretation theory.[81]

3.4.3 The Need for Criteria of Adequate Understanding

Gadamer's concept of the hermeneutical experience is over-optimistic. He always reckons with success in understanding.

Therefore the problem of distorted communication and the question whether the reader really understands a text do not arise for Gadamer. As long as these considerations do not enter the hermeneutical reflection, the fusion of the horizons must appear as a happy process. Yet once the suspicion arises that a reader might misunderstand a text, Gadamer's phenomenological description of the hermeneutical experience proves to be somewhat unsatisfactory. Moreover, his own principal suspicion against all kinds of methodological moves in hermeneutics makes it impossible for him to develop a set of criteria of adequate understanding. Also his effort to rehabilitate the 'ontological' dimension of language beyond the 'instrumentalist' confines of modern linguistic analysis makes him blind to the possibilities which such linguistic procedures provide for a more critical hermeneutical programme.

The title of Gadamer's *magnum opus* should really be 'Truth *or* Method' for he sees a radical conflict between his phenomenological approach to hermeneutics on the one hand and the host of modern methodological proposals for an adequate text-understanding on the other hand. But as we shall see in more detail in the following chapters, there need not be such a radical conflict between these hermeneutical departures. Instead, it would appear to me to be much more promising to combine Gadamer's hermeneutical concept with the critical moves provided by many important theorists of the last two centuries. Only the discussion of methods in text-interpretation allows a really critical test of individual hermeneutical performance without, however, necessarily being hostile towards the more transcendental questions of the hermeneutical experience raised by Gadamer.

Without a critical discussion of what actually happens during the process of the fusion of horizons, this concept remains utterly idealist and open to all sorts of ideological distortions. For example, any fundamentalist reader of the Bible will happily claim that his or her particular fusion of horizons has revealed the truth of the Scriptures and therefore urges all other readers to copy this particular material agreement with the text. As long as such a hermeneutical performance, which at best could be classified as 'monist', is not subjected to a radical criticism of both the horizon of the reader and the supposedly understood horizon of the text (including its authority and the authority of the tradition it incorporates), it remains ideological and misleading. Moreover, any defender of a particular 'tradition' will be able to use Gadamer's hermeneutics in order to stress the authentic value of text-interpretation, namely to confirm (rather than challenge) that 'tradition' (cf. below 7.2) As these examples demonstrate, 'conflict' will more often have to be the key word to describe our actual hermeneutical experience in this world. And the conflict of interpretations would need to be examined in every instance of an important process such as the opening of texts towards the truth, a truth supposedly mediated in this process.

3.5 RETRIEVAL AND SUSPICION: PAUL RICŒUR'S PHILOSOPHICAL HERMENEUTICS

The French philosopher Paul Ricœur (born 1913) has widened the hermeneutical reflection so as to include a discussion of the prevailing *Conflict of Interpretations*, as the title of one of his now famous books on hermeneutics indicates.[82] Ricœur has contributed a series of books and articles to the contemporary reflection on hermeneutics. He too has been influenced by Dilthey, Husserl and Heidegger. But unlike Gadamer, with whom he has often debated hermeneutical issues, Ricœur has welcomed the host of modern methodological proposals as potentially helpful suggestions on the way towards a truly critical concept of hermeneutics. However, he has not lost sight of the more fundamental philosophical implications of hermeneutical reflection. In fact, all his hermeneutical considerations must be seen as necessary 'detours' on his way towards a more comprehensive philosophical grasp of the human situation. While Gadamer has been motivated by a more platonic urge to disclose the truth by harmonising every interpretative act spirited by a like-minded attitude of goodwill, Ricœur has began with a reflection on the phenomenon of existence.

> I am, I think; to exist, for me, is to think; I exist in as much as I think. Since this truth cannot be verified like a fact, nor deduced like a conclusion, it has to posit itself in reflection; its self-positing is reflection; Fichte called this first truth the thetic judgement. Such is our philosophical starting point.[83]

But this point of departure is always already confronted with the problem of interpretation since all such positing demands an understanding of the self and the other. The way of reflection proposed by Ricœur has to come to terms with language because firstly reflection is language, and secondly reflection tries to understand the linguistic manifestations of other selves. Language, however, is always ambiguous. Therefore Ricœur has stressed the need for a theory of interpretation which would allow the interpreter to deal critically with the ambiguous nature of all linguistic events.

We shall first outline Ricœur's theory of text-interpretation as it can be distilled from his many writings on the matter, and then offer our assessment of Ricœur's contribution both to interpretation theory and to a critical theological hermeneutics.

3.5.1 Understanding and Explanation

Gadamer has considered the distance which exists between a contemporary reader and his or her text to be the result of historical alienation and proposed to overcome this distance through acts of renewed participation in the sense of the text. Whereas Gadamer has regretted this distance between a text and its reader, Ricœur has regarded this distance as the very foundation of the hermeneutical act of the reader's appropriation of the text. For Ricœur, the 'hermeneutical function of distanciation' consists in the autonomy which a written text receives at that moment when its author releases it onto the public. An autonomous text calls for new appropriations without obliging these to conform to the possible intentions of the text's author, its original communicative context and its original addressees.

Ricœur calls such an autonomous text a 'work', and thus highlights the fact that a text once it is released represents an independent composition which is open for ever new appropriations. Unlike Gadamer, Ricœur discusses different models of text-appropriation and seeks help in all methodologies related to his own hermeneutical aims, such as formalist, structuralist and Freudian psychoanalytical theories of interpretation. In discussing these theories, Ricœur acknowledges that there is no single interpretative move which could rescue the meaning of the text, but that there are conflicting aims, interests and methods which seek to appropriate the text. There are then radically differing horizons or perspectives through which a text can be approached, and the question arises how contemporary interpreters orientate themselves in this jungle of methodologies, interests and aims. Ricœur rejects any totalitarian claims by the different methodologies, and demands that all methodological proposals must prove their adequacy in the act of interpretation. Structuralist interpretation, for instance, is welcomed as a potentially enriching method of text-interpretation, but structuralism as a philosophical system is rejected because of its ideological implications. As method it might help to explain the structure of the text and thus contribute to the critical process of validating particular acts of reading, whereas as an ideology it inhibits the open and critical examination of a text by excluding the historical dimension from interpretation already before the actual interpretation has even begun.[84]

In accordance with this openness towards explanatory moves in interpretation, Ricœur rejects both Dilthey's separation between 'understanding' as the key concept of the humanities and 'explanation' as the key concept of the natural sciences, and Gadamer's anti-methodological ontological hermeneutics. Instead Ricœur insists that both, understanding and explanation, are necessary steps in every act of interpretation. They must be dialectically related to one another. That new view of the relationship between both moves makes it possible for Ricœur to consider the actual linguistic character of a text as a linguistic event, a task which Gadamer's hermeneutics was never able to accomplish since it viewed a text not in semiotic terms, i.e. as an actual structured semiotic whole, but only in philosophical terms as a semantic potential. Thus, to some extent Gadamer's call that hermeneutics ought to pay more attention to language has been better followed by Ricœur than by Gadamer himself!

The dialectics between understanding and explanation in Ricœur's model of interpretation allows modern hermeneutics for the first time since Schleiermacher to return to an examination of the dimensions of textuality. As we have seen, Gadamer treated texts also as carriers of sense [Sinn], but he never explained how texts actually carry such a sense. Schleiermacher (whom Gadamer considered to be a dated Romantic thinker) had begun to reflect on the problem of the textuality of a text. He described texts as structured wholes composed out of general patterns of language and an individual style.[85]

Only in this century have text-linguists and philosophers resumed and advanced this discussion. We shall treat of text-linguistics in Chapter 4. Here, however, it is important to appreciate that Ricœur, not unlike Schleiermacher, defends a dipolar theory of interpretation and thus provides a connection with the founder of philosophical hermeneutics. Both hermeneuts are aware of (1) the need for a detailed examination of a text's linguistic features which constitutes the 'objective' dimension in the act of interpretation; (2) the need for a thorough examination of the individual interpreter's perspective which constitutes the 'subjective' dimension of interpretation; and (3) that both dimensions are of equal importance in any act of interpretation. Of course, Ricœur's discussion of all three insights is more advanced, but to some extent its principal concerns are already anticipated in Schleiermacher's hermeneutics.

However, in terms of their description of the aims of interpretation Ricœur and Schleiermacher differ radically. In his book *Interpretation Theory* Ricœur defines his interpretative aims in this way:

> The sense of a text is not behind the text, but in front of it. It is not something hidden, but something disclosed. What has to be understood is not the initial situation of discourse, but what points towards a possible world, thanks to the non-ostensive reference of the text. Understanding has less than ever to do with the author and his situation. It seeks to grasp the world-propositions opened up by the reference of the text. To understand a text is to follow its movements from sense to reference: from what it says, to what it talks about. In this process the mediating role played by structural analysis constitutes both the justification of the objective approach and the rectification of the subjective approach to the text.[86]

While Schleiermacher wanted to understand the mind behind the text (when possible even better than that mind understood himself), Ricœur wishes to understand the meaning and the reference of the text itself in always new communicative contexts. Moreover, Ricœur, here following Heidegger, regards text-interpretation as an activity of existential significance. In the process of interpretation texts can open up new existential possibilities, new worlds or new 'modes-of-being-in-the-world'.[87] These modes-of-being are not, as in Gadamer's hermeneutics, gained by a harmonious entering into the horizon of the text, but they are disclosed in critical and self-critical acts of interpretation. We shall come back to this existential dimension of Ricœur's hermeneutics below (cf. 3.5.3).

Ricœur demands that every understanding of a text must always be complemented by acts of explanatory validation or correction. Put in terms of a formula one could sum up Ricœur's interpretation theory as follows:

Initial understanding (or guess) + explanation = critical comprehension

But as we have indicated already, Ricœur's explanatory moves are not limited to structuralist or linguistic analyses and considerations. They also include modes of suspicion following such propagators of modern suspicion as Freud, Marx, and Nietzsche.

Over against Gadamer's uncritical concept of understanding as entering into a tradition, Ricœur advocates the introduction of a critical dimension into the very centre of the hermeneutical experience. He thus agrees with Habermas on the need for a critique of ideologies and of possible systematic distortions of the process of interpretation. Yet unlike Habermas, Ricœur considers this critical dimension as a properly hermeneutical dimension. Understanding and the critique of ideology must penetrate each other.[88] Hence the emancipatory interests of the social sciences and the interests of philosophical hermeneutics to promote a critical retrieval of our human traditions are closely related. 'The moment these two interests become radically separate, then hermeneutics and critique will themselves be no more than . . . ideologies.'[89]

Incorporating the critical concerns of the human sciences, Ricœur's hermeneutics represents a clear advance over against his hermeneutical predecessors from Schleiermacher to Gadamer. Although none of these was explicitly hostile to the possibility of a critical dimension in human understanding, their concepts of understanding focused more on the agreement between text and reader. Only Schleiermacher, in good exegetical tradition, defended the need for a linguistic critique in text-interpretation. Yet of course, the critical concerns of psychology, of cultural anthropology, of the social sciences and of other related disciplines, were to emerge only after Schleiermacher's time. By insisting on the need to include retrieval and suspicion, Ricœur's hermeneutics represents the first effort in hermeneutics to integrate critical concerns into interpretation theory proper. Moreover he has demonstrated that these critical concerns are themselves essentially hermeneutical.[90]

3.5.2 The Conflict of Interpretations

As we have seen, Ricœur's contribution to the development of philosophical hermeneutics has already been very significant. Here we wish to sum up Ricœur's achievement and point out problems and remaining tasks:

(1) He has overcome the idealist confinement of Gadamer's ontological approach to understanding, however, without neglecting the existential-ontological dimension of hermeneutics. For Ricœur ontology describes a necessary goal, but a goal which cannot be reached in our human existence. An always 'broken ontology' is therefore all we can hope to achieve.[91] The circular nature of text-interpretation illustrates the limits of understanding. Without pre-judgements and initial risks the interpreter cannot begin the process of authentic understanding at all. Yet because of this subjective dimension every act of interpretation will be somewhat different. Important for Ricœur is now the introduction of critical checks which impose limits on the act of understanding precisely by testing its presuppositions from the perspective of the text. However, even the retrieval of textual perspectives constitutes an interpretative act. Thus, no single act of text-interpretation can ever yield anything like an 'absolute' ontology.

(2) Ricœur has introduced a strong and comprehensive critical dimension into interpretation theory. Now interpretation includes understanding and a host of explanatory procedures which attempt to validate or correct the initial acts of understanding. Hermeneutics is no longer confined to retrieval, as in Gadamer's concept, but it comprises also suspicion.

(3) Among these explanatory moves which Ricœur has suggested, linguistic considerations rank very highly. For the first time since Schleiermacher, the text as text and the dynamic character of texts begin to be taken seriously again in philosophical hermeneutics. Accordingly, the relationship between reader and text appears as a dynamic process. However, a more detailed description of this dynamic process would be needed in order to allow us to draw more precise conclusions as to how a text can transform its reader in the act of reading. Ricœur has identified the significance of this relationship between linguistic and existential aspects of interpretation theory, but has not yet examined it sufficiently.

(4) Ricœur's concept of the autonomy of texts has opened texts to a multiplicity of new appropriations through reading. But how are

we to assess the emerging pluralism of interpretations? Of course, the critical dimension in Ricœur's hermeneutics attempts to expose any reading as inappropriate which cannot be validated through explanatory moves. But Ricœur does not address the possibilty of conflicting readings which may all be validated by the respective critical moves. This problem will have to interest us throughout the subsequent chapters: what constitutes a legitimate pluralism of readings?

(5) Ricœur distinguishes between the sense of a text and its reference. 'To understand a text is to follow its movements from sense to reference: from what it says to what it talks about.'[92] As I have shown elsewhere in some detail, this distinction seems to me to be misleading. Ricœur limits 'sense' to the purely linguistic level of texts, and sees 'reference' as the actual bridge between the text as sign and the existential meaning of that sign. I understand our interpretative aim as the disclosure of a text's sense through the process of reading. One could say that the text's potential for sense is actualised in the act of reading. 'Sense' in my view already expresses this actualisation (through reading) of the combined referential power of the signs within the text. Precisely through this combination of referential acts within a 'text' a text is formed. Thus, it would seem best to define 'sense' as a quality of texts, but 'meaning' as a quality of those individual linguistic acts which together are able to form a network of references which produces a 'text'. Since every reader will understand the text informed and guided by his or her own personal reading perspective which then is tested through the various explanatory moves, the sense of the text thus emerging will always be shaped according to competence and performance of individual readers. It will refer to their understanding of the universe; therefore one would have to say that the text's sense is its reference, namely its reference to the world of the reader (which it might also transform).[93]

3.5.3 Existential and Theological Dimensions in Ricœur's Hermeneutics

We return now to the beginning of our discussion of Ricœur's hermeneutics. There we have seen that the consideration of interpretation theory was a necessary detour for Ricœur on his way towards a more adequate understanding of human existence in this universe. For Ricœur, the reflection upon this existential condition is not intuition, but rather 'the appropriation of our effort to exist and of our desire to be, through the works which bear witness to that effort and that desire'. This appropriation demands interpretation 'because I cannot grasp the act of existing except in signs scattered in the world. That is why a reflective philosophy must include the results, methods, and presuppositions of all the sciences that try to decipher and interpret the signs of man.'[94] Thus, Ricœur's hermeneutical reflection has always been motivated by existential concerns.

These existential concerns have moved Ricœur also in the direction of religious texts since they often represent very dense reflections on human existence. On a number of occasions, Ricœur has examined the possible worlds which religious texts are willing to disclose in the act of reading.[95] Although we shall come back to theological hermeneutics later (cf. Chapters 6 and 7), it is of great interest for us here to point to this theological dimension in contemporary philosophical hermeneutics. Our narrative of the history of philosophical hermeneutics began with a theologian, Friedrich Schleiermacher, who discovered that theological interpretation needed a thorough foundation in philosophical hermeneutics. Now the development of philosophical hermeneutics by Ricœur has revealed the need to include the interpretation of religious texts in an adequate human existential reflection. The symmetry between the theological endeavours of Schleiermacher and the philosophical enterprise of Ricœur is striking!

3.6 CONCLUSION

In this chapter we have reported and commented on the development of philosophical hermeneutics from Schleiermacher through Dilthey, Husserl, Heidegger, Gadamer, Habermas to Ricœur. At last, it seems that Ricœur's interpretation theory has provided the kind of philosophical hermeneutics which Friedrich Schleiermacher had called for nearly two centuries ago. But some questions and problems remain, especially the problem of a proper theory of text and reading. Therefore, we shall have to examine now in the following chapters (a) how Ricœur's theory can be modified and (b) to what extent such a critical hermeneutics could transform theological thinking.

4
The Written Text

4.0 INTRODUCTION

In Chapters 2 and 3 we have studied developments in theological and philosophical hermeneutics. Before we resume the discussion of the more recent career of theological hermeneutics, and particularly of its response to the developments in philosophical hermeneutics, we must clarify our own position in hermeneutics in order to outline the horizon from which we shall review the different positions in twentieth century theological hermeneutics. The best way to prepare ourselves for this critical assessment of contemporary theological hermeneutics seems to me to be a systematic discussion of the two poles of all interpretative activity, i.e. of text and interpretation. Such a systematic consideration will also provide us with an opportunity for discussing in more detail a number of issues which in our historical overview have been identified as vital for any hermeneutical programme. In this chapter we shall concentrate on text-linguistics and on its implications for interpretation theory, and in Chapter 5 we shall discuss important features of a theory of reading.

Here we begin our systematic consideration with a study of the nature of the written text and of the demands which this makes on the interpreter of the text. As we work out a theory of text we must be aware that we know texts only through our acts of writing and reading. These experiences of production and reception teach us that texts are never static, but dynamic entities. Texts come to life only when people become involved in them. A proper text-theory can therefore not be developed without due regard to this personal involvement of people in the production and reception of texts.

In oral communication we are generally quite aware of the dynamic nature of texts, as we are engaged in producing our texts in conversation with other text-producers and as we are listening to other texts. Here our voices, ears and even our eyes (which discern gestures) play a supportive role. However, while in oral communication the main channels are the hearing and sound-producing instruments of our body, in written communication these immediate facilities of speaking and reacting are not available. Here we can neither emphasise words as effectively as we can in oral communication through different shades of intonation, nor can we grasp messages through the sensitivity of ears trained to detect the slightest voice-variation and its possible significance in a particular conversational context in which we are present with our entire body. Nor can we clarify problems or emerging issues as immediately as is possible in oral communication.

However, it would be wrong to consider writing and reading merely as the second-best mode of human communication to be employed only in such situations where speaking and listening are not possible for whatever reason. Rather writing and reading are not the last resort in which people may take refuge either because they wish to overcome geographical separation or because they do not wish to face one another directly. Instead writing and reading ought to be appreciated as distinct modes of communication offering their own unique opportunities.

In this chapter we shall explore these unique opportunities. Although oral discourse is not the concern of this book, occasionally, for the sake of clarification and illustration, we shall draw parallels between written and oral communication.

The following questions shall help us to focus on our subject-matter 'the written text'. What makes a text a 'text'? Is a text the sum of its sentences or is it something more? What distinguishes one text from another? For instance, what distinguishes a novel from a poem? Both kinds of texts are 'texts', yet they differ in terms of their particular textuality. It appears that we employ certain textual models in order to express specific concerns. However, while using such models of textualisation we contribute to their continuous development. This dialectical relationship between textual models and their individual application will also occupy our attention in this chapter.

But before we begin our investigation into the particularities of the textuality of texts, we need to remind ourselves once more that we look at texts from the perspective of the user. How do we use texts in order to communicate something to somebody (text-production) and in order to learn something from somebody (text-reception)? The concern of the present chapter differs from that of the next in that here we shall reflect upon the communicative possibilities of texts in general, whereas in Chapter 5 we shall examine how we as readers may respond appropriately to the challenges of texts. We begin our analysis of the written text by considering the implications of 'writing' for human communication.

4.1 WRITING

There are many reasons for writing. Students take notes in order not to forget the main points made in lectures. Somebody may write to a friend to inform her about a recent personal experience. Every appliance which we aquire for our household carries a written instruction with it which tells us how to operate the appliance correctly. Such a leaflet may be particularly useful if we have failed to locate an experienced salesperson who could have instructed us orally. Here writing may indeed be a last resort after oral communication has failed. There are texts written to special people, such as the letter to a friend, and there are texts composed for an unknown readership, such as works of literature. Accordingly we may distinguish between private and public texts, while recognising, however, that in principle every text could become public even though it may have been written for a strictly limited readership. Therefore most contemporary societies have laws protecting the right to private communication. But no such law will ultimately be able to guarantee that private texts may never be read in public, since texts by virtue of their written nature are in principle accessible to every competent reader.

A written text can have a life of its own as soon as it is produced and released from the author's hand or word-processor, whereas an oral text usually dies in a certain sense after it has been uttered and received. More recently, however, the development of audio-visual instruments has allowed for the recording of oral statements, and has thus added new ways of 'inscribing' language. However, these new modes of preserving oral texts do not annihilate the basic difference between speaking and writing.

Writing is a conscious act of producing language for a distant audience. Speaking is usually addressed to a more specific and present audience. Writing ultimately aims at letting a text go into a mostly unknown future. Hence, writing represents always an act of 'distanciation', i.e. the author of a text has composed a piece of structured language in his or her personal style and lets it go to readers who will have to decode this structured linguistic whole. In order to do so these readers will have to be competent and willing to operate this decoding competence as well as their imagination and reading style. Every reader who appropriates a text by using these strategies makes the formerly alien text now his or her own.[1]

It is obvious that this process of appropriation must fail whenever readers are either unable or unwilling (1) to decode the linguistic signs which make a text and (2) to appreciate the particular structure with the help of which these signs have been ordered. Yet even more interesting for hermeneutics than the possibility of a radical failure of this decoding process are the following questions. Can any reader ever *fully* understand a complex text and what constitutes such a 'full' understanding? And do all readers of the same text understand it in the same way? However, before addressing these questions in Chapter 5, it is necessary for us first to familiarise ourselves with yet some further implications of writing.

Under 'writing' we understand the act through which an author expresses a text. This text, once it has been released by its author, may unfold its own dynamic life now outside the circumstances of its production. It may, for instance, reach readers for whom it was not originally intended. It may provoke readings which differ in some degree from the readings which the author had in mind while producing the text. We all are aware that we may still be able to read texts whose authors, whose original contexts and addressees we do not know. For example, nobody knows the exact circumstances out of which many of the biblical books emerged. Yet these texts are being read even today because they continue to promise a most stimulating reading experience.

Though it might be interesting for some readers in particular circumstances to know about the author of a text, such a knowledge is by no means always essential for an appropriate understanding of the text. The obsession to understand the author of a text first before addressing one's questions to the text is a rather recent phenomenon which may have to do with the rise of the individual consciousness since the Enlightenment.

In order to illustrate this point we may look at the *Gospel of John*. Nobody has any independent information about the author(s) of this New Testament text. We do not know who the author was, his or her name and backround still remain a mystery. But even without such information the reading of this Gospel does make sense to us today. Hence, texts can be read independently from their original conditions of production. Texts can function autonomously. Obviously the reading of some texts may benefit from such additional (extra-textual) information about the history of a text's production, whereas other texts, especially literary texts, are designed to convey their meaning to readers on the strength of their own communicative potential independent of its original circumstances.

The text's potential for disclosing its meaning to a succession of new readers is in fact one of the main attractions of literary forms of expression. A poem, for instance, begins its journey as an independent bearer of its own meaning to an unknown number of readers as soon as it is released by its author. From this moment of 'distanciation' from its creator onwards, the poem comes to life mainly through the energy given to it by its readers. They alone disclose its meaning. Even the poem's author can no longer claim any special prerogative of understanding the text better in virtue of having produced it. At the moment of distanciation, the poem has become a 'work' on its own; and its author becomes just another possible reader. From now on, every appropriation of the poem must find its authentication in the text and not behind it.

All interpretations of literary works which wish to be called 'adequate' (in terms of how they understand the texts themselves) must be faithful to the texts themselves and not to any extra-textual authority, such as 'I understand Samuel Beckett's texts better because I am his cousin or because I am studying at Trinity College Dublin where Beckett himself was once a student'. While any such circumstantial knowledge may be of help to a biographer of Samuel Beckett, it is not needed in order to appropriate the actual texts with some degree of adequacy. As now independent potentials of literary meaning, Beckett's texts solicit careful reading by the reader in order to free their meaning. Should no reader wish to disclose these texts, they remain only black ink on white paper.

Of course, literary texts as indeed all other kinds of texts may also function as documents. In such a capacity they will be able to point the historically minded reader of Beckett's texts back either to Beckett's life and working conditions or to the general period of history from which they have emerged. Similarly, John's

Gospel may be read as a document of one particular early Christian community, since it reveals many insights into the life and religious concerns of such a group of Christians. However, the question remains whether such an historical reading of a literary or biblical text will lead us to as adequate as possible a disclosure of the text's own communicative intentions.

A telling example of the futility of such a search for authorial assistance in interpretation is Beckett's elegant answer to the naïve question which was put to him about the truth of his play *Waiting for Godot*: 'If I knew it I would say it.'[2] Thus, interpreters of this play will have to concentrate anew on the text of the play instead of searching for hints in the life of the author or in his own secondary remarks.

However, not all written texts are literary texts. While instructions accompanying electrical appliances also function as independent texts, their authors remain accountable in the event of an error in the text of the instruction with possible tragic consequences for the users of the appliances. Here the authors remain responsible for providing a text which is clear and unambiguous.

Biblical texts constitute yet another category of texts. Although at present it seems to be fashionable to regard the New Testament texts either as predominantly literary texts or as merely historical documents, these texts transcend any such monistic classification.[3] They combine the features of both of these categories with their theological intentions. More accurately, their literary and historical features are coordinated by their theological intentions. Accordingly, any adequate interpretation of biblical texts will have to include due consideration of all these features, as we shall see in more detail in Chapter 5 when we discuss how reading perspectives are shaped by the text.

In the context of 'writing', however, it is important that we distinguish different kinds of texts according to their particular 'text-genre'. Producers of texts will always choose a particular text-genre according to the primary communicative perspective and function which their text is to perform in the universe of readers. Readers of texts will always have to identify the genre of the text (from the text itself) in order to understand the text with some degree of adequacy.

Yet before we pursue this aspect of text-theory any further we must ask the even more fundamental question: what makes a text a 'text', what is a 'text'?[4]

4.2 WHAT IS A 'TEXT'?

A text is more than the sum of its words or sentences. A text is a meaningful whole, a structured whole. Of course, in special circumstances even a single word may function as a meaningful whole. We might think of the function of traffic signs in this context. Here the single word 'Danger' does function as a small but powerful communicative entity containing a host of meanings. So, if one wishes, one can define 'text' as a structured whole of meaning which consists of at least one word. But usually our written texts are made of a number of sentences which are connected with one another. The connection is generally organised on three levels at once. Firstly, we expect texts to be characterised by a thematic [or semantic] progression; in other words we expect that a text pursues one theme or a couple of related themes.[5] Secondly, we expect texts to express this thematic unity through grammatical [or syntactical] devices, such as pronominal substitution.

> Example: *The mother came home at 5PM. She saw her children playing in the livingroom.*
>
> In this minitext, the second sentence substitutes 'the mother' through the pronoun 'she', and thus establishes a thematic unity.

Thirdly, we recognise written texts as texts also because of such a simple fact as this that a flow of black ink on paper comes to a halt, or that the book which we read has no more pages.

Thus, every text is organised on three different levels at once: on the level of meaning, of grammar and of printing. The three subdisciplines of linguistics dealing with these levels of organisation are named as follows:

> SEMANTICS studies the meaning of words and texts.
> SYNTACTICS studies the connections between words and sentences.
> PRAGMATICS studies the external conditions of linguistic communication.

The difference between the meaning of one single sentence and the meaning of a text is caused by the different systems of structure and reference operative in each of these linguistic entities. A *SENTENCE* usually consists of a subject and of a predicate. Both can be enlarged and thus further qualified by attributes etc., but the principal structure remains the same for all sentences. The precise extension of a printed English sentence is normally recognised because of the capitalisation of the first word of a sentence and because of the full stop after its last word. But most importantly, the meaning of a printed sentence is ultimately characterised by its reference within the wider system of meaning and reference, namely that of the *TEXT*.

In the context of our discussion of Ricœur's hermeneutics (cf. above 3.5.2) we have already defined what we understand by 'meaning', 'reference' and 'sense'. Accordingly a sentence in a text functions within the communicative structure of that text, while the reference of the entire text is directed towards some kind of reality outside the text in the world of the reader. This reference of the text to at least one aspect of the reader's world we called the 'sense' of the text. Hence, we can say that the reference of a text is its sense, whereas a sentence refers always to the textual whole. The sense of the text is what the interpreter ultimately wishes to disclose in the process of reading.

While the pragmatic dimension of textuality defines the actual extension of a text, it is the combination of syntactic and semantic dimensions which produces the communicative dynamics of the text in the process of reading. A single sentence has no real dynamics. It is a straightforward statement. Of course, it can refer to a past, a present or a future time within the context of the text, but in itself it always remains a static entity. But a text is different: it contains a development of communication, of different communicative perspectives, of confirmations, and of qualifications and negations which may challenge the statements offered in each individual sentence. As such the sense of the text transcends all individual statements out of which it has been composed.

The Latin noun *textus* and the verb *texere* refer to the act of weaving. As the sum of threads woven into a carpet transcends the individual threads and creates a new identity, so our sentences are woven into a new textual identity. But unlike the carpet, a verbal text does not offer a total picture. Rather the sense of the text is a mental entity which needs to be recomposed by every reader in the act of reading following the instructions contained in the text itself. Moreover, unlike the carpet's colourful visual identity, the text's identity exists only in the mind and memory of each of its readers and is unavoidably coloured by the imaginative powers of each of its readers. Thus, pictures have a somewhat more stable identity than written texts, because they offer a more stable potential for sense, whereas the text's sense is in itself a dynamic identity, an identity in process.

But this is not to say that the sense of a written text is a mysterious message somewhere *behind the text*. Rather it is, in Paul Ricœur's words, *in front of the text*: it is what the text itself conveys to the reader in the act of reading.[6]

In the light of our analysis of the dynamic nature of textual sense we may conclude that every text structures the act of reading in particular ways. Particular conventions or norms of how to weave a text help the author to produce the text for a particular occasion or with a particular function in mind. These conventions or norms will then be taken into account by the discerning reader. However, these norms and conventions of text-production offer only general guidelines to an author who then needs to adapt them to meet the specific requirements of his or her communicative intentions. This phenomenon of choosing a communicative norm and of adapting it to the specific communicative intentions we call *style*.

Having seen that every text is a structured whole, we shall now examine the extent to which a text is structured normatively on the one hand, and individually on the other.

4.3 GENRE AND STYLE IN TEXT-PRODUCTION

4.3.1 Genre

At first sight, we recognise a novel not only because of its length but also because of its particular narrative form. We recognise a poem not only because of the particular way in which it might be printed but also because of the particular rhythm which distinguishes all lyric from prose. We recognise a letter not only because it arrives in an envelope with a stamp attached to it but also because of its particular opening and closing rituals. These three examples illustrate how easily we identify particular *genres* of textual discourse.

When we wish to express ourselves in speech or writing we choose the genre of our expression very carefully because much of the initial reception of our text which normally structures the process of reading will depend on our choice of genre.

Verbal communication in all human societies is highly structured according to specific social norms or conventions which have been developed throughout the history of each society. The primary purpose of such norms and conventions is to facilitate communication. Accordingly, genres of writing indicate to the reader the major function of texts and thus help the reader to select appropriate modes of reading, i.e. appropriate 'genres of reading'. In Chapter 5 we shall discuss to what extent not only our writing but also our reading is structured according to such social norms and conventions.

When, for example, a reader opens a letter which begins as follows:

> *Sir, you are summoned to appear in court . . .*

he or she will immediately grasp that this text is neither a fairy-tale nor a love letter, but a legal text which requires serious and immediate reading and possibly speedy reaction. When, however, a letter begins like this:

> *My dear friend, it is a long time since we have heard from each other . . .*

the reader will quickly spot that the four pages which follow are likely to narrate the circumstances which have been causing the delay in communication in a writer who is well known to the reader; and the reader will have to decide with which degree of urgency the ensuing text ought to be read and reacted to.

Text-genres may, however, at times be deceptive. Finding a personal letter under your door, you expect it to be from a friend, but upon opening it you discover that some business operation has chosen to deceive you in this way in order to attract your attention for a few precious moments to a new product which otherwise you would not consider.

Occasionally literary authors use the device of a misleading genre in order to achieve a particular reaction in their readership or audience. For instance, Beckett's *Waiting for Godot* is staged as a drama so that the members of the audience in a theatre might expect a drama along the lines of the well-known conventions of classical drama: its usual five acts, its well-ordered development of action on the stage etc. Yet to their great surprise or shock the spectators are confronted with four bizarre figures on the stage who are involved only in pseudo-communication and who are not producing any kind of coherent action or development. Hence, this drama in two acts does not keep its conventional promise. Instead the two acts are more or less identical, and nothing at all happens on the stage in terms of plot or character development. The thus-negated genre of theatrical expression is perceived by the audience with confusion because they are unable to develop an appropriate perspective for the successful reception of this 'drama'. Their expectation is proven to be absurd. Eugène Ionesco, Wolfgang Hildesheimer, Thomas Bernhard and other authors of 'Absurd Theatre' have used similar deception techniques in order to demonstrate to the reader or viewer that their expectations of an ordered and meaningful development of sense are unjustified in the present world. This experience of frustration creates the recognition that life may be absurd.

Another example of genre deception is the use of 'pseudepigraphy' in antiquity in general and in the New Testament in particular. Pseudepigraphy means that a text was published intentionally under the name of an author who had not produced it. We know that some letters which claim the Apostle Paul as author do in fact originate from the hand of other authors. Such authorial claims were not uncommon in Graeco-Roman culture and were understood as an indication that a text should be read in a particular tradition or school of writing.[7]

On the whole we do trust the functioning of genres in our communication, and we use genres as we have been learning to do since our earliest childhood in order to achieve the intended results in communication. The effect of an intentional misuse of genre in the way illustrated above is in itself a sign of the normal efficiency of genres of writing. But as the examples of genre deception also show, genres are only as normative as we allow them to be. They are the result of communicative conventions, and thus by themselves they do not have any lasting authority. Moreover, we always have to adapt them to our particular communicative needs; that means we use them according to our own style.

4.3.2 Style

Everybody who writes adopts and adapts genres of writing, but according to his or her individual context and in his or her personal manner. When I write a letter to a close friend I am likely to begin my text with a more personal greeting than when I write to the Internal Revenue Commissioners. Thus, within the genre 'letter' I have a number of choices as to the general tone of the letter. This phenomenon of choice of expression we have already defined as 'style'.

The English word 'style' is derived from the Latin word *stilus* which refers to the instrument of writing, such as a pen or a pencil. Thus, even according to its origins, the word 'style' points to an individual activity of writing. Today, however, 'style' is often used to refer to the ornamentation of texts or works of art. In this usage the word has lost its original reference to the whole act of writing. Therefore, I wish to propose that we use 'style' again in the wider sense: style is the phenomenon of individual choice in the acts of text-production and text-reception. It refers to the individual application of such communicative norms as genres of writing, and correspondingly also to genres of reading.[8]

The process of composing a letter, a poem, a song or a novel contains in fact many choices: the choice of words, of syntax, of paragraph length, of headings and sub-headings, of colour of ink, kind of paper, etc. What, for instance, different novels have in common is a matter of genre, what distinguishes them is a matter of style.[9] Hence, we may define 'style' even more precisely as 'the principle of individuation'.

Of course, even our stylistic decisions are influenced by the stylistic conventions of our linguistic traditions. Thus, our choice of linguistic expression is always conditioned, though not determined, by our cultural horizon. Were it determined it could never happen that certain writers revolutionise the style of a whole epoch through their particular choices of expression. A 'period-style' is born whenever people happen to express themselves in a similar manner. We can also speak of the 'personal style' of a particular author when her or his texts witness to some continuity in modes of personal expression. Nevertheless, stylistic conventions or norms are always transitory because every member of a linguistic community may adapt these norms or conventions according to his or her particular needs and thus contribute to the transformation of these conventional modes of expression. Every creative use of language promotes stylistic change.

At times, the need for new ways of expression becomes so strong that a mere transformation of style will no longer be sufficient. Then a new genre of expression may need to be created in order to allow for the realisation of new communicative perspectives.

A good example of such an occasion is the birth of the genre 'gospel' in early Christianity. The newness of the experience of God's activity and presence in Jesus of Nazareth's life, death and resurrection led to a linguistic explosion of genre and style. The gospels constituted a new genre of writing because of particular communicative needs; and this new genre has been, and continues to be, a successful communicative device.[10] The fourfold realisation of that same genre 'gospel' in the New Testament demonstrates the effect of particular stylistic needs and activities in the respective communities. Thus, no genre ever exists as pure possibility, rather it is always already realised individually and concretely in a text.

The example of the gospels may also illustrate the fact that, although new needs for expression will give rise to new forms of expression, even these new genres must employ a sufficient measure of conventional forms in order to hope to achieve their communicative purpose for the reader and thus to be understood as new forms of expression. No reader can be expected to relate 'adequately' to some totally new form of expression. The various literary subforms within the gospels, such as genealogy, ordinary reporting, legends, narrative, parable etc., were all known to the reader of the time. We perceive new forms only when they both use and alter already established conventions. That again means that no communication can operate successfully on new ways of expression alone.

The consideration of the interplay between genre and style has provided us with the basic framework of text-production. However, we have not yet explored text-production in terms of how we actually shape specific genres. This leads us to the question of textual strategies.

4.4 TEXTUAL STRATEGIES

Textual strategies are those procedures which guide the process of text-formation. In our linguistic tradition we can observe four main kinds of textual strategies: narration, argument, description, and instruction. These strategies are rarely used in isolation. In most cases our text-production requires a combination of two or more of them.[11]

An *instruction* for an electrical appliance makes sense only when it also *describes* carefully which part of the appliance is to be fitted where. A letter of apology to a teacher not only *narrates* the story of the pupil's accident, but *argues* also that special medical treatment will require the pupil to be absent from school for another week.

The principal function of a text dictates to its producer the choice and possible combination of textual strategies. Other textual elements will then be chosen accordingly. For the reader it will be important to recognise the text's major communicative strategy in order to disclose the text's sense appropriately while being guided by an adequate reading perspective. On the whole, this overall communicative strategy of a text becomes clear to the reader as soon as he or she grasps the particular genre of the text.

For example, the pragmatic dimensions of reading, i.e. the discovery that a text is very long and contains a certain progressive order of communication, together with a first discernment of the strategy of such a text as narrative, would suggest immediately that we are confronted with a work of fiction or of historical writing, such as a 'novel' or a 'biography'.

After such a basic recognition, the reader will be able to concentrate on the concrete development of the text's sense. That means the reader will have an initial grasp of a perspective which allows him or her to follow the communicative dynamics of the text. Formally speaking, this textual dynamics is structured by the main perspective of the text and the respective strategies which together direct the semantic and syntactic texture of the text. Whether this initial grasp proves to be correct or requires modification will become clear only during the further process of reading.

As we shall see in greater detail in Chapter 5, it is not always easy to discover the network and order of perspectives in a text. Yet the process of reading can work successfully only when the reader does structure his or her reading through some organisation of perspectives. Hence, the concern for adequate reading is largely a concern for the grasp and subsequent use of the most adequate reading perspectives. These reading perspectives can only be called adequate when they correspond to the text's own communicative perspectives. If they do not the text will be misread.

4.5 CONCLUSION

In order to recognise the textuality of texts it is essential that we appreciate the communicative potential of every text and also its sophisticated perspectival structure. One major communicative perspective determines the composition of a text, i.e. the choice of genre, of textual strategies, and of all other semantic, syntactic and pragmatic features of the text.

How all of these features are working to form a structured whole, a text, which provokes reading, how the reader grasps the sense of the text, and what may happen to a reader in the act of reading will be our concerns in Chapter 5.

However, already in this chapter it should have become clear how essential these text-linguistical considerations are for the development of an adequate text-hermeneutics. For far too long hermeneuts have not appreciated the necessity of engaging in such formalist discussions while claiming at the same time to have the answers to all interpretative questions. Ricœur deserves much credit for rediscovering the need to take linguistic procedures seriously for the first time since Schleiermacher. Everybody interested in hermeneutics ought to welcome the insights into our communicative praxis offered by formalists, structuralists and text-linguists.

In this chapter we have shown that 'text' is one of the two essential categories of any text-hermeneutics. The other category is 'reading' or 'interpretation'.

5

The Transformative Power of Reading

5.0 INTRODUCTION

This chapter should be understood as the complement to the previous one. There we considered various aspects of writing. Here we are going to discuss the dimensions of reading and the implications of reading for our human self-understanding. As in Chapter 4, our discussion of reading will require a few conceptual and technical clarifications. Reading is an interpretative activity. In terms of its clarification I would like to define all acts of reading as interpretative acts, though there are obviously interpretative acts other than reading, for instance the reception of pictorial works of art. But on the basis of this clarification I shall use 'reading' and 'text-interpretation' synonymously.

5.1 THE DIALECTIC OF TEXT AND READING

Reading is first of all an act of communication in which a given set of written signs is decoded; as such it is always an act of response to a prior act of writing. Already at the beginning of Chapter 4 we wondered to what extent a reader can hope to understand a text through reading. In order to find an answer to this question, after having studied the conditions of writing and the strategies available to authors of texts, we need to attend to the conditions of reading and to the strategies available to readers of written texts.

Schleiermacher described understanding as an 'art'. Similarly reading as one particular form of understanding could be described as an art. Such a description may highlight the fact that we are dealing here not only with a purely technical process whose requirements one could learn to master and subsequently apply at any moment. Rather in addition to the mechanical skill of decoding the signs out of which a written text is made, the reader needs to be able to relate imaginatively to the sense of the text. But, as we shall see, according to their particular genre, texts require different measures of imagination from their readers.

The sense of a text emerges only when the reader re-creates it out of the wealth of meanings assembled in the text. This creative dimension of reading is captured when we call reading an art. However, it would be misleading to overemphasise the artistic dimension of reading and to take the mechanical dimension of reading for granted. First of all, the latter dimension represents the foundation of all understanding of texts, and secondly, any reconstruction of textual sense must be validated in the text and thus requires from the reader a thorough competence in lexical and syntactical decoding.

A phenomenological description of the act of reading seems to be called for in the context of theological interpretation in order to retrieve the general dimensions of reading before allowing the particularly theological imagination to enter the process of text-interpretation. Such a phenomenological treatment of reading then may free theological interpreters to realise anew their dependence on ordinary means of human communication. Moreover, the recognition of this dependence urges the critical theologian to participate in the discussion of theories of reading. Theology must have a lively interest in this particular discussion, otherwise its dealings with texts would be guided by unreflected and possibly inadequate theories of reading. Therefore, most of this chapter is devoted to an examination of such theories.

However, before approaching these theories it is essential that we recall from our examination of text-theories that texts and reading can only be approached 'dialectically'. That means that we can never study the phenomenon of reading without giving due consideration to the nature of texts; nor can we study texts without discussing theories of reading since any approach to texts is always guided, consciously or not, by such theories. In order to stress this dialectical relationship between text and reading, I shall name the dimensions of reading in accordance with the names which I have given to the dimensions of writing. Thus, as I have distinguished between 'genres' and 'styles' in text-production, I shall also distinguish between 'genres' and 'styles' in text-reception. Text-production and text-reception are determined by both conventional patterns and individual intentions and perspectives.

As we have seen in Chapter 4, a text-genre individually applied by the text's author and the particular way of structuring the text determines the production of a text. Likewise, the act of reading is guided by a genre of reading. This reading-genre is shaped by an individual style and motivated by the particular expectations which the text-genre has provoked in the reader. The act of reading then must not be seen to be propelled by mere subjective motivations. Rather these motivations are at least to some extent already responses to the text's own provocation. Although we will have to study this subjective element of reading more closely, it should already be clear from our discussion of philosophical hermeneutics in Chapter 3 that a purely objective reading is as impossible as a purely subjective reading. Therefore, the question which a theory of reading needs to address is this: under which conditions may a particular act of reading be called 'successful' or 'adequate'.

5.2 THE SPECTRUM OF CONTEMPORARY THEORIES OF READING

Here we cannot discuss in detail the various contributions to the continuing debate on reading. Rather, I wish to provide some orientation by exposing the major issues in this debate.

5.2.1 Determinism and Relativism in Reading

E. D. Hirsch's theory marks the one pole in this debate, Roland Barthes' proposal the other. According to Hirsch's objectivist theory of interpretation, the verbal meaning is determinate, it never changes.[1] The reader, therefore, must be concerned to decode the text with a view to grasping and stating its clearly determined original meaning. Hirsch does not leave room for the individual reader's imagination or suspicion during the act of reading. Rather against 'intuitism', 'positivism', 'perspectivism', Heidegger's hermeneutics, and Barthes' analysis of the pleasure of reading, he defends the objective accessibility of verbal meaning.[2] He imagines the task of interpretation as the establishment of 'an interpretive hypothesis'.

> An interpretive hypothesis is ultimately a probability judgment that is supported by evidence. Normally it is compounded of numerous subhypotheses (i.e. constructions of individual words and phrases) which are also probability judgments supported by evidence. Hence, the objectivity of interpretation as a discipline depends upon our being able to make an objectively grounded choice between two disparate probability judgments on the basis of the common evidence which supports them.[3]

Hirsch is adamant to point out that an author's original meaning can never change. What may change is a text's significance, but not its meaning.[4] For Hirsch textual meaning seems to be exactly the same as any other linguistic meaning, i.e. the meaning of a word or sentence. The qualitative difference between a text on the one hand and a word or sentence on the other completely escapes his attention.[5] Thus, he frequently refers to the act of representation in a sentence as example for the construction of textual meaning. But as we have seen in Chapter 4, texts are much more complex structures of meaning in which different strategies of linguistic concatenation operate. As a result, different receptive strategies are required when we are interpreting textual meaning (or sense) than when we are interpreting the meaning of an individual word or sentence.

On the other side of the hermeneutical spectrum, Roland Barthes (1915–1980) diagnosed an endless space for the reader's imagination. He encourages the reader initially to deal with the text as an object of pleasure. 'Pleasure is a critical principle.'[6] But he then examined the instability of pleasure and proposed to treat of texts in terms of the bliss which they evoke in the reader. He used sexual images to point to the blissful and orgiastic character of the meeting between the erotic reader and the text.

> *Pleasure of the text*. The pleasure of the text can be defined by praxis (without any danger of repression): the time and place of reading: house, countryside, near mealtime, the lamp, family where it should be, i.e. close but not too close . . . This pleasure can be *spoken*: whence criticism.
> *Texts of pleasure*. Pleasure in pieces; language in pieces; culture in pieces. Such texts are perverse in that they are outside any imaginable finality – *even that of pleasure* . . . No alibi stands up, nothing is reconstituted, nothing recuperated. The text of bliss is absolutely intransitive.[7]

However, Barthes' interest in interpretation theory must be seen in the context of his overall critique of forms of cultural expression. As a semiologist, i.e. an analyst of signs of whatever nature, Barthes devoted his critical attention not only to linguistic communication, but also to such expressions as fashion and photography. His critical eye was always keen to expose hidden structures operative in the expression of cultural signs. Thus, unlike Hirsch, Barthes analysed also the dark side of language. In one of his last writings he described language as 'fascist'.[8] 'As soon as it is uttered, even in the deepest interior of the subject, language enters into the service of a power.'[9] Strictly speaking, then, Barthes did not advance a programmatic theory of reading, rather he offered a critical description of reading and tried to expose its often hiden assumptions and aspirations.

Both Hirsch and Barthes have contributed to our understanding of the process of reading. On the one hand, every reader who seriously wishes to grasp a text's sense will agree with Hirsch to the extent that one ought to search for a determinate sense [Hirsch speaks of the 'meaning' of a text], but will disagree that a complex literary text will release one and the same identical sense or meaning to different readers. Thus, the issue at stake in the debate with Hirsch's objectivism is not that a diligent reader ought to look for a determinate meaning, but whether or not such a meaning can be identified once and for all. On the other hand, Barthes stressed the role of critical imagination in the process of reading and vividly illustrated the nature of the pluralism in text-interpretation. The question we have to put to this and any related theory, then, is not whether or not critique and imagination are necessary in acts of reading, but whether or not we have to reckon with a total relativism of imaginative readings which alone satisfy the critical and the bliss seeking individual.[10]

Such a relativism would mean, for instance, that a community which sees itself based on a particular text or set of texts could not hope ever to experience an identity through interpreting these writings. Rather these writings would create an ever increasing Babel for their readers.[11] Hirsch's total determinacy of a written text would provide such a central focus for a community, but at the cost of destroying any serious subjective engagement on the part of the reader during the act of reading and thus excluding the possibility of a pluralism of readings altogether. Moreover, both of these theories of reading distort the dialectic between text and reading in some way: Hirsch denies the productive role of reading, Barthes limits the effect of the actual text on the reader by raising the imagination of the reader, i.e. the experience of bliss, over the text. Moreover, two very different functions of reading appear here. Hirsch values reading as a search for a hidden meaning, Barthes critically examines reading as a search for pleasure, and ultimately bliss. We shall have to come back to the diversity of functions and genres of reading later in this chapter (cf. below 5.3.3).

Of course, both types of reading theories have found a number of followers who share their respective promises. Thus, for example, for those theologians who wish to proclaim the inerrancy of Scripture or of papal statements, a theory like Hirsch's will represent an ideal vehicle. For those theologians who propagate a radical individualism in biblical interpretation, a theory like Barthes' may offer some support. However, for those theologians who search for ways of understanding the dialectic between text and reader and its implications for the community of Christians that searches for some form of focus through biblical interpretation, neither model seems satisfactory. Rather a dialectical understanding of text and reading calls for a different kind of reading theory. In this respect the proposals made by two very closely related contemporary movements seem to promise more help: one is generally referred to as 'reader-response criticism', and the other is called 'theory of aesthetic effect'.

5.2.2 Theory of Aesthetic Effect and Reader-Response Criticism

Both of these clusters of theories aim at attending to the texts themselves rather than to the objectivist (cf. Hirsch) or subjectivist (cf. Barthes) impositions on the texts by respective interpreters. Thus, unlike Barthes and Hirsch, the representatives of the two movements in reception theory, inspired by the phenomenological tradition, are interested first of all in examining what a text does to its readers, i.e. what effect the text exerts on the reader in the act of reading. Understandably, these theories are also keen to study the entire communicative situation in which texts are read, but they focus primarily on the way the text discloses its communicative potential to the reader during the act of its reception.

Wolfgang Iser, a prominent propagator of the theory of aesthetic effect, sees the disclosure of meaning in a literary text as a combined effort of both text and reader.[12] For Iser the text does not yet represent a definite sense, rather it depends on the reader for the production of such a sense. Thus, since the reader in a way could be said to be always already 'implied' in a literary text, Iser can speak of 'the implied reader'.[13] The text provides the actual reader with a set of signals, gaps and other incomplete qualities which in turn provoke the reader's imagination and participation.

While Iser spends much time studying these mechanisms present in the literary (or fictional) text itself, the representatives of reader-response criticism focus more on the reader's reaction to the text and on the social conditions for such reactions, without, however, losing sight of the demands of the text itself.[14] In spite of these variations of focus, both movements have contributed much to a better understanding of the basic dialectic between text and reading: Iser and his colleagues[15] have helped us to see how the text promotes this dialectical movement in the act of reading, while the promoters of reader-response criticism could show how the reader responds to the text's own invitation to participate in its disclosure.

Both of these reflections on reading have been influenced by the phenomenological movement in philosophy and its insights into the method of examining the phenomena of human life in general and of human communication in particular (cf. above 3.3.1).[16] Thus, in a sense we could say that Husserl is also god-father of these phenomenological studies.

In the context of our discussion it is especially important to combine the phenomenological insights into the processes of reading and writing with the philosophical examination of the process of human understanding which we have outlined in Chapter 3. This combination of philosophical reflection and detailed phenomenological examination seems to me to provide us with a very solid foundation for an adequate theory of text-interpretation. But before we attempt to present such a theory and reflect on its significance for human self-understanding we ought to comment on some other developments of great importance for any consideration of writing and reading.

5.2.3 Structuralism, Post-structuralism and Formalism

It is Paul Ricœur's great achievement to have included structuralist analysis into his interpretation theory. As we have seen (cf. above 3.5.1), Ricœur has welcomed the insights of structuralism into human communication while at the same time rejecting the philosophical claims of structuralism as an attitude or *Weltanschauung*. For Ricœur, the structuralist study of human writing could contribute to those explanatory measures which he has demanded from every responsible interpreter, so as to provide a critical test of his or her initial understanding of the text's sense.[17]

At this point of our discussion we should return to *structuralism* in order to assess how its further development should influence our hermeneutical programme. Here we cannot provide a detailed study of the structuralist movement with its many sub-directions and concerns. Such concise studies are already available.[18] But we need to indicate in what way structuralist thinking is important for our hermeneutical project.

The structuralist movement began with the Swiss linguist Ferdinand de Saussure's (1857–1913) thought. After his death, the sum of his work was published as *Course in General Linguistics* (1916 [English translation only 1959]).[19] Over against the then predominant historical interest in language, the diachronic perspective of linguistic research, de Saussure favoured an examination of the systemic features of language, i.e. the systematic or synchronic perspective.

Thus, the structuralist movement must be credited with the retrieval of general linguistic problems and concerns. As we have seen in our report on the development of philosophical hermeneutics, Schleiermacher was the first modern hermeneut to reflect upon general linguistics and its importance for hermeneutics. His interpretation theory was based equally on grammatical interpretation and psychological interpretation. Also his reflections on text and style document his intention to ground his hermeneutical programme on a thorough investigation of linguistic procedures. But these linguistic concerns were not promoted by his successors in hermeneutics.[20] Only in response to the structuralist programme did Paul Ricœur in his hermeneutics return to linguistic topics. And as we know from our report on the development of theological hermeneutics in Chapter 2, Augustine already insisted that a thorough theory of text-interpretation must be firmly grounded on general linguistic observations. His semiotic analysis represents in a way a first synchronic study of language, while his philological analysis aimed at bridging the historical gap between different generations of linguistic performance (cf. above 2.2.3).

De Saussure's distinction between language as system, *langue*, and language as performance, *parole,* can be seen then also as a significant development of older insights. Nevertheless, the new emphasis on *'langue'* promoted the modern study of semiotics. Like Augustine, de Saussure distinguished between the phonetic or acoustic aspect of a sign and the semantic aspect, i.e. what a sign means. The first aspect he named the *signifiant* [signifier], the second aspect the *signifié* [signified]. This last distinction allowed de Saussure to draw attention to the arbitrariness of our linguistic signs. While Augustine held that all signs point to a thing (*res*), he overlooked that a language as a semiotic system includes signs whose primary function is to link with other signs. Structuralists therefore argue that we do not order our language according to our semantic needs, but that we are always already structured by the particular way in which our language as linguistic system works. The need for a structure is universal, but not the given structure itself. There are many linguistic structures operative in the world of human communication. One must compare them without judging one to be better than another.[21]

Looking at a sign from the perspective of its systemic context, i.e. how it functions in the semiotic system of a particular language, de Saussure can define it in terms of its difference, i.e. what it is not:

> *In the language itself, there are only differences.* Even more important than that is the fact that, although in general a difference presupposes positive terms between which the difference holds, in a language there are only differences, *and no positive terms.* Whether we take the signification or the signal, the language includes neither ideas nor sounds existing prior to the linguistic system, but only conceptual and phonetic differences arising out of that system. In a sign, what matters more than any idea or sound associated with it is what other signs surround it.[22]

This analysis of a sign points to the fact that every sign has its semiotic and semantic value only in the context of a system of signs. The semantic dependence on the context has been known by some of the Church Fathers as we have seen. But the semiotic dependence on the system has been discovered and analysed only since de Saussure. This insight into the sign's semiotic dependence on the system has inevitably led to a relativistic view of linguistic expressions. For on the basis of this insight there cannot be such a thing as an absolute, i.e. context-free, linguistic meaning. Similarly, as the Danish linguist Louis Hjelmslev put it, there is no universal structure or formation, but only the universal principle of linguistic formation.[23]

This semiotic relativity is of great importance for hermeneutics, since both the process of text-production and the process of text-reception are dependent on semiotic systems.

One of the main targets of structuralist reflection was the interpretation of literary texts. Here it could particularly undermine 'the naïve but endemic view that literature, like other art-forms, is essentially self-expression, because of its insistence that one "self" may be mediated to another only by means of a common, objective system of signs.'[24] Over against this traditional treatment of literary texts, structuralists propagated an immanent mode of interpretation. That means before we attend to the possibility of a text's external references we should attend very closely to the text's internal way of generating meaning. The text constitutes its own semiotic and semantic system within the linguistic system of a particular culture.

Here the concerns of structuralists meet with those of the *Formalist Movements* in Eastern and Central Europe. The formalists too wanted to rehabilitate the particular text as the primary object of interpretation. Their strong interests in the mode in which a text as text produces meaning has advanced the theory of text-linguistics which we have studied in some detail in Chapter 4. Precisely because the formalists have known that texts can be made to function somewhat differently in different contexts, they wanted to find out whether texts have a potential for meaning prior to such functions. The Prague Formalist Jan Mukařovský identified a host of functions in which a text can be read.[25] He discussed a number of functions, such as the communicative, the religious, and the aesthetic. He concluded that these functions are usually organised in a hierarchical way.[26] According to our terminology, we would rather speak here of 'genres of reading'. Many such genres are possible, but which ones are adequate in a given act of reading? Can we develop criteria of adequacy? Can we appeal to any extra-textual criteria for guidance in our search?

The representatives of the so-called *post-structuralist movement* of more recent years, for instance Jacques Derrida (born 1930) and Michel Foucault (1926–84), have stressed the need for a proper study of the text. 'There is nothing outside of the text.'[27] All texts point to themselves and one another, but not to some presence beyond. This self-referential nature of all texts invalidates classical metaphysical theories and philosophical ontologies. Texts are all we have. According to Derrida, the creation and retrieval of meaning ought to be seen as a never ending process in which meanings and systems are always by necessity fluid. 'The absence of the transcendental signified extends the domain and the play of signification infinitely.'[28] However, Derrida insists that 'we cannot give up this metaphysical complicity without also giving up the critique we are directing against this complicity'.[29]

But since we cannot appeal to any semantic authority outside the text, post-structuralists point to the necessarily inter-textual nature of interpretation. We understand one text because we differentiate it from other texts. Hence, the differential system of sounds and words studied by de Saussure and structuralist linguistics has now been transposed onto the level of texts. But at the same time the notion of 'text' has shifted.[30] A text is no longer a clearly confined, but a fluid, phenomenon.

> Since each text becomes itself in relation to other texts, no text is self-contained. . . . There can no more be a text-in-itself than there can be independent signifiers. Texts, like the signs which comprise them, ceaselessly cross and criss-cross in a perpetual process of interweaving. As a result of this oscillating interplay, texts are neither stable nor static, but are transitory.[31]

Derrida's importance for interpretation theory lies in his radical challenge to extra-textual foundations for reading written texts, and closely related to this, in his rehabilitation of writing as a semiotic activity in its own right, no longer judged to be only the second best form of linguistic communication. In written language, he argues, there is no presence, there is only movement of differences. As a result, Derrida feels compelled to deconstruct all those myths of presence in the Western tradition. Even structuralism depended on the myth of presence, i.e. the presence of a structure according to which a text had to be read. Thus, structuralism, too, operated teleologically, i.e. moved by an extra-textual goal.[32] Yet Derrida's deconstruction goes even further. By insisting that language itself is the real locus of meaning, he deconstructs all assumptions of presence in the subject, and hence challenges the traditional assumptions of the very nature of the reading subject.[33] It is not only the text which emerges from Derrida's thought as a new and fluid entity, but also the reader. Not only theories such as reader-response criticism would not survive Derrida's approach untransformed, but much of the hermeneutical tradition which we have outlined in this book would emerge as a creation myth of a subject full of illusions about itself. Ultimately, Derrida envisages a general or universal 'text' of which all written texts are only traces. But this general text never appears as such, instead it disappears.[34]

If we were to subscribe fully to Derrida's theory we would need to announce the end of traditional theological hermeneutics at this point and bring our discussion to a close. But instead I suggest that we assess the foundations of Derrida's own anti-foundationalist theories. Charles Taylor has strongly criticised the 'poverty' of Derrida's position. 'Nothing emerges from this flux worth affirming, and so what in fact comes to be celebrated is the deconstructing power itself, the prodigious power of subjectivity to undo all the potential allegiances which might bind it; pure untrammelled freedom.'[35] Yet as we have seen Derrida has not advocated a kind of textual nothingness, rather he has criticised the limitations of the traditional concept of text. Thus, it would seem to me important to take Derrida's critique of the traditional hermeneutical assumptions more seriously, though not to the point of abandoning text-interpretation altogether. One of Derrida's main contributions to hermeneutics lies precisely in his powerful warning against any form of absolutist or authoritarian reading of texts.

We may learn from Derrida, then, to appreciate the difference between speaking and writing, and thus concentrate anew on the interpretative possibilities which a text's semantic autonomy entails. And we may agree with him that a naïve linguistic positivism, i.e. the belief in the successful process of signification from words to things, needs to be challenged. But we realise that our human communication, oral as well as written discourse, is based on the shared expectation of all of its participants that some form of meaning can be expressed and is, in fact, expressed and communicated. Thus, the more concrete expectation of some readers to find existential meaning or sense in the act of reading also seems justified. Of course, after Derrida's deconstruction job is done, no meaning or sense disclosed in an act of reading can claim any longer to be validated by any uncritical appeal to a metaphysical authority. But the search for *possible* meaning does not need to die with the end of traditional metaphysics. Nor does the search for tentative ontologies and preliminary metaphysical formulations. Moreover, the insight into the social nature of language and its acquisition points to a larger context for text-production and text-reception, and hence for hermeneutics. In other words, I am saying that we ought to respect the critical intentions in Derrida's work without, however, subscribing to his proclamation that the end of possible meaning – emerging from the reading of individual texts – has come.[36]

Similarly, we ought to be grateful to Michel Foucault for his insistent reminder that texts and readings may represent instances of oppression. In order to expose the authoritarian claims of cultural expressions Foucault set out to explore their origins. His 'archaeological' work can be described as an 'ethnology of our rationality, of our discourse'.[37] Such a critical enterprise provides diagnostics and therapy for any interpretation theory.[38] Thus it represents a necessary dimension of hermeneutics, rather than the dissolution of hermeneutics.

So far we have concentrated mostly on linguistic considerations. But at this stage we should have become aware that even language itself can be studied as one among many phenomena of human existence. Post-structuralism has shown us that we cannot hope ever to achieve a determinate meaning or lasting act of signification, and thus it has exposed the fragility of all meaning emerging from human communicative activity as well as the fragility of the reading self. Paul Ricœur has repeatedly pointed to Freud, Marx and Nietzsche as masters of suspicion who have undermined the certainty of the writer and interpreter by problematising the psychological, socio-political and cultural conditions of human communication. More recently, the feminist movement challenged even more radically the traditionally patriarchal context of text-interpretation, and of Western thinking in general. To these wider considerations I must return before being in a position to attempt to formulate a coherent hermeneutical programme.

5.2.4 Reading as Socio-political, Psychological and Cultural Activity

It is certainly correct that the primary ambition of structuralist and formalist linguistics has been to study the texts synchronically as sub-systems of linguistic systems. But within the wider structuralist movement we find also studies which focus on the phenomenon of culture which includes, but also transcends, purely linguistic concerns. Culture is discussed as a social system, and even the unity of all cultural systems is considered. The most famous representative of this branch of structuralism, usually referred to as 'structuralist anthropology', is Claude Lévi-Strauss (born 1908). This branch of structuralism aims at understanding the phenomenon of culture, and thus shows close affinities with both the phenomenological movement and hermeneutical thinking. It is therefore imperative to include the concerns of structuralist anthropology in any examination of contributions to the project of hermeneutics. However, such an inclusive treatment of structuralist concerns in hermeneutics remains critical of structuralist ideology. Following Lévi-Strauss, text-hermeneutics must try to understand its task in this wider context of culture. Texts are products of culture and contribute to its transformation. Therefore they will have to be considered in this natural context, and not only as autonomous linguistic systems or purely self-referential entities. But Lévi-Strauss' proposal to understand all creations of a culture as fully determined by the rules of the cultural system must, of course, be rejected on the basis of our insight into the creativity of both the writer and the reader within a communicative situation. Thus, in spite of opening our horizon to cultural considerations, Lévi-Strauss destroys the dialectical movement between culture and its products in favour of a cultural determinism.[39]

The exposition and subsequent rejection of this ideological aspect of structuralist analysis also teaches us that critical hermeneutics must remain sensitive towards any effort in our world of communication which tries to determine either the production or the reception of cultural products such as texts and works of art. The civil, economic and clerical power structures not only in those still existing totalitarian societies but also in the so-called free world, represent a massive threat to the free unfolding of the process of communicative and hermeneutical activity. Censorship is not a phenomenon of a distant past, rather it manifests itself in often very subtle forms. For example, in the West the actual publication of literary texts, such as Salman Rushdie's *Satanic Verses*, or of theological texts, such as Hans Küng's *Infallible?*, could no longer be prohibited today as they were in the past. Nevertheless even in the West the process of reception of such texts has been profoundly influenced by the respective power groups interested in controlling the texts' effective history. Threatening an author with death or with the withdrawal of his or her teaching licence are still contemporary ways of interfering in the hermeneutical process.[40]

In view of such interference it is essential for hermeneuts to reflect upon the power structures operative in the communicative situation in which they consider and propose certain models of understanding. Therefore hermeneuts are indebted in particular to thinkers such as Michel Foucault and Jürgen Habermas who have attempted to analyse the socio-political conditions of interpretation today.

As we have indicated already above (cf. 3.4.2), Habermas has paid particular attention to the problems of distortion in communication and to the requirements for a non-repressive communication. He has also examined possible criteria of communicative competence. His work is of great importance for hermeneutical inquiry because it emphasises the need to investigate the actual conditions of communication and to establish a list of necessary conditions for a type of human communicative praxis which one can justifiably call 'emancipatory'.[41] According to Habermas, only such a continuous reflection on the conditions of human communication can ensure the possibility of constructive social and existential transformation, that which in the Enlightenment would have been called 'progress'. Hence Habermas ought to be appreciated as an advocate both of critical enlightenment and of a liberating and emancipatory human progress through non-repressed communicative action.

Michel Foucault's approach to communicative praxis past and present is characterised by a more negative perspective. He has diagnosed an almost ontological repression in human discourse. Every discourse aims to influence, to win and to subject the communicative 'partner'. Therefore all 'partners' in communication ought to be seen as potential victims. Foucault attempted a structural analysis of the various conditions and intentions of communicative oppression. He saw a need to investigate the individual communicative structures without presupposing an implicit metaphysical continuity which would suggest that each such structure could be understood from the historical continuum out of which it has arisen. The presupposition of such a continuity is itself the result of a particular interest in viewing human life, an interest which Foucault wished to expose and dismantle. 'We want historians to confirm our belief that the present rests upon profound intentions and immutable necessities. But the true historical sense confirms our existence among countless lost events, without a landmark or a point of reference.'[42] The writing of history, he argued, results from a kind of conspiracy of those who exert power and authority. 'It is no longer a question of judging the past in the name of the present, but of risking the destruction of the subject who seeks knowledge in the endless deployment of the will to knowledge.'[43]

Both thinkers, Foucault and Habermas, have provided us with important insights into the politics of communication. Foucault's achievement lies more in the effort to make us sensitive to the misuses which operate in cultural hermeneutics, and especially in historiography [the writing of history]. Habermas' merit lies in his proposal of criteria for a non-repressive communication. However, Habermas and Foucault contradict one another on one crucial point. While Foucault saw a structural evil in all human communication and in its historically mediated identity, Habermas continues to believe in the principle of the emancipatory nature of human communication and in the potential of therapy. He has proposed, as we have seen, a depth-hermeneutics. Foucault proposed no method of retrieval, instead he advocated the most radical suspicion. For him 'power' had assumed the position of a foundationalist concept which directed his critical analysis of human reason and communication.[44]

In the context of examining cultural influences on reading it is important to pay particular attention to the feminist contribution to hermeneutics. Recent feminist hermeneutics has not only examined the patriarchal power structure which has been operative in traditional theology and biblical interpretation,[45] nor does it add just one other dimension to the ongoing post-modern deconstruction of the Cartesian self.[46] Rather feminists such as Julia Kristeva challenge some of the aspects of the very critique of traditional hermeneutics itself as put forward by Derrida and fellow post-modernists. Kristeva is committed to the liberating praxis of psychoanalysis, and therefore interested in examining how analysis could lead to successful therapy. In view of these aims, she rejects Derrida's purely negative concept of truth. 'Relativizing all notions of truth, deconstruction cannot account for the experience of truth in analysis.'[47] It is significant that this kind of feminist critique reintroduces the political dimension into the post-structuralist and the post-modernist debates and thus reminds their respective participants that the praxis of liberation makes urgent demands on the hermeneutical discussion and focusses it anew on the questions of communicative praxis, interpretative accountability and ethics.

Such an orientation on the demands of liberating praxis has also been characteristic for Marxist theoreticians such as Terry Eagleton. He has reminded us of the social nature of our communicative existence. On the basis of his insights into the social nature of all linguistic production and reception he has levelled strong criticisms against Husserl's pure phenomenology and against Heidegger's hermeneutical philosophy. 'How I can possibly come to possess meanings without already having a language is a question which Husserl's system is incapable of answering.'[48] And he attacks Heidegger for his failure 'to overturn the static, eternal truths of Husserl and the Western metaphysical tradition by historicizing them. All he does instead is set up a different kind of metaphysical entity – *Dasein* itself. His work represents a flight from history as much as an encounter with it; and the same can be said of the fascism with which he flirted.'[49] In fact, Eagleton is very critical of the entire hermeneutical discussion of this century for its failure to reflect upon the social context of communicative activity. According to him any form of pure literary theory is nothing other than an 'academic myth'.[50] Every theory of reading is already political, whether its representatives like it or not. The question is, however, which ideological path it follows. 'The idea that there are "non-political" forms of criticism is simply a myth which furthers certain political uses of literature all the more effectively.'[51] Eagleton himself generally favours a socialist programme with the particular emphasis on liberating strategies. 'Any method or theory which will contribute to the strategic goal of human emancipation, the production of "better people" through the socialist transformation of society, is acceptable.'[52] And on this basis he is prepared to welcome the 'valuable insights' of structuralism, semiotics, psychoanalysis, deconstruction, and reception theory, and to condemn other hermeneutical approaches.[53]

Eagleton is, of course, right to emphasise the social nature of human communication and to define the liberating praxis as a desirable goal of reading. The question is, however, if his own strategic programme is the only possible alternative to traditional critical hermeneutics which he rejects so forcefully.[54]

It is interesting to observe that Eagleton does not treat of Ricœur's hermeneutics. He thus misses the opportunity to link his own social and emancipatory concerns with the critical but constructive retrieval of the great hermeneutical tradition of the West. Ricœur's hermeneutical model which we have discussed already in Chapter 3 is open both to retrieval and suspicion, yet combines both moves in a thoroughly constructive manner. It is emancipatory in the sense that it wishes to promote real understanding and subsequent transformation, and it is radically suspicious of all kinds of distortions which threaten to undermine the hermeneutical process. Ricœur devoted an entire book and many essays to the need for such suspicion. In his *De l'Interprétation: Essai sur Freud* [the English translation reverses title and subtitle: *Freud and Philosophy: An Essay on Interpretation*] and in a number of related articles, Ricœur examined the role of the masters of suspicion, i.e. Marx, Nietzsche, and especially Freud, for the process of interpretation.[55] His particular concern in this regard was to demonstrate the problems of the interpreting self. The traditional view, for instance of Descartes and his followers, has been that the subject can be presupposed not only as the given, but also as the secure point from which a process of thinking can unfold. However, the masters of suspicion, but particularly Freud, could show that such an anthropological constant cannot be taken for granted. Instead, Freud exposed the various substructures of the human ego as a highly complex and unstable, and thus most unreliable starting-point for reflective processes. Following Freud's awareness of this problematic nature of the human self, though not always Freud's method, Ricœur postulates that hermeneutical reflection must also be necessarily a process of self-reflection since the human self cannot be taken any longer as a secure point of departure for human reflection and text-interpretation. Ricœur's observation, then, makes it necessary to consider reading now also as an existential activity.

5.2.5 Reading as Existential Activity

Reading, i.e. the disclosure of the sense of texts, is one of the interpretative activities through which the human being can gain some awareness of himself or herself. A reader who truly aims at understanding a text must open himself or herself to it. Only then can the text unveil the existential possibilities which it may entail, and only then can the text transform the self of the reader. Reading leads then to a double disclosure, namely the disclosure of the text's sense and at the same time the disclosure of 'new modes of being in the world', the revelation of new modes of self-understanding.

> [W]e must say that the subjectivity of the reader is no less held in suspense, no less potentialised, than the very world which the text unfolds . . . . in reading, I 'unrealise myself'. Reading introduces me to imaginative variations of the ego. The metamorphosis of the world in play is also the playful metamorphosis of the *ego*.
>
> In the idea of the 'imaginative variations of the ego', I see the most fundamental possibility for a critique of the illusions of the subject.[56]

Reading has a transformative power. It may transform our understanding of the world and, at the same time, our understanding of ourselves, the readers. However, transformation is also an ambiguous concept. Therefore strategies of suspicion are essential in order to review the nature of the transformation affected during the act of reading. As we have seen, Ricœur, Habermas, Foucault and others have discussed such strategies. But their discussion is restricted to possible structural and systematic distortions of reading. The ethical problem of attending to a text and disclosing its sense has not been reflected adequately by these philosophers. Questions such as these have not been asked: should I as a reader allow every text to transform my self-understanding and my understanding of the world? At what stage in the process of interpretation should the critique of the text begin?

Acts of reading do not happen in a social, political, psychological, cultural or existential vacuum, nor do they occur in an ethical vacuum. Hence, we need to reflect upon possible criteria for an ethics of reading. Such criteria are not meant to limit the reader, but rather they ought to be able to help the readers in their assessment (a) of the text, (b) of their own reading performance, and (c) of the conditions of communication in which text and reader meet.

When we now try to formulate our own hermeneutical proposal we have to pay special attention to this ethical dimension. Elsewhere I have tried to develop a hermeneutical programme which, though following Gadamer and Ricœur in its principal approach, takes account of this need for an ethical dimension in interpretation theory.[57] Here I wish to sum up my previous argument and carry it further.

5.3 TEXT-INTERPRETATION: A METHODOLOGICAL PROPOSAL

5.3.1 The Problem of the Starting-Point

At various stages of our discussion of the development of theological and philosophical hermeneutics we have become aware of the need to clarify what we mean by 'understanding a text'. Neither concept, 'understanding' and 'text', can be taken as clearly defined by ordinary language and therefore call for some further reflection.

Particularly since the seventeenth century the very basis of our interpretative activity has been shattered. The emerging modern world-view does not know any longer the security which previous generations of interpreters could presuppose as long as the Aristotelian world-view was intact. Moreover, the Cartesian retreat to the human self as the starting-point for the interpretation now of both the texts and the horizon of the interpreter itself has proved illusory. Ever since Freud we know that the self is itself a fragile and unreliable construction. As a result hermeneutical activity has become even more complex. Interpreting a text involves now at least simultaneously a threefold act of interpretation: interpretation of the text, interpretation of the world of the interpreter, and interpretation of the self of the interpreter. Each one of these three aspects of interpretation needs to be discussed further.

The first aspect, *the interpretation of the text*, could mean a number of things, as we have emphasised earlier in this chapter. It could mean that a reader wishes to understand the author behind the text (cf. Schleiermacher). It could mean that a reader wishes to understand the structure of the text (cf. the structuralist interpretation). It could mean that a reader wishes to understand the effect of the text on a community of readers (cf. Gadamer and the theory of aesthetic effect). It could mean that a reader wishes to understand the effect of a text on the understanding of understanding (cf. Post-structuralism). It could mean that a reader wishes to understand how the understanding of a text promotes the programme of human emancipation and liberation from all kinds of oppression (cf. political, social, and feminist criticism). It could mean that a reader wishes to understand the history of the text, i.e. how it was composed, handed on, received at different times and places etc. (cf. the traditional modes of biblical exegesis and literary criticism).

The second aspect, *the interpretation of the world of the interpreter,* also could mean more than one thing. It could mean the interpreter's effort to understand his or her interpretative horizon. It could mean that the interpreter has seen the need to be necessarily involved in a continuous reinterpretation of the starting-point for text-interpretation. For instance, should the starting-point in biblical interpretation be either purely Christian or should it be an awareness of religious pluralism. Moreover, it is essential to discover which are the major factors which at a given point condition, explicitly or possibly even in a concealed fashion, the reading perspective in a community of readers. Thus, 'the world of the interpreter' could mean the community of interpreters in which a particular reader lives and reads; or it could mean the more or less private world of a particular interpreter. But since no interpreter can opt out of the network of communication, he or she will always have to reckon with some hidden or open influence of such a communicative context on his or her activity of reading.

The third aspect, *the interpretation of the self of the interpreter*, points us to the need for every interpreter to become as aware as possible of her or his presuppositions which may be challenged, corrected and possibly transformed during the process of reading. Here it is important to assess with Ricœur whether the interpreter acts on the basis of a determined ego or opens the ego for a possible metamorphosis.[58]

All three aspects characterise every act of interpretation. That does not mean that every interpreter will always be conscious of all three. But it does mean that any adequate theory of interpretation has to deal with them since there is no universal starting-point in interpretation. One could say that one of the characteristics of our age is precisely the absence of such a universal starting-point, as Derrida in particular has repeatedly emphasised. Hence any search for meanings and sense in text-interpretation is in a way a new beginning both in terms of a possible new disclosure of a text's sense, but also in terms of a new beginning in interpretation as such.

After our consideration of this fundamental predicament of all interpretative activity we shall now discuss the various dimensions of text-interpretation.

5.3.2 The Dimensions of Text-Interpretation

In spite of the differences in their hermeneutical programmes, Schleiermacher, Dilthey, Husserl, Heidegger and Gadamer would all agree that every text-interpretation aims at producing an understanding of sense. Thus, for them *understanding* is the goal of hermeneutics. Schleiermacher, however, had already called for some explanatory move in interpretation when he demanded that grammatical interpretation should be considered to be as important as psychological/technical interpretation. Thus, the explanation of the principles of text-composition was for him an essential move in interpretation. The same is true for Ricœur. As we have seen, he too demands a second step in text-interpretation following the first act of understanding. Unlike Gadamer, he regards the explanatory move as a necessary step in interpretation. *Explanation* provides the critical test of the interpreter's initial understanding.

In our discussion of reading as existential activity (cf. above 5.2.5), we have already become aware of the ethical dimension of interpretation. Every reader operates consciously or unconsciously in an ethical context. That is to say that every interpreter of texts is involved in a process of decision-making. The decision whether or not to read a book is of ethical significance, as is the reader's decison to open himself or herself to the sense potential of the text which may well prove to have a transformative effect on him or her. However, as we have seen, 'transformation' cannot be regarded as an unambiguous experience. Instead the reader will have to consider whether a possible transformative experience is truly liberating or oppressive. Of course, the criteria which help us to distinguish between 'liberating' and 'oppressive' transformation also need to be developed in a particular communicative situation. Since there is no neutral point of discussion outside a communicative situation, all aspects of human communication call for an ethical assessment.

In view of this nature of all acts of human communication I propose to acknowledge an ethical dimension in *every* act of interpretation. Therefore, our proposal for a theory of text-interpretation must include some form of *assessment* besides the dimensions of understanding and explanation. This dimension of assessment would then provide the hermeneutical process with a proper recognition of both its opportunities and limitations and its ethical implications beyond the consideration of the mere technical concerns of 'explanation'.

Unlike Ricœur, I do not speak here of interpretative 'steps' but of 'dimensions' of interpretation. It appears to me to be misleading to distinguish a number of subsequent steps in every act of interpretation, since explanation, understanding and assessment are so closely linked at every moment of text-interpretation. If, for instance, an interpreter waits with the critical and self-critical assessment until a text is understood and explained, the sense potential of the text would have had already an opportunity of unfolding itself in the reader, possibly in a transformative way, however, without being adequately assessed. Moreover, since the reception of all texts and especially of such complex texts like novels depends, as Wolfgang Iser has emphasised (cf. above 5.2.2), on the co-operative imagination of the reader, the reader's assessment will become operative at the very moment when his or her imagination is provoked. This early activation of assessment does not, of course, exclude another level of assessment at the end of an act of reading, namely when a reader 're-flects' upon the act of reading as a whole. But it is important for us to realise that the reader's critical and self-critical faculties ought to become active at the very outset of an act of reading.

Elsewhere I have called for a double critique in every assessment, i.e. a material critique of the text and a critique of the reading self.[59] This call was put into question by Klaus Berger. He argued that the modern reader of an ancient text, for example, has not sufficient access to the content of the text so as to criticise this content. Instead he proposed to open a relationship between the ancient text and the modern reader's understanding of the world.[60] I think Berger misunderstood to some extent what I meant. I never suggested that a reader could 'have' the content of a text. Rather I suggested that every approach to a text's sense should be accompanied by a critical move. What else could a critical reader do? I was and continue to be concerned to point out possibilities and limitations in the act of text-interpretation. First of all, the emphasis on the need for the dimension of assessment in every interpretative act stresses precisely the limitations inherent in all interpretation and thus warns the reader against any form of unreasonable hope of fusing completely with the text. Secondly, the dimension of assessment tries to respond to the great line of critical voices from Nietzsche to Foucault which have unsettled any form of interpretative certainty.

Understanding, explanation and assessment are, then, three essential dimensions of every act of reading. The dimension of understanding stresses the existential aspect of disclosing a text's potential for sense. The dimension of explanation underlines the methodological aspect of text-interpretation. A number of explanatory moves are necessary in order to validate or correct our perspectives and the results of understanding. And the dimension of assessment points to the need for both a critique of particular texts and readings and for an ethics of reading in general.

5.3.3 Towards an Ethics of Reading

At this point in our reflection it may be useful to collect our thoughts on criteria for an ethics of reading. We have seen that reading meets the need for ethical dimensions at a number of levels. First of all, the level of attention which a reader brings to the text is ethically significant. The reader may wish to interpret the text or use the text as a spring-board for further reflections. Both procedures are legitimate as long as the respective claim corresponds to the task fulfilled. However, a reading which claims to have interpreted the *text*, yet in reality has either only interpreted a section of a text outside of its textual context or used the text or fragments of it in order only to promote the reader's own thoughts, must be considered as fraudulent. But this level of ethical reflection in hermeneutics does not really pose many problems. Everybody will be able to identify very quickly whether or not a reader has *tried* to do justice to the text.

A more intricate ethical problem emerges in relation to the question whether or not a particular genre of reading is adequate. In order to illustrate this question, I wish to refer back to our previous discussion of reading-genres, reading-styles and reading-functions (cf. above 5.1 and 5.2.3). There we noticed that such genres and styles of readings emerge in response to the genres and styles of texts. A text whose primary communicative perspective is aesthetic can be expected to provoke an aesthetic genre of reading. A text whose primary communicative perspective is theological can be expected to provoke a theological genre of reading. And a text whose primary communicative perspective is instructive (e.g. an instruction of how to connect an electrical appliance) will normally provoke an obedient genre of reading. However, as the Prague Formalists correctly observed, a text can be made to function in many contexts. Thus, the question arises whether or not it could be said to be legitimate that a particular text may be made to function in any context of reception.

For example, is it legitimate to suppose that biblical texts are treated solely as historical documents even though their own communicative perspective far transcends the historical concern? Is it legitimate to interpret a literary text theologically, for instance Beckett's *Waiting for Godot*? Of course, this play contains a number of theological passages but they function in the text only as subperspectives and are controlled by the overall fictional aesthetics. That a theological reading of this play is possible, nobody will debate. But it needs to be asked whether such a reading alone is fully adequate.

The two related problems which we are facing here are (1) the problem of interpretative adequacy towards the text, and (2) the problem of interpretative aims. A purely immanent reading will be very strict in claiming that any perspective which does not fully respond to the communicative intentions of the text ought to be rejected as inadequate. However, we have seen already why such a radically immanent reading is not really possible. Every reading is conditioned by the communicative situation in which it operates. No reader can escape totally the limitations and influences of his or her inherited linguistic tradition. Nor will a text be able to unfold its sense potential without the co-operation of readers whose receptive competence will always be coloured by their linguistic, social, political, existential, i.e. their cultural, context. Already Friedrich Schleiermacher knew that no reading of a complex text will ever be able to claim to have exhausted the text. Hence, a total adequacy of reading is impossible and it would be wiser to work for a 'relative adequacy'.[61]

Such a relative adequacy, then, we could define as being achieved when a text is read through perspectives which seem appropriate to its generic and stylistic identity, and when the reader aims at responding critically to the text as far as possible without claiming to have exhausted the text.

Finally, we must clarify the qualification 'critically' in this definition of relative adequacy in reading. An ethics of reading does not only attempt to cover the text against fraudulent acts of reading by exposing them, but it also must protect responsible readers against possible repressive attacks from the texts themselves. The unmasking of both types of distortions, i.e. the distortions of the text by the reader and the distortions of the reader by the text, must be the concern of the entire community of readers in which an individual reader participates. Of course, interpretative communities may at times prove to be distorted, as for instance Hitler's German readership or Stalin's Soviet community of interpreters, but a community of interpreters whose intellectual competence and public performance has not been manipulated by a totalitarian regime normally provides at least a wider public context for properly critical and self-critical reading.

5.4 CONCLUSION: PHILOSOPHICAL AND THEOLOGICAL HERMENEUTICS

In this and the two previous chapters of this book we have been dealing almost exclusively with problems of philosophical hermeneutics and the general linguistic and cultural conditions of text-interpretation. It is now time to return to the theological focus of this book, that is to theological hermeneutics. At the beginning of Chapter 3 we were led by Schleiermacher to accept that theological hermeneutics is first of all a special hermeneutics and as such dependent on the rules and methods of general hermeneutics. Such a general hermeneutics, Schleiermacher had identified as 'philosophical':

> Since the art of speaking and the art of understanding stand in relation to each other, speaking being only the outer side of thinking, hermeneutics is part of the art of thinking, and is therefore philosophical.[62]

By insisting that theological hermeneutics has to reflect upon and respect the principles of philosophical hermeneutics, he freed theological hermeneutics from any ecclesiastical tutelage and opened up a whole new era of hermeneutical thinking. As a result, all humanities, and indeed all human efforts at interpreting written texts, were called to enter into the interdisciplinary discussion of hermeneutics. However, this discussion was to take place on philosophical foundations.

We have tried to report on the development of these efforts and have highlighted in particular the emerging philosophical and linguistic contributions to the discussion of hermeneutical principles. We have discussed the radical challenge brought to hermeneutical activity by the masters of suspicion and deconstruction. And we concluded this report with our own methodological proposal which tried to do justice not only to the existential and explanatory moves in text-interpretation but also to the necessity of ethical reflection from which no critical human thinking can be exempted. We have accepted that a relatively adequate text-interpretation can foster human liberation from oppressive situations and transform human self-understanding for the better. But we have also warned that such acts of interpretation must be open for public consideration by a wider community of interpreters in terms of adequacy both to the text and to the community of readers themselves.

In the two remaining chapters of this book we shall have to examine first the more recent developments in theological hermeneutics and the relationship between theological and philosophical hermeneutics in the twentieth century, and finally the significance of a philosophically based and critical theological hermeneutics for reflection upon the identity of Christian faith in this world.

6

The Development of Theological Hermeneutics (II): Barth, Bultmann, and the New Hermeneutic

6.0 INTRODUCTION

In the twentieth century, the attention to theological hermeneutics has reached a new height. The reasons for this can be found both in the intense discussion between theologians and contemporary philosophers and in a new departure in the practice of biblical interpretation itself. These reasons are, of course, related, since the search for new exegetical methods in the twentieth century has directed theological attention by necessity again towards philosophical reflection on the principles of text-interpretation. But in order to understand the influence which philosophical reflection has had on theological thinking we must take into account especially the enormous impression which Martin Heidegger's philosophical insights have made on protestant theologians such as Bultmann, Ebeling, and Fuchs.

After the disaster of the First World War had disavowed the nineteenth-century liberal theological tradition, Heidegger's phenomenological-existentialist approach was welcomed by theologians as a promise of a new method of reflection. The purely historical approach to biblical exegesis and theology which had emerged in the nineteenth century (cf. 6.1. below), proved unable to yield concrete proposals for a Christian way of life in a world confused by radical political and scientific challenges. At this point, Heidegger's philosophy promoted a new concentration on the anthropological foundations which transcended any solely historical attention to texts and religious developments (cf. above 3.3.2). Now a new creative synthesis between the biblical message and the reinterpreted human *Dasein* in this world seemed possible and able to provide the desired solution to the existential quest of many contemporary Christians.

But not all theologians shared this enthusiasm for this kind of new methodological departure in theology. The Swiss-German theologian Karl Barth (1886–1968) who, together with his fellow theologians, held a negative view of protestant liberalism nevertheless rejected his colleagues' theological reception of Heidegger's philosophical hermeneutics. For Barth, any close co-operation between theology and philosophy represented a severe danger to theology. Thus, our critical consideration of the relationship between theological and philosophical hermeneutics in this century has to begin with a discussion of the most radical challenge to this very relationship, a relationship which, for the first time in modernity, Schleiermacher had tried to promote with great conviction (cf. above 3.1).

In our discussion of the Barth-Bultmann debate on hermeneutics in this chapter we shall therefore have to address the principal issues of the foundations of theological hermeneutics once more before we attend to the detailed hermeneutical proposals offered by both Barth and Bultmann. Then we shall introduce the major concerns of the subsequent or second wave of hermeneutical discussion in this century which is generally referred to as 'The New Hermeneutic' and which is characteristic of protestant theological thinking of the fifties and sixties. This wave was dominated by the influence of the later Heidegger's philosophy of language (cf. above 3.3.3) and by a generally more positive reception of Bultmann's insights into the hermeneutical foundations of theological thinking. It also documents the growing influence of American thinkers in the continuing hermeneutical discussion.

But before embarking upon a discussion of theological hermeneutics in the twentieth century we must focus briefly on the situation of biblical interpretation in the nineteenth and early twentieth century. For it is this interpretative praxis and its theological framework which both Barth and Bultmann rejected and against which they developed their own approach to theological hermeneutics.

6.1 OVERCOMING HISTORICISM IN THEOLOGICAL HERMENEUTICS

6.1.1 The Challenge of Historical Consciousness to Biblical Interpretation

The approach to text-interpretation both in theology and in the emerging literary sciences which characterised much of the nineteenth century is usually called 'historicism'. This more recent term already includes a negative assessment of the purely historical approach which has dominated text-interpretation for a long period and which continues to influence many biblical scholars today.

To many theologians of the late eighteenth and the nineteenth century the historical-critical study of biblical texts seemed the only respectable academic way of dealing with the ancient texts of the Jewish-Christian tradition. Thus, historical-critical scholarship of the Bible must be seen as one response to the challenges to theology by rationalism and by the emancipatory thrust of the Enlightenment.[1] As we have seen already, the new science and its rapid progress led to a rationalist critique of the foundations of the biblical world-view (cf. above 2.2.6). This challenge made it necessary for theologians to redefine both content and method of theological thinking. And the emancipatory nature of the Enlightenment critique of all unfounded authority provoked theologians to demonstrate the authority of their research both in terms of their sources and methods and in terms of their freedom from the tutelage of religious institutions. Those theologians who wished to respond to these challenges, such as Semler (see above 2.2.7), saw themselves caught between the emerging ideal of a critical science on the one hand, and loyalty towards their respective religious traditions on the other. Was it still possible for a theologian to be faithful both to the demands of reason in which critical research is grounded and to the demands of a tradition which called for absolute loyalty to the sacredness of its foundational texts and ancient modes of interpretation?

This question became even more acute when it was made known that the biblical texts could not only not be trusted any longer as scientifically adequate descriptions but that even their status as reliable historical documents witnessing to God's revelation in time and space began to be shaken. Thus, after scientific research had already demanded a first reassessment of the nature of biblical texts and their interpretation, a second such reassessment seemed unavoidable when it became obvious that the chronology even of the account of the very life of Jesus as provided by the gospels could not be taken as sacrosanct. Moreover, the painfulness of the impression that the gospels occasionally contradicted one another in their report of events called for further critical studies and could no longer be reduced by any easy reference to the traditional dogma or the general human inability to understand divine matters. By now the human mind had reached a state of self-consciousness which no longer accepted such references.[2] Therefore the question had to be answered, how one had to deal with contradictions between the so-called truths of history and tradition on the one hand and the truths of reason on the other.

This question received its lasting formulation by Gotthold Ephraim Lessing (1729–1781). How can we deal with the broad ugly ditch between the truths of history and the truths of reason? Surely, Lessing argued, we cannot trust the accidents of history to be the conveyors of necessary truths.[3] Thus, although Lessing himself fostered the development of historical-critical research on the Bible, he put already a radical question-mark upon the theological significance of such research. Historical research alone cannot provide necessary criteria for establishing the truth of Christian faith. Nevertheless, the historical treatment of biblical texts proved to be the best method in which the old supernatural claims of Christian religion could be destroyed. But since this historical treatment of the biblical texts could not ground human faith in God, further theological moves in biblical interpretation were necessary.

Friedrich Schleiermacher tried to respond both to Lessing and to Immanuel Kant. The latter had also argued against the possibility of any metaphysical foundation of religious belief and that the value of religion ought to be found in its ability to organise a morally sound human community. Schleiermacher now agreed that the basis of religion was not metaphysics, but against Kant he stated that it was not morality either.[4] For Schleiermacher, religion could ultimately be based only on direct human experience of the divine and on the interpretation of this experience through the light provided by the documents of the religious tradition. Therefore he offered a new model of theology which tried to be faithful to both institutions, scientific reason and Christian faith, while cultivating a critical distance from each of the two by developing his hermeneutical reflection. As we have seen, his hermeneutical model included a radical critique of any a priori claims for the holiness or inspiration of any particular biblical text, but it also included a radical negation of any over-optimistic ideal of text-interpretation. The interpretation of texts will never be more than approximation (cf. above 3.1.1). Because of his singular combination of explanatory moves (grammatical aspect) and individual aims (psychological aspect) in interpretation, Schleiermacher could continue to hold that the scientific study and the personal appropriation of a religious text are not only not enemies, but that they presuppose one another. From our perspective today it would appear that this synthesis should have been well able to foster the bond between our understanding of *ratio* and our understanding of *fides*, but the actual development of biblical scholarship was not prepared to adopt Schleiermacher's methodological proposals. Instead the split between 'biblical scholarship' and 'biblical faith' increased.

Ironically, it was another effort to reach a synthesis between faith and reason which accelerated the split between the two even further: Georg Wilhelm Friedrich Hegel (1770–1831) tried to overcome this conflict between a religion, based on historically doubtful biblical sources, and critical human reason in his way. He aimed at transcending the sources through extrapolating certain religious ideas from them and synthesizing them into the larger system of an all embracing historical spirit. Hegel portrayed this spirit both as the principle of development and as its final goal. However, once this ideal of a spiritual reconciliation between religious ideas and human reason had lost its attraction, Hegel's concept of historical development nevertheless remained influential for generations to come. But now, the aim of philosophical and theological research was no longer the speculation of how the historical process reaches its ultimate completion, but rather to examine the origins and developments which have led to certain mental or physical results. Thus, historical research moved away from Hegel's teleological concept of history, towards a more and more detailed study of the human past. For Hegel, 'history' was a term which indicated a particular result of the philosophical interpretation of biblical texts, but after Hegel 'history' became the framework of all biblical interpretation.[5]

Just as the rise of science had caused a revolution in theological thinking, so did now the rise of historical consciousness. Both frameworks, i.e. the scientific and the historical-critical, questioned the authority of the dogmatic traditions of Christianity, and therefore at first met with strong ecclesiastical opposition. The scientific world-view had shattered the ancient Christian concept of the world and hence challenged the horizon in which the biblical texts used to be understood. Now the historical-critical consciousness questioned the order of events and sometimes the events themselves to which the biblical texts refer. Hermeneutically speaking, first the horizon of the interpreter was challenged, and now the reliability of the sources of theological thinking themselves, i.e. the biblical foundations of Christian faith and theology, were also questioned. No wonder that many Christian people saw in these attacks nothing short of the work of the devil who was undermining their faith. However, as with the scientific revolution before, a number of theologians grasped the significance of the new historical matrix for theological thinking and then embarked on historical-critical research of the biblical texts. But the question of how to integrate the results of such historical-critical research into theological thinking was not yet answered. Instead of trying to address this question, historical-critical text-examination developed mainly alongside or even outside theological thinking proper. Biblical exegesis and systematic theology went different ways once again.

A book on the development and significance of theological hermeneutics is not the place for a detailed analysis of the course which historical-critical exegesis has taken during the last two centuries. Historians of biblical exegesis such as Hans-Joachim Kraus, Robert Morgan, John Barton and others, have attempted this task and narrated the process of that branch of biblical research.[6] The different orientations and emphases of historical-critical research, i.e. history of traditions, history of religions, history of literary forms, history of redaction etc., are well known. Instead our concern in the present book must be to reflect on the importance of historical-critical interpretation as such for theology. Wherein lies the contribution of that particular approach to theological hermeneutics and what are its limitations?

6.1.2 Historical Criticism as One Aspect of Theological Hermeneutics

The 'turn to history' in modern human thinking is, of course, irreversible. But the necessary awareness of our existence in time does not necessarily constitute an historicist attitude to human life and its linguistic expressions.

An important illustration of the limitations of a purely historical analysis of biblical texts is the famous 'life-of-Jesus research'. Throughout the nineteenth and until the early twentieth century, a great number of theolgians undertook to reconstruct the life of Jesus on the basis of their historical-critical research on the Bible. But as Albert Schweitzer (1865–1965) concluded in his report on this movement, there were as many lives of Jesus as there were researchers.[7] Historicism in biblical studies, then, represents a methodological failure on at least two accounts. First it cannot overcome the ditch separating history and faith; and secondly it rests itself on the illusion of pure and objective research. However, as we have emphasised in our previous chapters, no reading perspective is free of interests, and therefore every reading must be tested against its possible ideological features.

The methodological and theological limitations of a purely historical-critical approach to text-interpretation are thus obvious. A text is not yet 'understood' when its origins have been critically analysed. The historical-critical exegesis of biblical texts is not identical with a critical text-interpretation as such; rather it must be seen as one aspect of the larger interpretative effort. Hence, we may sympathise with both Karl Barth and Rudolf Bultmann when they demanded from the historical-critical researchers a more critical attitude towards their own exegetical method.[8]

Of course, a biblical text may be studied by anybody with any kind of interest; and it is perfectly possible to apply a purely historical perspective to such a text. However, in text-interpretation we must be careful not to identify the overall process of responsible reading with the application of one and only one aspect of reading. Thus, historical-critical reading may very well help the reader in his or her overall process of interpreting a text, but a purely historical-critical reading of a text can never claim to have done full justice to the text. Of course, both text and reading are historical phenomena (which phenomena are not historical?), but at the same time they are also conditioned by other aspects of reality, as we have seen in the previous chapter when we discussed the various possibilities of reading. Therefore it is essential at this point to reject any historicist attitudes with equal vigour as we have rejected before other ideological attitudes towards texts. Historicism is an ideology, whereas an historical consciousness may lead towards a critical attitude in text-interpretation.

How did Barth and Bultmann attempt to overcome this historicism in biblical interpretation?

6.2 THE BARTH-BULTMANN DEBATE ON THEOLOGICAL HERMENEUTICS

We have already pointed to the new context of theological thinking after the First World War. The suffering of millions of people, the horror of the war, hunger for bread as well as hunger for meaning in this confused time – such pressing phenomena of human life could no longer be tackled by theologians with the answers of the old liberal protestantism. The synthesis between human morality and Christian faith had proved to be false. Either Christian faith could say something new to this shattered world or it would have to share the fate of the old political empires and of the ideologies which had supported their militaristic way of existence.

Also theology as an intellectual exercise needed a new reflection upon its biblical foundations after the old theological mode had been discredited because of its affinity to German imperial politics which in a sense made it co-responsible for the war and its horrors. Now the mere historical reference to a certain biblical or post-biblical development did not yet offer a meaning for troubled Christians in post-war Europe who searched for ways of reordering their shattered lives. If the Bible was to disclose any meaning to those people at all, a different kind of approach to the biblical texts was necessary both on the side of the preacher and on the side of the theologian.[9]

This new context of Christian existence provoked a number of Christian thinkers to reflect anew on the principles of biblical interpretation in particular and text-interpretation in general. In our discussion we shall focus our attention on the two most influential theologians of the first part of our century, Karl Barth and Rudolf Bultmann. Since our sympathies generally lie more with the aims of Bultmann's hermeneutics, we shall organise our discussion through concentrating first on Karl Barth, thus trying to balance our own interpretative perspective.

6.2.1 Theological Hermeneutics According to Barth

Karl Barth began his theological career in the pulpit. The young pastor in a Swiss village was faced with preaching the Word of God to his congregation. This task directed his attention in a fresh way to the texts of the Bible, and this direction was to remain the context for Barth's life-long theological reflection: his rediscovery of the biblical texts and his interpretation of these texts for his troubled times.[10] Among the first fruits of this rediscovery were his talk 'The Strange New World Within the Bible'[11] and the two editions of his commentary on Saint Paul's Letter to the Romans.[12] Moreover, all the volumes of his major work, the *Church Dogmatics*,[13] were written with this same intention: to serve the church in its proclamation of God's Word. Barth the Professor always remained faithful to the concerns of Barth the Pastor; his academic theology deals with the task of responsible preaching. His theoretical efforts always aimed at renewing the praxis of the church. Like the Fathers of the church, especially Augustine and the Reformers, whom he always admired, Barth did theology for the sake of the church. Of course, the university teacher gained a greater awareness of the heritage of his own Reformed Tradition, especially of the powerful scriptural emphasis of the Reformers. Yet, the exploration of the background of the Reformed Church did not add a new qualitative dimension to his theological programme. Barth's task was from the beginning, and remained thereafter, 'evangelical theology'.[14]

At various places in his theological writings Barth discussed this practical task of biblical interpretation in a more theoretical way. In our analysis we shall concentrate mainly on such theoretical statements in both parts of Volume I of his *Church Dogmatics*, i.e. the prolegomena for a church dogmatics, where he treats the hermeneutical problems in great detail.[15] But we shall also consult his *Epistle to the Romans*, especially the various prefaces,[16] and we shall look at the dialogue with his life-long friend Rudolf Bultmann which gave rise to many discussions of hermeneutical problems.[17]

It is essential for us to appreciate that the hermeneutical question for Barth does not arise originally from a conscious methodological concern, i.e. how to devise an appropriate theory of text-understanding. Rather the hermeneutical question entails for him the ultimate material question of theology, namely: who is God and who am I? Thus, Barth's hermeneutics is not an introductory reflection before actual theology begins. It is part of theology proper, and thus part of dogmatics. Therefore Barth begins his *Church Dogmatics* with the hermeneutical-theological question: What is the Word of God and who am I in relation to God's Word? The hermeneutical question is for Barth the question of how to talk adequately about God's revelation in history, i.e. how to proclaim God's Word today so that it is truly talk of God (CD I/1: 187ff.).

Barth's particular revelation-hermeneutics may be better understood if compared with Bultmann's approach to hermeneutics.[18] Influenced by his one-time colleague at the University of Marburg, Martin Heidegger, Bultmann searched for an adequate description of the human situation in which the biblical texts are allowed to speak today and in which these texts confront individual human existence. As we shall see in greater detail below, Bultmann thus attempted to clarify the formal (i.e. linguistic, philosophical, cultural, geographic, historical, etc.) and perspectival conditions (*Vorverständnisse*) of the process of biblical interpretation. He insisted that there cannot be an understanding of these texts without such particular presuppositions. Therefore, he suggested, following Heidegger's recommendation, that the reader must recognise these conditions in order to become better aware of the various obstacles in his or her way of reading these texts.[19] However, Bultmann, like Barth, believed that the final understanding, the ultimate appropriation of God's Word in Jesus Christ by the reader is in fact God's own achievement in the reader. Yet Bultmann saw God at work in the human process of interpreting the biblical *kerygma* [proclamation].[20] Although both theologians agreed in their critique of the old theological liberalism and in their call for a new understanding of God's otherness, Bultmann held a much more positive view of the world and of history and of the mediating role of philosophy than Barth.[21]

Barth rejected Bultmann's hermeneutical approach to the biblical texts. He considered Bultmann as a victim of philosophical and other decisions which had led him to the illusion that any human method of interpreting the Bible could be sufficiently adequate to grasp God's revelation. God must never become the object of our methods, of our hermeneutics, our interpretations.[22] For Barth, God must always remain the subject who interprets us.[23] As God speaks in history, God interprets history. According to this order, the human activity called for here is not an appropriation of the Word of God, but a way of corresponding best to it while submitting to being interpreted by the Word of God. Thus, 'revelation is not a predicate of history, but history is a predicate of revelation' (CD I/2: 58).

Already in the various prefaces to his *Epistle to the Romans*, Barth had described our relationship to the biblical texts by the old Germanic term *Treue*.[24] This faithfulness to the text does not exclude a critical awareness of the general relativity of all human words, even those of Paul. Here Barth and Bultmann could agree.[25] Yet Barth's concern was not limited to a detailed historical and exegetical study of words, sentences or concepts. Rather he aimed at bringing to light the subject-matter of the text. Therefore he demanded that the historical-critical exegetes should be more critical in order to be able to discern what the subject-matter of this text really is and what it demands from us.[26] According to Barth, the historical-critical exegetes are too modest in their hermeneutical efforts.[27] Barth understood the ultimate theme of the biblical texts as follows:

> God is in heaven and you on earth. *This* God's relationship to *this* man, *this* man's relationship to *this* God is for me the theme of the Bible and the sum of philosophy at once.[28]

Barth's hermeneutical reflection began where Bultmann's hermeneutics might eventually lead to, namely with the recognition of God's revelation in history. Barth understood the Bible as witness to God's freely given revelation. Thus, he was clear about the overall material content of the Bible before he actually interpreted any particular biblical text. Like Augustine and Martin Luther, Barth's hermeneutics is characterised by a pre-apprehension of the Bible's overall theological meaning: what was 'love' for Augustine, 'justification by faith' for Luther, is 'God's otherness' (yet closeness) for Barth. But unlike Augustine, Barth did not engage in a thorough reflection on the linguistic conditions of the communication of God's Word in the Bible, and unlike Bultmann, Barth did not consider the particular anthropological-philosophical context of biblical interpretation in his time.

Bultmann tried to analyse the process of human understanding first. In the sense that we can say that while Barth's hermeneutics is material, Bultmann's is formal. Barth rejected the imposition, as he saw it, of any formal hermeneutical principles on the human appreciation of God's revelation. Bultmann rejected the material imposition, as he saw it, of a particular theological dogmatics on every effort to begin the process of understanding.[29] To use the distinction introduced above (cf. 1.2), Barth started with a macro-hermeneutics, Bultmann with a micro-hermeneutics which Barth rejected as too modest.

For Barth, an appropriate reading of the Bible must avoid engaging in human talking, *eisegesis*. Rather, the interpreter should listen to the human words of the Bible through which God's Word *might* reveal itself. 'God's revelation in the human word of Holy Scripture not only wants but can make itself said and heard' (CD I/1: 471). But how did Barth know that God's revelation can and does make itself heard through the mediate and never immediate witness of these texts? He answered:

> We believe in and with the Church that Holy Scripture as the original and legitimate witness of divine revelation is itself the Word of God. (CD I/2: 502)

This faith must precede our exegesis and our theological reflection. Therefore Barth could say that theology is always 'under' the Bible.

When the Scriptures do become for us the Word of God, God's revelation, then this is itself, according to Barth, a miraculous event of God's freedom. It can only be accepted in faith (CD I/2: 506). Outside this faith and the Word which has called for faith there is no firm ground. Barth condemned that biblicism which wrongly identifies the letter and the spirit of the text (CD I/2: 506–12). The Bible is not infallible, it is a human book, yet a book which witnesses to God's transcending Word. The presence of the Word of God transforms the reality of the book, but this transformation does not mean that it is by the power of the book that revelation actually happens. The authority of the Bible is grounded in the fact that this revelation can happen, but the event of revelation is God's free activity and not the Bible's. Barth supported this insight with his doctrine of the Holy Spirit: 'the witness of Holy Scripture is therefore the witness of the Holy Spirit' (CD I/2: 538).

The only appropriate response to the event of revelation is obedience (CD I/2: 543), and the church as the community under the Word of God must therefore be a church of obedience (CD I/2: 575f.).

Barth underlines the written nature of the Bible. Because of it the Bible can continue to resist all efforts of domestication and distortion, and the Bible's openness and potential for reformation of the church is protected (CD I/2: 583ff.).

Freedom under the Word of God is the freedom of all Christians. All Christians are invited to participate in the explanation of the biblical texts. Yet all Christians must accept the fundamental rule for all appropriate explanation of the Bible: 'the freely performed act of subordinating all human concepts [*Vorstellungen*], ideas and convictions to the witness of revelation supplied to us in Scripture' (CD I/2: 715). Thus, the basic mode of biblical interpretation for Barth is subordination. Barth qualifies this rule further when he says that subordination did not mean disposal and destruction. Rather it 'presupposes that that which is subordinated is and remains present as such. However, subordination means *Hintanstellung*, discipleship, flexibility of the subordinated to the superior'.[30]

Subordination and obedience are the key terms which Barth used in order to stress the absolute priority of Scripture over against all our emotions, axioms, systems, philosophies etc. No method of interpretation, no hermeneutics could ever disclose God's revelation. Therefore, the only remaining response for the reader of the Bible is obedience and the willingness to let the Bible interpret himself or herself, to let the Holy Spirit speak the word of judgment about the reader through the text. Barth finds the reason for this principle of biblical interpretation in the content of Scripture. 'The content of the Bible, and the object of its witness, is Jesus Christ as the name of the God who deals graciously with man the sinner.' (CD I/2: 720) For Barth the recognition of this content excludes all autonomous activities of our own thinking.

> [T]he testimony of the Bible . . . and the autonomy of our own world of thought is an impossible hermeneutical programme. (CD I/2: 721)

This principle of biblical interpretation also determined the three practical steps which Barth now recommended for the detailed explanation of the biblical texts. (1) *Observation* aims at the literary and historical presentation of the structure and sense of the text (CD I/2: 722ff.). (2) *Reflection* aims at thinking along with the text and assessing the text (CD I/2: 727ff.). Here Barth agrees that no reader can think along with the text without certain hermeneutical keys. The crucial point here for Barth is not that we do approach the text with certain modes of thought [*Denkweisen*] or even philosophies, but that these philosophies are only of an experimental nature, and that they must not determine our reading.

> I shall have to bear in mind the difference between my mode of thought and that of Scripture, the essential unfitness of the means employed by me. I shall have to remember that grace is implied if

> my attempt and therefore my mode of thought can become useful to this end. (CD I/2: 731)

(3) *Appropriation* (CD I/2: 736ff.). This third step of biblical interpretation corresponds to the classical concept of *usus scripturae*, the different uses of Scripture (cf. above 2.2.4). It is concerned with the application, and that means with assuming the biblical witness into one's own responsibility. Application does not mean, however, that we *use* the Scriptures for our own purposes but, rather, that we should allow ourselves to be taken over by the Scriptures for God's purposes. Total faith is the only adequate human response to the Word of God.

After this presentation of Barth's hermeneutical thought we need to discuss the problems and implications of that approach to biblical interpretation and locate Barth's proposal in the context of the development of theological and philosophical hermeneutics. Again, as we shall see, the comparison between Barth and Bultmann and further references to the debate between the two theologians will help us to gain a clearer picture not only about the development of hermeneutics in our century, but also about the requirements of a more adequate theological hermeneutics than either Barth or Bultmann have provided. Thus, we shall first have to ask how critical is Barth's hermeneutics, and then focus on Bultmann's own proposal for a critical theological hermeneutics.

6.2.2 How Critical Is Barth's Hermeneutics?

Karl Barth's hermeneutics is a passionate hermeneutics. Barth was passionately concerned with protecting the biblical texts against the 'uncritical' claims of those historians and exegetes who pretended to have understood a text when they have analysed it as an historical document. Barth demanded a better criticism. For him, true criticism meant to take the sense of the text seriously, and, in the case of the biblical texts, that was to take seriously that the text is critical of the reader. The biblical text causes a crisis in the serious and attentive reader.

Eberhard Jüngel could show how Barth gained the material criterion for his hermeneutics through his reading of Paul's Epistle to the Romans. Barth's particular interpretative experience of this text led him to accept the axiom that 'God is God' which he then applied to all the biblical texts. Jüngel reminds us that this axiom is in fact an insight of natural theology. But, unlike in the tradition of doing so-called Natural Theology, Barth's tautology 'God is God' certainly did not act so as 'to secure the existence of a godhead, of a divine essence, but to emphasise the radical difference between the divine essence, the Godness of God, and all ungodly essences.'[31]

This axiom of the divinity of God is the axiom through which Barth wanted us to read every text and not only biblical and religious texts. That is why he could say that we did not really need a specific theological science (*Wissenschaft*) and that all the sciences which are engaged in explanation and understanding could ultimately do the business of theology. In other words, biblical hermeneutics does not need to be different from general hermeneutics. Only because general hermeneutics does not agree with this basic axiom do we need biblical hermeneutics in order to be reminded of the subject-matter of all honest understanding (CD I/2: 725–7).

This axiom 'God is God' conducted Barth's reading of *Romans*, whereas his *Church Dogmatics* was increasingly guided by the axiomatic insight that God revealed himself in Jesus Christ in order ultimately to show us his eternal love for us human beings. This latter insight is no longer born from natural theology, but from Barth's particular hermeneutical experience with the New Testament texts. Thus, while the major reading perspective of *Romans*, his earlier work, was more or less apologetic, the guiding perspective of his *Church Dogmatics* was based on his own particular reading experiences. However, here too an axiom was at work which provokes our critical attention, namely the axiom that the biblical text interprets itself. This axiom we have already encountered in our examination of the Reformers' hermeneutics (cf. above 2.2.5). There, however, it did not entail an overall rejection of human reason; rather it was used as a criterion against ecclesiastical impositions on and distortions of biblical interpretation. Barth, however, applied this axiom now not only against Liberal Theology, but also against philosophical reflection on the condition and methods of biblical interpretation as it was undertaken by theologians since Schleiermacher and more recently by Rudolf Bultmann, Gerhard Ebeling and others.

It is important for us to realise that Barth and his hermeneutical adversaries all agreed that the subject-matter of the biblical texts must be allowed to make itself known to us, the modern readers. Barth differed, however, from the other hermeneuts in so far as he claimed to know the only possible outcome of all truly biblical interpretation: the obedient witness to the self-revelation of God in the Logos [Word]. Over against Barth's material determination of the believing reader's hermeneutical experience with the biblical text, Bultmann suggested that we ought to engage in biblical interpretation in order to see what these texts have to say to us today. Both theologians wished to protect the texts against *eisegesis* [reading into the text], Barth through his effort of unmasking all ideological misreadings, Bultmann through his call for the interpreter's self-conscious and self-critical openness to the text. Both hermeneuts were aware of the human condition of reading. Both reflected upon the necessity of a connecting-point between God and us. But they differed sharply in their starting-point: for Bultmann the connecting-point between God and us is the hermeneutical process itself, whereas Barth begins already with the positive fact of God's revelation as witnessed to by the text. Barth starts *extra nos*, Bultmann *intra nos*.

Yet texts can only begin to witness to something when they are read. Therefore we have to ask how we can control Barth's own interpretative experience if not by participating in the process of text-interpretation itself? But such a participation must be protected against possible ideological distortions as well as against any kind of dogmatic pre-determination of new acts of reading. It seems to me that there is no possibility of a shortcut to the meaning or sense of the biblical texts. Texts need to be interpreted in order to be understood. Hence, in order to see whether or not Barth's universalization of his own hermeneutical experience is legitimate we must go the long way through the texts themselves. There can be no critical macro-hermeneutics without critical micro-hermeneutics! Without such a continuous test Barth's criterion for biblical interpretation, i.e. God's self revelation in Jesus Christ, remains indeed mere positivism, as Bonhoeffer had suggested.[32]

In his hermeneutics Barth was also not concerned with any formal linguistic considerations. Unlike Schleiermacher he did not discuss the dimensions of human communication, nor did he tackle the problems of misreadings, misunderstandings of the texts etc., for he was not interested in a reflection on how language functions. Instead Barth rejected Schleiermacher's hermeneutics because it lacked the theological axioms which he, Barth, insisted must be accepted before good interpretation could begin.[33] Barth's lecture on Schleiermacher did not even begin to deal with Schleiermacher's theory of the dipolar nature of text-interpretation (the grammatical and the psychological interpretation of the text).[34] As Eberhard

Jüngel correctly remarked, Barth's hermeneutics was a hermeneutics of revelation and not a hermeneutics of signification.[35] But how can we talk about God's Logos if not through the medium of our language and its often ambiguous processes of signification? Although Barth himself presupposed and used these functions of language, he neglected to appreciate their significance, character and implications for our interpretation of texts. Here he lacked the genius of Augustine whom he so admired. Instead of bothering about semiotic problems, Barth aimed at the whole, at the interpretation of the universe in the light of his particular hermeneutical experience of revelation. Through his own reading of the Scriptures, his own observations, reflections and appropriations, he arrived at the theological and ontological axioms for his interpretation which he then recommended to us. But without any critical reflection, these axioms must remain dogmatic and they already determine too much of the outcome of our own reading.

Undoubtedly, Barth's great achievement was to have drawn our attention to the *theological* message of the biblical texts. Using the language introduced above (cf. 4.5), we may say that he rediscovered the communicative perspective of the biblical texts. The biblical texts are first of all theological texts, they communicate a theological message. But Barth did not help us to grasp how we can disclose this message today, how we can read these texts, and how we might cope with the claim that there may be a legitimate plurality of biblical readings.[36] Barth did not address the general problem of the cultural conditioning of reading contexts, such as the particular Eurocentric nature of most of Christian theology including his own. Moreover, why should his reference to the activity of the Holy Spirit in the world exclude our critical reflection upon the most adequate method of studying the biblical texts?[37] Barth's passionate vote for the difference between God and human beings might not only have failed to appreciate the importance of the humanity of God, as he later admitted,[38] but also the basic hermeneutical condition in which we recognise this difference.[39]

Barth's legitimate fear of all the philosophical and other possible impositions on biblical interpretation which he saw at work in Liberal and Natural Theologies alike led him to misunderstand Bultmann's equally legitimate reflection upon the conditions of human understanding. The exchange of views between the two theologians in 1952 shows with great clarity how Barth rejected

Bultmann's reflections on the hermeneutical condition as an illegitimate determination of the text.[40] As Barth had outlined already in his earlier book on Anselm, the foundation of any good theology must be the prevenient *credo* of the theologian.[41] Accordingly Barth felt compelled to reject any theological programme which started below or outside this determination by faith. Bultmann recognised correctly that Barth's ontological presupposition differed radically from his own. And with Bultmann we too must ask Barth[42] why an open discussion of the presuppositions of any approach to texts would need to be seen as *determining* our understanding of these texts. Of course, all interpretative efforts are *conditioned*. But there is a big difference between conditions and determinations! As long as our discussion of the interpretative conditions is a truly open discussion, one fails to see why God's Spirit should not be able to lead us towards an always deeper appreciation of the truth of the Bible precisely through such discussion.

The radical distinction between God and the world in Barth's thinking has made it impossible for Barth to address the double need of theological hermeneutics which we have identified as the result of the philosophical and scientific revolutions since the sixteenth century, namely the need to develop an adequate theory of text-interpretation and at the same time to develop an adequate theory of world-interpretation. Both influence each other: the latter provides the context in which the former works, and the former participates in the establishment of the latter. Instead of contributing to this twofold hermeneutical task which characterises our period as 'modern', Barth limited himself to the defense of a particular form of theological hermeneutics and refused to accept the legimitacy of other ongoing interpretations of culture in modernity. This self-limitation which reminds us of the Protestant and Catholic Orthodoxies (cf. above 2.2.6) has earned Barth's theology the attribute 'neo-orthodox'.[43]

6.2.3 Theological Hermeneutics According to Bultmann

As we have seen already at various occasions in our discussion, Rudolf Bultmann did not limit his hermeneutical focus to purely material, i.e. theological, aspects of biblical interpretation. Rather he recognised the importance of reflecting upon the nature of the connecting-point between God's self-revelation and our human understanding of God's activity among us. Therefore he attempted to clarify the conditions of human understanding and thus felt the need to enter into the discussion on philosophical hermeneutics. Bultmann's reflection on philosophical hermeneutics stands in the tradition of Schleiermacher. Both theologians engaged in philosophical hermeneutics in order to improve theological hermeneutics. We have already pointed to the affinity between Bultmann's approach to theology and Heidegger's earlier work on existentialist hermeneutics. Bultmann's hermeneutical programme and his search for authenticity in Christian existence owe much to Heidegger's philosophy. From Heidegger he adopted his insight into the existentialist quest and from him he also derived his own existentialist rhetoric. But that is not to say that Bultmann's own thinking were nothing more than a simple application of Heidegger's philosophy on theology. Such a reductionist view could never do justice to Bultmann's important attempt to develop a theology which was involved both in a critical dialogue with other methods of text- and world-interpretation and in a critical interpretation of its own textual sources and traditions.[44]

Moreover, it would be wrong to condemn Bultmann's hermeneutical insights altogether because of the problematic nature of his particular programme of 'demythologization'. As we are going to see in this section, Bultmann's hermeneutics contains many important insights which must be considered and developed further; but at the same time we must examine very critically what may be inadequate in his programme of demythologizing the biblical texts.

Bultmann addressed hermeneutical issues throughout his career as a teacher and writer at the University of Marburg.[45] Like his friend Karl Barth he was dissatisfied with historicist exegesis. Instead of finding out what was said at some stage in the Christian tradition, Bultmann wanted to know what such a text meant for his own time. For him the decisive question was 'whether we confront history in such a way that we acknowledge its claim upon us, its claim to say something new to us'.[46] However, after being united in rejecting the objectivist illusions of historicist exegesis, Barth and Bultmann parted company and developed radically different approaches to biblical interpretation. While Barth, as we have seen, advocated a closed theological circle in which the interpreter was to move, Bultmann acknowledged the complex situation of the modern interpreter of the Bible. Especially in his article 'The Problem of Hermeneutics' (1950)[47] he sought systematically to clarify the conditions under which modern man confronts the biblical texts.

Here, Bultmann referred to both Schleiermacher and Dilthey who long before him had tried to reformulate the problem of modern hermeneutics but whose efforts had not been fully appreciated by subsequent theologians. He particularly praised both thinkers for their realisation that a mere analysis of the formal constituents of a text does not yet lead to a real understanding of what the text means. An additional move was seen to be necessary, a subjective move in which the interpreters grasp the subject-matter by relating it to themselves. Schleiermacher had called that aspect of interpretation 'divination', and Dilthey saw the common experience of human life as the ground on which any particular expression could be understood. Schleiermacher's objective was the understanding of the human mind behind the text, Dilthey's was the understanding of life as such in its various forms. Precisely by sharpening such an objective, both thinkers emphasised the need for some kind of perspective through which to approach a text (cf. above 3.1 and 3.2). Bultmann now stressed that there are quite a number of interpretative perspectives possible other than those two employed by Schleiermacher and Dilthey, but that each act of interpretation ought to imply the use of such a particular perspective. Without a particular question on the text, we have no focus for our understanding of what the text wishes to communicate. 'Therefore, interpretation always presupposes a life relation to the different subject matters that – directly or indirectly – come to expression in texts.'[48] In other words, any interpretation is fuelled by a particular preunderstanding, or, as Bultmann said elsewhere,

> [*N*]*o* exegesis is without presuppositions, inasmuch as the exegete is not a *tabula rasa*, but on the contrary, approaches the text with specific questions or with a specific way of raising questions and thus has a certain idea of the subject matter with which the text is concerned.[49]

'Objective', 'perspective', 'presupposition', and 'preunderstanding' – each of these concepts points to the fact that every interpreter is always already moving in a hermeneutical circle. Above we have distinguished two levels of the hermeneutical circle: the circle of preunderstanding and understanding the subject-matter of the text, and the circle of understanding the whole through the parts and vice versa (cf. above 1.3). Bultmann's hermeneutics attempted to clarify in particular the first level. He listed a number of possible interests which could motivate an interpreter in his or her reading, such as psychological, aesthetic, and historical, and he then concluded:

> Finally, the objective of interpretation can be given by an interest in history as the sphere of life in which human existence takes place, in which we acquire and develop our possibilities, and in which, by reflecting on these possibilities, we each come to an understanding of ourselves and of our own possibilities. . . . The texts that most nearly lend themselves to such questioning are the texts of philosophy and religion and literature. But in principle all texts (like history in general) can be subjected to it.[50]

The existential concept of reading which Bultmann postulated here was not only not anti-historical (as is still quite often claimed), but it followed from the very insight into the nature of our human historicity. Bultmann repeatedly stressed this point. 'If we approach history alive with our own problems, then it really begins to speak to us.' But he also did not get tired of stating that 'historical knowledge is at the same time knowledge of ourselves'.[51] Thus, Bultmann wanted to destroy the objectivist pretensions of some (biblical) historians, but not the historical task of the theologian. Rather, the theologian was to be made fully aware of the implications of historical thinking.

As we have seen already, Karl Barth saw Bultmann's programme of an existential hermeneutics as an imposition on the biblical texts and on their subject-matter, whereas Bultmann, like Schleiermacher before him, claimed that 'interpretation of the biblical writings is not subject to different conditions of understanding from those applying to any other literature'.[52] The Bible needs to be approached with all philological rigor and the tools of formal analysis, but also with a critically examined preunderstanding of its subject-matter. Against Barth, Bultmann emphasised that even the realisation of God's self-revelation in our human history depends on some form of preunderstanding. Such a preunderstanding is provoked by our existential knowledge of God.

> There is an existential knowledge of God present and alive in human existence in the question about 'happiness' or 'salvation' or about the meaning of the world and of history, insofar as

> this is the question about the authenticity of our own existence.[53]

Since all human knowledge of God is interpreted knowledge, it is important that the theologian who reflects on this process of interpretation discusses the conceptual framwork in which he interprets. Bultmann's framework was the existentialist undestanding of existence, and he summoned Barth to declare what was the source and meaning of his conceptuality.[54]

In a later article, 'Is Exegesis Without Presuppositions Possible?' (1957), Bultmann formulated five consequences which followed from his hermeneutical programme: (1) The exegesis of biblical texts must be free from prejudice (he had previously contrasted 'prejudice' and 'presuppositions', whereby prejudice referred to a wilful, dogmatic imposition on the text); (2) however, it is never without presuppositions, 'because as historical interpretation it presupposes the method of historical-critical research'; (3) a life relation between exegete and the biblical text and a resulting preunderstanding is presupposed; (4) this preunderstanding is not closed, but open for transformation; and (5) the understanding of a text can never be taken to be definitive, thus 'the meaning of the Scriptures discloses itself anew in every future'.[55]

Like Barth's hermeneutics, Bultmann's interpretation theory challenged the historicist approach to the Bible as well as the split between biblical exegesis and systematic theology.[56] But in spite of Barth's strong protest, Bultmann's hermeneutics reconnected theology again with the movement of philosophical hermeneutics which Schleiermacher had initiated more than a hundred years before. However, whereas Schleiermacher and Dilthey aimed at the imaginative reconstruction of the text's original sense, Bultmann, developing Schleiermacher's and Dilthey's approach now in the light of Heidegger's existentialist hermeneutics, shifted the hermeneutical goal towards retrieving the subject-matter of the biblical texts.[57] Thus, in Bultmann's hermeneutics we can see the fruits of all philosophical hermeneuts from Schleiermacher to Heidegger, while in Barth's hermeneutics we can see an effort to avoid allowing theology to come more fully to terms with the hermeneutical conditions of all text interpreters.

Our rejection of Barth's negative verdict of Bultmann's interpretation theory does not, however, imply that Bultmann's entire hermeneutical reflection was free from problems and contradictions.

Particularly his concept of demythologizing the texts of the New Testament rightly provoked much criticism. To this debate we have to turn before we shall be able to arrive at an overall assessment of the significance of the Barth-Bultmann debate on theological hermeneutics for the further development of theological thinking.

6.2.4 The Programme of Demythologizing the New Testament

Bultmann presented his theory of demythologization in a number of essays and books following its first formulation in 1941 ('New Testament and Mythology') which caused a storm both of enthusiasm and severe criticism.[58] At times the debate on this concept took the form of intellectual warfare. While we cannot follow this debate here in detail, it is important for us to realise that it was in fact a debate on theological hermeneutics. Of course, many aspects of Bultmann's hermeneutical programme are outdated today, but the major concerns of his hermeneutical reflection seem to me to be of lasting significance for any discussion of theological hermeneutics. In this section, therefore, I wish to explain Bultmann's main ideas of demythologization, appreciate their hermeneutical significance and offer appropriate aspects of criticism.

Bultmann's method of demythologization followed from his overall hermeneutical convictions which we tried to present in the previous section of this chapter. There we saw that Bultmann criticised any interpretative effort which was not sufficiently aware of its own hermeneutical conditions, i.e. its conceptuality, preunderstandings and underlying world-view. His method of demythologization represented his own effort to make his particular hermeneutical conditions explicit, especially in relation to the modern horizon or world-view through which he approached the texts of the New Testament. The ancient mythological way of speaking about God's activity in the world which had also influenced the origins of Christianity could not be transposed easily into our own scientific way of explaining the world. It needed a critical translation, that means it needed a critical interpretation.

> This method of interpretation of the New Testament which tries to recover the deeper meaning behind the mythological conceptions I call *de-mythologizing* – an unsatisfactory word, to be sure. Its aim is not to eliminate the mythological statements but to interpret them. It is a method of hermeneutics.[59]

Thus, in no way did Bultmann wish to get rid of those parts of the New Testament in which we encounter mythological language, but he insisted that these myths required a special hermeneutical effort on the part of the theological interpreter. While our ordinary religious imagination may be well able to relate to these mythological passages in the biblical texts, our systematic theological reflection must first of all admit that in the act of reading these texts two radically different world-views confront one another. This confrontation makes it necessary to understand how myths functioned in the ancient model of the world, what meaning they have in the context of the text, and how we can relate to this meaning in the context of our own modern world and our religious quest.

Looking at the development of theological hermeneutics we ought to appreciate that Bultmann tried to take seriously both the biblical texts and the modern scientific world-view, and thus was among the first theological hermeneuts to respond constructively to the hermeneutical challenges which had emerged since the sixteenth century. Whatever critique of Bultmann's particular hermeneutical proposals and his understanding of the concept of myth may be necessary, his great merit lies in his clear acknowledgement of the hermeneutical conditions in which modern theologians must attempt to interpret the biblical texts in the age of reason and science.

Bultmann never claimed that the scientific world-view was good or preferable to any other, but he defended both the duty of the theologian to translate the Christian faith into our modern world-view and the actual possibility of such a translation. 'To de-mythologize is to deny that the message of Scripture and of the Church is bound to an ancient world-view which is obsolete.'[60] Thus, he freed the Christian from the bizarre effort of trying to sacrifice his or her intellectual integrity, to change world-views and to think in the way a second century Christian might have done.[61] Like Augustine and Schleiermacher before him, Bultmann distinguished thoroughly between the Bible and the sense of the Bible. We do not believe in the Bible, but in what it has to say to us today. Moreover, he insisted that the only way we can be certain to acknowledge God's otherness and God's incomprehensibility is by recognising the contingent nature of all human talk about God (whereas Barth seemed to suggest that we actually can attain to non-contingent talk of God). Therefore, we may in fact be on our way to understanding God's 'Godness' better when we have understood that no world-view will ever be able adequately to express God's nature. In order to stress this point even more vigorously, Bultmann underlined the fact that such a demythologizing attitude appears already in the New Testament texts themselves, when, for example, Paul and John reinterpreted Jewish eschatological hopes by pointing to the 'now' as the time of decision.[62]

These concepts and distinctions provided the matrix for Bultmann's concrete interpretation of the supernatural language present in biblical texts. Biblical images such as 'kingdom of God', 'begotten of the Holy Spirit', 'born of a virgin' etc. are mythological. That is not to say that they make no sense, but that these expressions produce sense in a way which needs explaining and translation for a modern reader of the biblical texts.

Bultmann was repeatedly attacked by Karl Barth and other theologians for supposedly imposing a particular philosophy on the Bible. In response to these attacks Bultmann pointed once more to the necessity of declaring one's hermeneutical framework. Every hermeneutical framework is grounded on some kind of philosophy. Hence, the question is really which is the 'right' philosophy, i.e. 'which philosophy today offers the most adequate perspective and conceptions for understanding human existence'.[63] As we have seen in the previous section, Bultmann adopted Heidegger's existentialist philosophy beacuse it provided him with a clear focus on the existential quest for religious meaning and on the need for existential praxis.

> It would be a misunderstanding to think that the existentialist analysis of love can lead me to understand how I must love here and now. The existentialist analysis can do nothing more than make it clear to me that I can understand love only by loving.[64]

According to Bultmann the method of demythologization of the biblical texts leads to an existential intensification of God's call on the individual believer. However, this call is mediated though the church, i.e. the community in which God's word is preached and received. Thus, ultimately Bultmann, like Barth, wished to serve the act of proclaiming the Word of God; but unlike Barth, he insisted on a proper analysis of the conditions in which such a proclamation is to take place.

6.2.5 Assessing Bultmann's Contribution to Theological Hermeneutics

There can be no doubt that Bultmann's interpretation theory calls for a thorough critique today. But the datedness of that theory and its various limitations must not be allowed to conceal an appreciation of the significant progress which this hermeneutics represented. Following Schleiermacher, Bultmann recognised the need to develop an interpretation theory which was able critically to relate the meaning of the biblical texts to today's scientifically-minded world. He defended convincingly the philosophical character of theological hermeneutics and opted himself for a particular philosophical framework without, however, claiming that his option was the only possible or legitimate one. Thus, he opened a conversation between theology and philosophy which must continue as long as theology wishes to engage in its primary duty, namely the translation of the sense of the Bible into the respective world-view of human listeners.

Paul Ricœur has praised Bultmann for developing his hermeneutics beyond Schleiermacher and Dilthey towards a hermeneutics of meaning instead of a hermeneutics of the author's intention. But at the same time Ricœur has criticised Bultmann for not having gone far enough in his hermeneutical reflection. He blamed Bultmann for having taken a short-cut from texts to existential meaning instead of having embarked on the long road of interpretation.[65] What does Ricœur mean here?

First of all he notices that Bultmann was prepared to interpret myths as objectifying expressions, but that he did not propose any theory of interpreting the non-mythical parts of the Christian proclamation (the *kerygma*). 'Bultmann seems to believe that a language which is no longer "objectifying" is innocent. But in what sense is it still a language? And what does it signify?'[66] Thus, Bultmann's opposition between objectifying mythical expression on the one hand and faith on the other is naïve. Interpreting myth is promoted, but interpreting other faith statements is not considered. Therefore, Ricœur warns that the *sacrificium intellectus* which Bultmann wanted to avoid by recognising the mythical nature of many biblical texts, is in a way now demanded from a believer who no longer needs to interpret the non-mythical sections of the Bible when he or she relates existentially to them.[67] In other words, we could say that Bultmann's hermeneutics is not hermeneutical enough.

Secondly, Ricœur warns us that this too exclusive attachment to the opposition between myth and *kerygma* obscures the more important distinction between objective meaning and subjective understanding. In an illuminating comparison, Ricœur calls Bultmann's problem with meaning the opposite of the structuralists' problem with signs. Bultmann stressed the 'speaking' side whereas structuralism has stressed the 'language' side. And while the structuralists need to think about language as event, Bultmann lacks thinking about language as a system of signs.

> If there is no objective meaning, then the text no longer says anything at all; without existential appropriation, what the text does say is no longer living speech. The task of a theory of interpretation is to combine in a single process these two movements of comprehension.[68]

The real problem with Bultmann's hermeneutics, then, is not, as Barth had suggested, an objectification of faith or, in other words, a dissolution of faith into talk about human existence. Bultmann did not aim at either. Instead the really serious problem is that Bultmann's hermeneutical reflection runs short and ends too quickly in a decison of faith, before all the implications of the biblical text are sufficiently considered. Thus, against Bultmann we must insist that the existential decision is critically grounded only then when the process of interpretation has allowed the text to disclose its full challenge. This disclosure of the text's sense provokes faith and theological reflection. But this disclosure is a painful process which entails much explanatory labour as we have seen in the preceeding chapters. Either the text confronts me as an *objectum*, i.e. as something which lies in my way and to which I can refer, or it is not protected against an easy dissolution into my mere opinion of what it represents. Hence, critical hermeneutics needs to include a theory of language in general and of textual signification in particular.

The fact that Bultmann had used Heidegger's philosophy in developing his interpretation theory ought not to be held against him. As we have seen he was prepared to see any adequate philosophical system enlightening the theologian about his or her conceptuality. However, that he did not address the later Heidegger's philosophy of language (cf. above 3.3.3) and then, in critical dialogue with this philosophy, offer his own critical theory of language, must be noted with surprise and theological suspicion.[69]

6.2.6 Conclusions from Our Discussion of the Barth-Bultmann Debate on Hermeneutics

At this stage it may be helpful to sum up the state of theological hermeneutics in the light of the Barth-Bultmann debate. First, it has become obvious that in the interest of assessing a theologian's approach to hermeneutics we have to ask whether or not and to what extent he or she does make explicit his or her hermeneutical framework. In the case of Barth, the principles of text-interpretation and the challenge of the modern interpreter's horizon were not critically reflected. In the case of Bultmann, the horizon was discussed but the critical reflection on hermeneutics was not supported by a critical theory of language.

Secondly, we have seen how Barth rejected the entire hermeneutical enterprise as initiated by Schleiermacher out of fear it could distort the self-revelation of God's Word, whereas Bultmann critically and constructively developed Schleiermacher's and Dilthey's hermeneutical insights and suggestions in order to enlighten the theological interpreters about their need critically to reflect on their interpretative conditions and aims.

Thirdly, we noted that Bultmann connected theological thinking anew with the long tradition of critical reflection on the philosophical principles of exegesis in the Christian movement and that he reopened the dialogue with classical and contemporary philosophical reflection (especially Heidegger) on hermeneutics.

Fourthly, we appreciated that Barth and Bultmann were both critical of historicist interpretation of the Bible without, however, neglecting the historical dimension of all biblical interpretation.

Finally, it is of great importance to be mindful that Barth and Bultmann were both united in their attempt to protect the transcendence of God in view of all theories which claim that 'God' was only another term for meaning. In the case of Bultmann, the search for meaning prepared human beings to listen to the texts that speak about God. Given Ricœur's critical amendments, the biblical texts are able to address us anew and challenge us to think about God. In the case of Barth, one listens to the biblical texts in order to hear anew the Word of God which may make itself heard through the proclamation of God's revelation in these texts. Thus, both Barth and Bultmann vigorously claimed that in principal the biblical texts are able to funotion as mediators of God's revelation. As such both scholars attributed anew a communicative authority to these texts and kept the interest in their proper interpretation alive.

How this hermeneutical interest developed after Barth and Bultmann, though thoroughly influenced by both is the subject-matter of the remaining section of this chapter.

6.3 THE NEW HERMENEUTIC

6.3.1 Beyond Barth and Bultmann

By now 'The New Hermeneutic' has become a technical term which refers to the hermeneutical movement which emerged after Barth and Bultmann. Its main philosophical characteristic was its orientation to the later Heidegger's philosophy of language, its main theological characteristic was its unique combination of this new philosophical departure and a retrieval of the Reformational understanding of the power of the Word of God. While the Barth-Bultmann debate was, of course, closely followed outside its Germanic context, the New Hermeneutic remained no longer confined to this context; instead it attracted not only a more international audience, but also a more international circle of participators. In particular, theologians in the United States, such as James M. Robinson, John Dillenberger, Robert W. Funk, John B. Cobb, Jr. and others, began to enter into the hermeneutical debate. Significant for this new geographical horizon of hermeneutical reflection in theology was a congress on the New Hermeneutic in America (at Drew University in 1962) and the subsequent publication of its papers on both sides of the Atlantic Ocean under the title *The New Hermeneutic* (1964), edited by James M. Robinson and John B. Cobb, Jr., both of them American theologians.[70] The chief protagonists of the New Hermeneutic, however, still were German theologians, namely Ernst Fuchs (1903–83) and Gerhard Ebeling (born 1912). Both of them were former students of Bultmann at the University of Marburg, and later on each of them was to head an institute of hermeneutics, Fuchs in Marburg and Ebeling in Zürich. They co-operated closely with one another and were responsible for many creative impulses in the theological development after The Second World War. Due to Fuchs' difficult literary style, he remained less known outside the German-speaking world, whereas Ebeling's work has been translated into many languages and won him lasting international acclaim.

In spite of their close co-operation and their agreement on many aspects of theological hermeneutics, their starting-points differed somewhat. Fuchs was influenced in particular by the later Heidegger and attempted to correct Bultmann's hermeneutical programme in the light of Heidegger's later emphasis on language. Ebeling also has been influenced strongly by Heidegger, but he attempted to create a synthesis between Heidegger's philosophy of language on the one hand and Luther's theology of the Word on the other. He has also conversed with Hans-Georg Gadamer's hermeneutics and thus must be seen as the most influential representative of the New Hermeneutic today. In view of this continuing prominence of Ebeling's contribution to hermeneutical thought, it would seem only appropriate to devote most of our attention in this section to his work. Since, however, on the whole the contributions by Fuchs have remained rather inaccessible to those students of hermeneutics who have not mastered the German language, it may be useful here to point at least to some aspects of his hermeneutical proposal in some detail.

6.3.2 The Later Heidegger and Theological Hermeneutics: Ernst Fuchs

Fuchs developed his own approach to hermeneutics in a number of essays and most prominently in his book *Hermeneutik* (1st ed. 1954).[71] Unlike Bultmann who had applied Heidegger's earlier philosophy of existence to theology, Fuchs was also influenced by the later Heidegger's philosophical concern with language. Thus, while the crucial question for Bultmann was how the human being could achieve authenticity in his or her existence, the leading question for Fuchs was how the human being could learn to listen again to the undisturbed language of being.

We recall here that in his later writings, Heidegger was more and more moved by insight into the language of being (cf. above 3.3.3). Language speaks of being, therefore we have to listen to its call, 'the call of being', and to respond to it. For Heidegger, language could never be defined adequately by pointing only to its semiotic character, i.e. to the fact that it can signify something. (Augustine had described the nature of language like this, as we have seen above in 2.2.3.) Instead, language ought to be described as the event [*Ereignis*] of Being itself. But Heidegger added that such an event of Being could not be grasped fully. Rather language reveals and conceals Being at the same time. Applying the earlier Heidegger's particular language on the later Heidegger's programme, we could say that 'authentic existence' happens wherever human beings listen and respond to this call of Being in language. In this context, Heidegger payed special attention to the poets whose highest task he understood to be that they ought to call us back into Being by making us listen to the best expression of the voice of Being itself.

In his still very valuable report on 'Hermeneutic Since Barth' in *The New Hermeneutic*,[72] James M. Robinson pointed out with great clarity how Fuchs, following Heidegger, saw language no longer only as an objectification of human self-understanding, as did Bultmann, but now as the very constitutive factor of human self-understanding.[73] Accordingly he could define truth as '*Spruch des Seins*' [expression of being].[74]

Moreover, Fuchs appreciated Heidegger's complaint about the inauthenticity of most language as the negative folio into which true language could break:

> For the lament as *language* no longer belongs to lostness, but rather supplies man with the plus that as the *essence* of language reminds him that he belongs to a communication, a . . . *nearness* to the power at work in language prior to all human participation. For it is not true that man has given birth to language. Rather man is born out of language. That man then has made language a means of usurped existence merely proves that man is accustomed to exist in daily life having missed the mark.[75]

Fuchs discovered authentic language in Jesus' language of love, and thus identified the goal of Heidegger's quest for authentic language with the christological experience as witnessed to in the New Testament texts. Therefore, for Fuchs the hermeneutical problem is how we can *listen* properly to God's language in the texts of the New Testament.

> So we must find out to what extent our mental activity, our seeing, is bound to a hearing. That is the hermeneutical problem. It is posed for us every day anew. This is the point of departure for the New Testament.[76]

Listening to God's Word is, however, not easy for human beings in the twentieth century. Language has been too restricted by scientific concerns.

> The difficulty is not a false methodology, but a lack of conscious experience, and this on the part of the exegete of today. We cannot conceive of there being a life after death. We assume we are obligated to fit the divine within the limits of our scientifically investigated world of facts. And of course that does not succeed.[77]

In this situation of speechlessness the New Testament helps us to recover our language. 'The New Testament is itself a textbook in hermeneutic. It teaches the hermeneutic of faith – in brief, the language of faith – and it encourages us to try out this language ourselves, so that we may become familiar with – God.'[78]

Fuchs proposed a retrieval of ordinary language because such a language alone could help us to relate to the meaning of the New Testament texts. He concluded:

> The norm of our interpretation is preaching. The text is interpreted when God is proclaimed! So we should attempt to let ourselves be addressed by the text and to go with the text to the place it wishes to take us. But this is daily life. In the interaction of the text with daily life we experience the truth of the New Testament. And the remarkable thing is this, that this book shines brighter and brighter the more difficult daily life becomes. God intends to remain God. Perhaps this is the fundamental hermeneutical statement precisely for our time.[79]

This quote documents the close relationship between Fuchs and both Barth and Bultmann. All three theologians attempted to formulate a hermeneutical programme which was to enable the modern person to listen anew to the proclamation of God's Word in the texts of the Bible, and all three wished to restore the respect for God's godness. Their respective approaches to hermeneutics differed, however, in terms of their philosophical reflection. Barth rejected any philosophical imposition on biblical interpretation. Fuchs saw – at least in theory – the need for a general hermeneutics and thus followed Schleiermacher in this regard, whose hermeneutical intentions he saw taken up especially by Heidegger.[80] Fuchs not only hoped to learn from Heidegger's concept of language, but went so far as to identify true 'language' ontologically with God's Word. Moreover, he insisted with Bultmann that the biblical texts (or rather the New Testament texts, since neither showed much concern with the Hebrew Scriptures!) had to be interpreted for our human existence today and as statements which came out of an existential condition. The biblical texts are not just documents, but texts of existential significance.[81] At the same time, this act of interpretation brings the truth of our existence today to light.[82] Apart from these differences, however, Fuchs' hermeneutical programme culminated in the same recommendation as the one offered by Karl Barth: God wants to be proclaimed as God, and the matrix of our text-interpretation is the proclamation of God's self-revelation in our world. Thus, he can say that a proper hermeneutics is a *'Sprachlehre des Glaubens'* [language-teaching of faith].[83]

In spite of Fuchs' critique of various aspects of Barth's hermeneutics, his overall affinity to Barth's concerns remained quite strong. Fuchs presented basically a hermeneutics of faith, i.e. a materially oriented hermeneutics.[84] Although he mentioned the need for a general hermeneutics, as we have seen, he quickly proceeded to a discussion of the theological nature of any authentic search for meaning and referred us to the existential interpretation of the New Testament texts.[85] However, just by claiming an identity between a certain philosophical insight and a theological conviction the latter is not yet submitted to critical scrutiny.

As we have seen in the two previous chapters of this book, critical hermeneutics requires a critical and self-critical philosophical reflection on language, on its condition and its performance, as well as a thorough theological critique of the texts themselves. Fuchs' reception of Heidegger's ontological concept of language remained uncritical of the problems inherent in Heidegger's thought. The mere demand that we should go with the text where it would like to have us, does not yet offer a satisfactory proposal for critical interpretation. Fuchs may well have been right that a modern religious reading of the New Testament texts ought to be more firmly rooted in our everyday experiences, but he did not reflect enough either on the question how we could most adequately understand these everyday experiences, or on possible appropriate moves for a truly critical interpretation of the texts themselves.

6.3.3 Gerhard Ebeling's Theological Hermeneutics

No other theologian in this century has devoted so much of his energy to the reflection on and propagation of hermeneutical issues in theology as Gerhard Ebeling. His doctoral thesis at the beginning of his theological career dealt with Luther's hermeneutics[86], and since then he has not stopped thinking, lecturing and writing about hermeneutical problems in theology.[87] Many of his contributions to hermeneutics have helped greatly to focus the theological debate on this topic, especially his articles 'Hermeneutik' in *Religion in Geschichte und Gegenwart*,[88] 'The Significance of the Critical Historical Method for Church and Theology in Protestantism',[89] 'Word of God and Hermeneutics'[90] and 'God and Word'.[91] While the first of these presented the results of the hermeneutical discussion in Christianity and philosophy until the 1950s, in the other articles Ebeling has developed major aspects of his own approach to theological hermeneutics.

6.3.3.1 The Hermeneutical Nature of Theology

In these and his other publications in the field Ebeling has attempted to formulate a coherent and critical hermeneutics for Protestant theology in the twentieth century. Like Fuchs, he has been influenced by the later Heidegger's ontological understanding of language; but he has tried to combine Reformation theology with this new concept of language more clearly and forcefully than Fuchs. Ebeling was aware of the hermeneutical shortcomings of the Protestant Reformation; and he recognised the limitations of Luther's insight into the hermeneutical problem. Luther did not advance the reflection on theological method as such, nor was the Reformation in general sufficiently conscious of its temporal distance from Early Christianity.[92] According to Ebeling, the hermeneutical question for contemporary protestant theology therefore ought to be how to allow revelation to become contemporaneous with us today.[93]

Ebeling showed that the reformational doctrine of justification by faith alone (*sola fide*) contained already the rejection of any lasting or 'secure' effort of making revelation contemporaneous, but it also contained already an understanding of the personal dimension of any such encounter with revelation in the context of history.[94] Yet it lacked a clearer reflection on its linguistic nature. Even Bultmann's hermeneutics did not offer such a necessary reflection, as we have seen above (cf. 6.2.5).

At this point, Heidegger's ontological understanding of language comes to help. Following Heidegger, Ebeling rejects a purely instrumentalist view of language as too limited: 'To regard language exclusively as a technical instrument is to cut it off from that which is the constant source of its life – namely, the element of time.'[95] The event-character of language is lost in such a narrow approach. What has to be retrieved, therefore, is the foundational nature of language. Applied to our hermeneutical reflection, this means that '[t]he primary phenomenon in the realm of understanding is not understanding *of* language, but understanding *through* language'.[96] Heidegger spoke of the call of language, Ebeling speaks of the depth dimension of every linguistic event. He diagnoses in every word event 'a depth dimension which is indicated by the word "God" . . . as a hidden and tacit word event to which every word owes its existence'.[97] Unfortunately today, this basic situation of human existence is no longer part of public perception. As a consequence, speaking of God happens in the ghetto of private discourse and appears as a linguistic problem to those who are not themselves engaged in such language.

> Indeed the phrase 'Word of God' itself appears to be such a linguistic problem. In contrast to this understanding, which indeed readily suggests itself, the very criterion of a right understanding lies in whether God's Word is understood as assurance-giving language which has a saving effect in history, as the constant granting of the gift of language, as an authority for the Word which is superior to the powers that render us speechless.[98]

The biblical texts (the Old Testament by virtue of the New Testament) witness to this universal linguistic event. However, they must not be identified with that event.

> Word of God, according to the biblical tradition, thus seeks to be understood as a word event that does not go out of date but constantly renews itself, does not create closed areas of special

interest but opens up the world, does not enforce uniformity but is linguistically creative.'[99]

According to Ebeling, interpretation is called for whenever the normal function of the Word is disturbed. But he hastens to qualify the limits of such interpretation: 'The aim of such interpretation cannot, however, be anything other than the removal of the obstacle which prevents the Word from mediating understanding by itself.'[100] Here the essence of Ebeling's concept of theological hermeneutics becomes clear: theological hermeneutics is necessary because all theology is fully hermeneutical! In other words, the purpose of theology is the always new attempt at freeing the way for the Word of God in the act of text-interpretation. Elsewhere Ebeling defines theology as that 'which calls us to accept our responsibility for the Word'.[101] Thus, the task of hermeneutical theology is to make human beings more responsive and more responsible towards the Word of God. But this task includes a critical assessment of our own word situation: do we recognise the fact that God has already addressed us in his Word?

Ebeling concludes that the Word of Holy Scripture discloses the basic situation of human beings: a) a divided reality whose signature is the tension between the enigmatic and the mysterious; b) a reality of word which in all its complexity and variation addresses the human being 'laying hold of him at the point of his verbal responsibility and causing him . . . to cry out to Him whom he entreats and from whom he receives . . . the grace of a word that grants life'; and c) a reality which demands faith and which ultimately stands under the promise of the authoritative word of Jesus.[102]

6.3.3.2 *How Critical Is Ebeling's Hermeneutics?*

Undoubtedly, Ebeling's hermeneutical thought represents an enormous achievement in Protestant theology. Even more than his colleague Fuchs, Ebeling has thought through the hermeneutical insights of the entire Christian tradition and of contemporary philosophy. His knowledge of these developments is unrivalled in contemporary theology. Unlike Barth, he has recognised and defended the need for a close dialogue between theology and philosophy on hermeneutical matters. And he has appreciated the hermeneutical and related methodological problems which Protestant theology had inherited from the Reformation.

However, Ebeling has not cultivated the creative tension between philosophical and theological hermeneutics. Instead he has identified their mutual source in the Word of God and thus has combined the analysis of the conditions of human communication with his theological understanding of the nature and future of the universe. The critical reflection on the hermeneutical implications of human communication in general and of text-interpretation in particular on the one hand, and the critical reflection on the hermeneutical nature of theological thinking on the other, are no longer engaged in a productive dialectical relationship. Ebeling has sublated this dialectics in his own theological synthesis which owes its nature to the Protestant tradition of theology of the Word. If one accepts this tradition without asking critical questions, then Ebeling's synthesis must surely provide the best hermeneutical proposal for theology. However, if even the very tradition of the theology of the Word and its particular hermeneutical presuppositions are to be examined critically, then Ebeling's principal approach to hermeneutics would also need to be addressed more critically.

Since Ebeling reckons all the time with the power of the Word to reveal itself once the respective communicative condition has been made receptive for such acts of revelation, the possibility of an interpretation of the biblical texts outside the context of faith does not emerge in his reflections. For him the only real hermeneutical correspondence is the one between Word and Faith.[103] The correspondence between text and interpretation is only relevant for him in so far as it points to this theological correspondence between Word and Faith. Hermeneutics is then a function of theology and does not enjoy the status of an – at least initially – autonomous discipline with the aim of reflecting on the dialectical relationship between text and interpretation and its implications.

Hence, Ebeling has turned away from Schleiermacher's project of an independent philosophical hermeneutics, and ultimately totally subjected the discussion of philosophical hermeneutics to his particular theological needs. This move then implies that theology has opted out of the interdisciplinary effort of reflecting on hermeneutical problems and now concentrates solely on its own hermeneutical needs which are determined by its particular theological tradition. The effect of this limiting of the hermeneutical focus is, of course, that the particular tradition which has thus determined the hermeneutical horizon of theology, in Ebeling's case that is the tradition of theology of the Word, is itself no longer an object of hermeneutical suspicion. Accordingly, Ebeling could affirm that 'hermeneutics as a theological doctrine of understanding is then a doctrine of the Word of God'.[104] The primary task of theological hermeneutical thinking is accordingly the formulation of a 'theological doctrine of language' [*Theologische Sprachlehre*].[105]

Even though Ebeling has insisted that the task of a systematic theology, now newly understood as hermeneutical, is ultimately not the transmission of a set of definitive doctrines of a closed system, but the mediation of the ability of judgment in regard to theological thinking and the studying of the mode in which responsible theological statements come into being,[106] he never questions the tradition of theology of the Word. Hermeneutics for Ebeling remains characterised by its service function within the terms of this tradition. He appreciates the critical function of hermeneutics, but only within this tradition.

6.4 CONCLUSION

In this chapter we have reviewed a major part of the development of theological hermeneutics in this century.[107] We have seen that all the hermeneuts discussed here tried to overcome the ideological limitations of historicist interpretation of the Bible. The Barth-Bultmann debate on hermeneutics, however, illustrated that, as a result, two different types of theological hermeneutics emerged: Barth's hermeneutics with its radical subordination of hermeneutical questions under his own theological insights; and Bultmann's hermeneutics which tried to maintain at least in principle the critical tension between philosophical considerations of human understanding and his particular existentialist interpretation of theology. The shortcomings of Bultmann's hermeneutics, i.e. the problems with his concept of demythologization and the absence of a critical theory of language, however, do not devalue his principle achievement, namely to propose a dialectical relationship between philosophical and theological hermeneutics.

The movement called 'The New Hermeneutic' did not maintain this dialectic. Instead its chief representatives Fuchs and Ebeling proposed an inner-theological hermeneutics, i.e. a hermeneutics of faith, which was to benefit from philosophical hermeneutics but which was ultimately interested in it only in so far as it helped to foster the particular Reformation tradition of theology of the

Word. More precisely, within this tradition the goal of theological hermeneutics was to help promote proper preaching and not the establishment of a more adequate epistemological foundation of theological thinking.

Thus, in spite of its affinities to Heidegger's philosophy, especially his ontological understanding of language, the New Hermeneutic has not offered a contribution to the development of hermeneutics as such. It neither engaged in the linguistic discussions of the 1960s nor in the emerging critique of the hermeneutical tradition (cf. Ricœur, Habermas, Barthes, Foucault, Derrida), both of which were quite critical of Heidegger's philosophy of language. Also the question of an ethics in interpretation has arisen for Ebeling only within the context of the particular Protestant tradition. Ebeling has stressed the responsibilty of the interpreter towards the Word [*Wörtverantwortung*].[108] Therefore, in spite of its many valuable theological insights, the New Hermeneutic has more in common with Barth than with Bultmann, and remains on the whole within the confines of Neo-orthodox theology.

In Chapter 7 I shall discuss the impact of hermeneutical thinking on the theological question of determining the identity of Christian movement.

7

The Development of Theological Hermeneutics (III): Hermeneutics and Christian Identity

7.0 INTRODUCTION

In this final chapter I wish to examine the significance of hermeneutics for theological thinking today. That hermeneutical thinking is of importance for theology hardly any theologian doubts today. Thus, the crucial question is not whether or not we need hermeneutics, but which hermeneutics may be considered to be adequate for a particular kind of theological thinking. Moreover, nobody in contemporary theology would wish to question the necessity of proper exegetical methods as far as biblical interpretation is concerned. Yet the effect of the choice in favour of a particular method of interpretation on the self-understanding of the interpreter or of the interpretative community as a whole is often not appreciated with equal clarity. Thus, theology's actual commitment to hermeneutical thinking is not always quite comprehensive. This becomes particularly clear when we contrast those efforts in hermeneutics which are motivated by the goal to establish 'correspondence' with the Scriptures with those efforts which are aiming at a mutually critical 'correlation' between the interpretation of biblical and other religious texts on the one hand and the existing plurality of interpretation theories on the other.

7.1 HERMENEUTICAL PARADIGMS IN THEOLOGY TODAY

In the last decade a number of books on 'biblical hermeneutics' have appeared. Their primary interest has been to study the classical interpretative approaches to the Scriptures and to develop contemporary methods of reading the Bible. Through their writings biblical scholars such as Peter Stuhlmacher, Duncan Ferguson, Robert Morgan and John Barton have contributed significantly to the clarification of many burning issues in biblical interpretation and have made their readers fully aware of the critical demands which New Testament exegesis today imposes on the contemporary reader.[1] However, it is interesting to note that in different ways these approaches to biblical hermeneutics usually pursue the course of correspondence with the Scriptures. Thus, their primary aim is to use general hermeneutical thinking for their purpose of approaching the Scriptures. Normally, they do not see themselves called to contribute to the general discussion of hermeneutics in the light of their own particular interpretative experiences. While a 'special' biblical hermeneutics has, of course, its place and legitimacy, it can also be examined in terms of its relationship to 'general' or philosophical hermeneutics. Such an examination may provide insights into the actual nature of the hermeneutical thinking of the respective scholar.

Peter Stuhlmacher offers a very impressive discussion of the development of biblical interpretation since its beginnings. However, his discussion is dominated by his effort to develop a hermeneutics of *Einverständnis* [agreement] with the Bible.[2] For him, the Bible has an advance in truth [*Wahrheitsvorsprung*] to which the biblical interpreter must be an obedient servant.[3] Stuhlmacher considers the historical-critical method as the best available exegetical method, and welcomes Gadamer's invitation to join the tradition through interpreting its texts as a timely reminder to biblical scholars to develop 'a hermeneutics of agreement with the biblical texts which is based on the reflection on method and effective-historical consciousness'.[4]

However, from our discussion of Gadamer's hermeneutics (cf. above 3.4) and our reflection upon contemporary reading theories (cf. above 5.2), it should have become clear that neither the appeal to tradition nor to the historical-critical method can satisfy the contemporary reader who has learned to question both the cartesian self-certainty of the 'modern' interpreter and the constructs of historical thinking. While I have no problem in agreeing with Stuhlmacher that all interpretative efforts must aim at an understanding of the message or sense of the text in question, I see a problem in his hermeneutical starting-point. The hermeneut who integrates his or her formal hermeneutical reflection too quickly into his or her material discussion of the texts (in this case the biblical texts) runs the danger of losing the epistemological distance, which is necessary for the proper reflection on our hermeneutical conditions. In other words, the expected result of our concrete interpretative efforts should not structure our discussion of the nature of interpretation itself. Ultimately Stuhlmacher has opted for a special biblical hermeneutics which seeks information from those philosophical efforts which promise to enrich his understanding of biblical interpretation.[5]

Duncan Ferguson follows a similar approach. He too informs the reader competently about the hermeneutical tradition and draws conclusions from the discussion on philosophical hermeneutics which he then applies to his project of a faith hermeneutics. 'It is faith guided by historical study that supplies the clue to the interpretation of the Christian revelation.'[6]

Robert Morgan and John Barton are more interested in the recent development of biblical interpretation since the Enlightenment. They emphasise the need to take literary approaches to the Scriptures more seriously in any discussion of religious identity. They suggest 'that a literary framework, which includes the results of historical and linguistic research, is today more promising for the study of religion and for theology than the historical framework (which includes literary study) that has dominated New Testament studies in particular since the 1830s'.[7]

The question how linguistic and literary approaches shape our identity as Christians has also been George Lindbeck's primary concern in his theological reflection on *The Nature of Doctrine*.[8] Lindbeck favours a descriptive model of theological thinking. Taking the conditioning force of language seriously, he argues in favour of a cultural-linguistic description of religious thought and its doctrines. Accordingly he wishes to interpret texts 'intratextually'. 'To describe the basic meaning of these books is an intratextual task, a matter of explicating their contents and the perspectives on extratextual reality that they generate.'[9] By limiting the interpretation of texts to the level of an 'intratextual task', Lindbeck has defined reading in rather restrictive terms. Reading, however, can be more than an activity which operates only within a cultural-linguistic system. Reading can also develop into an experience of overcoming such intratextuality. It includes the potential of a transformational activity in which attitudes towards the world, towards one's own linguistic socialisation and competence, and towards one's own culture and religious preunderstandings may be (at times radically) altered. Thus, by offering such new intellectual experiences, the act of reading ancient and foreign texts may lead to all kinds of conversions of world-views.

Moreover, Lindbeck has suggested that a literary reading of the Bible is the most adequate approach, and he calls for a theology which uses explicitly biblical imagination to shape contemporary religious praxis.[10] He has opposed as 'foundationalism' the attempt to promote a formal and independent consideration of hermeneutics, and instead tried to re-introduce a specifically theological hermeneutics.[11] He thus has rejected the importance of a general or philosophical hermeneutics for theology. The result of a similar method – in spite of other strong differences – we have studied already when we considered Karl Barth's hermeneutics in Chapter 6. Not unlike Stuhlmacher, though now on a theological level, Lindbeck makes good use of gene al hermeneutical thinking in order to develop his cultural-linguistic model of interpreting theological statements, in order then to dispose of this general hermeneutical thinking in favour of a specifically hermeneutical model, i.e. his intratextual text-interpretation.

As we have seen in Chapter 6, at times dogmatic considerations are allowed to override hermeneutical insights. In the context of the Christian church this is the case when on the one hand church authorities acknowledge the duties of the professional interpreter to help the community of Christians to understand its tradition through an interpretation of its texts, but on the other hand refuse to listen to the results of such interpretative efforts. But dogmatism occurs also whenever interpreters for fear of upsetting old dogmatic balances fail to come to terms with the possible plurality of adequate approaches to a foundational text. These and other occasions of crisis in a religious tradition or in a culture as a whole necessitate a more fundamental revision of hermeneutical theory and interpretative praxis. 'A crisis of interpretation within any tradition eventually becomes a demand to interpret this very process of interpretation.'[12] Some systematic theologians and exegetes are united in diagnosing that Christianity seems to experience such a crisis at this time in history, and therefore requires a thorough reflection on its hermeneutical foundations.

The New Testament scholar Klaus Berger, for instance, has

insisted that the hermeneutical question must remain an open one.[13] Moreover, he has encouraged the mutually critical dialogue between general philosophical hermeneutics and special biblical hermeneutics.[14] And systematic theologians such as David Tracy and Hans Küng have stressed the need for such a mutually critical dialogue.[15]

As far as the significance of hermeneutics is concerned there are then at present three camps in Christian theology. (1) There are those Christian thinkers like Tracy, Küng, and Berger who favour an open-ended dialogue on method between Christian interpreters and other thinkers interested in hermeneutics. Generally speaking, they wish to assess the particular Christian vision for this world in the context of a great conversation with all other groups of human thinkers who care for the people of this world and for the universe in which we live. (2) There are those Christian thinkers like Stuhlmacher, Lindbeck and the late Hans Frei who feel that they ought to determine the specifically Christian vision predominantly from inside the church and biblical theology.[16] According to Lindbeck a dialogue with other religious or secular intellectual forces can happen on the basis of comparing different religious stories and their grammars.[17]

Both groups agree on the need for interpretation theory, but only the first group is willing to be engaged radically in the hermeneutical reflection on its methodological foundations. For the second group interpretation theory enters only on the level of micro-hermeneneutical concerns with specific Christian texts. In other words, interpretation theory is to help to receive confirmation from particular readings of such crucial texts as the Bible and differing sets of church doctrines.[18]

And finally (3) there are those Christian thinkers who call again for an 'orthodox' approach to the Scriptures. Obviously, such a dogmatic approach to the texts of the Christian tradition is not in favour of contemplating the insights of philosophical hermeneutics for its own interpretative work. Instead it rejects this 'alien' interference and claims thus to protect the integrity of its sacred texts. Karl Barth is as representative of this approach as is the current Magisterium of the Roman Catholic Church. The underlying thesis is, of course, that divine revelation does not need human methods or philosophical sophistication to do its job successfully. Christian thinking is understood to confront the world on the basis of its particular reception of the Word of God or of divine knowledge, whereas the world has access only to ordinary language and natural reason, however philosophically purified.

Apart from the questionable theology which supports this two-tier system of knowledge this last approach to text-interpretation betrays the rich Christian tradition of hermeneutical reflection which we tried to outline above in Chapter 2. Until the dawn of modernity Christian thinkers, often in co-operation with their Jewish and Muslim colleagues, reflected on the epistemological conditions of text-interpretation and on the dialectic between text-interpretation and world-understanding. Only when the traditional horizon of world-understanding had collapsed in the seventeenth century, did we encounter the phenomenon of hermeneutical refusal in Christian theology. The illusions of being able to offer a timeless body of truths which are beyond interpretative needs or of having access to the heart of the Bible without engaging in the messy job of actually and consciously interpreting its many texts are a modern phenomenon. They cannot claim much support from the earlier Christian tradition. They point to a fear and anxiety of the world in some theologians and to their deeper theological lack of courage in coming to terms with the developments of human knowledge. Rather than approaching the emerging world-views with critical reason, the various representatives of a theological 'orthodoxy' have circumvented, bedevilled, or replaced reason by authoritarian behaviour of one kind or another.

There are then at least three principal theological paradigms of engaging in hermeneutics today: one which defends dogmatic certainty, another which develops its own theological mode of participating in the wider human conversation on adequate theories of text-interpretation and world-interpretation, and a third which ultimately limits itself to intratextual considerations. In this chapter I do not wish to dwell any longer on the reasons for the first group's refusal to engage in critical and self-critical hermeneutics, nor on the third group's hermeneutical self-limitation. Rather I would like to show what Christian theology may have to gain for its own self-understanding by getting involved in the contemporary conversation on hermeneutics. Thus, I do advocate a return to the traditional theological occupation with questions of method.

In order to illustrate the significance of hermeneutics for Christian theology I shall take the example of the theological problem of interpreting the Christian tradition. The discussion of the hermeneutical dimensions involved in this theological activity may achieve two things at once. It may help the reader of this book to see a hermeneutics of retrieval and suspicion at work, and it may point once more to the necessity of such a methodological reflection for Christian theology. David Tracy has discussed at length the importance of hermeneutical thinking for the intellectual self-understanding of theology in the academy.[19] And Paul Ricœur, Jürgen Habermas and others have convincingly emphasised the significance of hermeneutical reflection for the development of the individual human being as well as for the emancipatory discourse of society as a whole.[20] However, the significance of hermeneutical thinking for the self-understanding of the Christian movement, i.e. the church, may need further clarification. Thus, in the following sections of this chapter I wish to offer some thoughts on the impact of hermeneutics on the method of ecclesiological thinking.

7.2 INTERPRETING THE 'CHRISTIAN TRADITION'

In a theological context, 'tradition' has at least two different though related meanings: it may refer to the extra-biblical apostolic heritage in the church or it may refer to the whole development of the Christian church until the present time.[21] While the narrower first meaning will also have to be dealt with in the course of our discussion, the overall focus of our reflections in this chapter is on the development and present situation of the Christian church.[22] Yet our reflections will not primarily concentrate on the history of the different branches of the Christian church. Rather I would like to attempt a systematic analysis of the criteria through which we may assess this development, its achievements and failures and the need for reform and change. Such a critical assessment of the Christian tradition is necessary especially today in the light of the stimulus for church reform coming from the ecumenical movement, and because of the continuous suspicion about the theological legitimacy of our present ecclesial traditions both from outside and inside the Christian movement. These and other questions concerning the identity of the Christian church have directed the attention of many theologians and church leaders towards a re-interpretation of the Christian tradition. Now once more the Christian tradition has become an object of interpretation, and at the same time interpretation theory itself has become the focus of theological attention.

However, no interpretation can be free of interests. Thus, we find a great number of approaches to this tradition. The spectrum of the plurality of interests is characterised on the one end by those approaches which attempt to examine the present situation of the Christian church critically, and on the other end by those approaches which aim at supporting a given ecclesial *status quo* at all costs. Thus, attitudes towards particular questions and problems in the different Christian Churches vary enormously as illustrated by the number of debates at present (cf. the debates on such issues as the participation of lay-people in the church, the role of women in church and ministry, the hierarchical constitution of ministry, the nature and authority of doctrines, the content and form of religious education, the attitudes towards homosexuals and lesbians in the church and ministry etc.) In all these conflicts and debates 'tradition' has been used to protect the *status quo* of ecclesial positions as well as to question it. Different appeals and interpretations clash with one another.

In such a state of confusion it must be the task of theologians to serve the Christian community by attempting to clarify the issues as far as possible and to develop an adequate method which will allow them to offer possible criteria for a critical and constructive examination of our common Christian heritage. The simple appeal to tradition in favour of or against a particular ecclesial or theological position can never replace critical and faithful argumentation. The Christian faith must be appropriated, and not just repeated, by all Christians and in every generation anew. The handing on of the gospel, a process called *'paradosis'* in the New Testament (cf. 1 Peter 1:18), and the act of appropriating it is never a smooth process, but always entails the emergence of new tensions. 'La querelle entre les anciens et les modernes', nowadays referred to as the 'generation gap', is a general human phenomenon to be observed in all dimensions of our culture, and of course, also in our religion.[23] Therefore, the legitimacy of any given doctrinal, liturgical and communal manifestation of our tradition has to be examined again and again. This process adds new life to the Christian movement and protects it against all forms of traditionalist incrustations.

Yet how can we judge the theological legitimacy of both old and new appropriations of the Christian message of salvation? What are our criteria for the examination of current claims to authenticity in the church? In order to tackle these questions we must first look briefly at the history of ecclesiological thinking in the Christian movement. Then we shall return to the contribution of hermeneutical reflection to theological method. This reflection may provide us with a critical approach to our questions.

7.3 THE FORMALISATION OF TRADITION

7.3.1 The Search for Criteria of Orthodoxy

The recognition of the ambiguous nature of written texts and the corresponding hermeneutical challenges are much older than the Christian movement, as we have seen in Chapter 2. But it was also the particular concern of the early church to establish itself on a secure and public basis which led very early to the development of theories of interpretation which could guarantee the authentic use of biblical texts in the church. Various movements, later judged as 'heterodox', such as Gnosticism, Marcionism, Montanism, Donatism, Arianism etc., forced the theologians of the early church – most of them leaders – to defend the integrity of their Christian faith and to clarify ways in which every human being could see with sufficient certainty which particular tradition (of doctrine, worship, community organisation etc.) was authentically Christian and which was not. The definition of 'orthodoxy' depended on a coherent set of convincing criteria.

The process of canonisation of the Hebrew Scriptures and later on of the twenty-seven New Testament texts did not yet offer such a sufficient criterion because all the 'heretics' were engaged in the interpretation of the same corpus of Scriptures.[24] The generally accepted method of allegorical interpretation made possible the emergence of very diverse references to the biblical texts as proofs for individual and communal attitudes, beliefs and self-understandings among Christians. Thus, although the canonisation of the New Testament and the acceptance of the canonical status of the Old Testament produced eventually a material constant for the *paradosis* of the Christian gospel and as such the basis from which to identify the historical and theological foundation of Christian faith, these normative texts could still be interpreted in very different ways, so that the new canon could remain a source of potential conflict. Particularly in view of the given philosophical and – since Constantinian times – political context which demanded that ultimately only one perception of Christian identity should be right and legitimate, the crisis of Christian identity produced by conflicting interpretations of the Christian tradition became even more problematic for the theologians of the early church. They were now challenged to develop criteria which would allow them to distinguish more clearly between authentic (orthodox) and inauthentic uses of and references to the Scriptures. At this time all of these new criteria had to do with a demonstration of the intact preservation of the original apostolic tradition.

As we have seen above (cf. 2.2.2) Irenaeus was one of the first theologians to develop such a set of arguments. According to him, the church's authenticity can be demonstrated on a number of levels at once: the church tradition is in itself in uninterrupted continuity with the apostolic beginnings which are normatively communicated by the Scriptures. As such the church is the living *regula veritatis*, the rule of truth.[25] In fact, its roots go back further, namely right to the beginning of God's revelation to humankind; the chain of authoritative witnesses to God's Word reaches from Moses to the Prophets and the apostles right to the present bishops and presbyters.[26] This historical continuity presents yet another proof for the church's authenticity besides its unquestionable apostolicity. Yet another guarantee for this authenticity can be seen in the uninterrupted succession of bishops in the church, exemplified by Irenaeus through the list of Roman bishops.[27] The principle behind all these 'guarantees' can be summed up like this: he who reaches the apostles has the truth.[28] Accordingly, Irenaeus legitimised himself as a student of Polycarp who in turn had claimed to have been a student of the apostles.[29]

These criteria of thematic (= biblical) and successive (= episcopal) apostolicity are complemented further by Irenaeus' identification of the realm of the true church with the realm of the Holy Spirit's presence: 'For where the church is, there is the Spirit of God; and where the Spirit of God is, there is the church and every kind of grace. The Spirit is truth.'[30] And ultimately, what could be more 'reasonable'[31] than to take refuge in the church and to be educated in her midst and nurtured by the writings of the Lord?[32] Thus, biblical interpretation can be done successfully only in the truth of the church. The church alone guarantees that the truth of the gospel can be adequately grasped.

After Irenaeus, other Church Fathers such as Origen, Tertullian, Augustine, and Vincent of Lérins contributed to the debate on the ecclesial foundations of adequate biblical interpretation as shown above in Chapter 2. Vincent could be called the most successful of these since his definition of authenticity has had the most influential impact on future generations of Christians. His criteria were not only universality and antiquity, but also the consensus among Christians.[33] This later criterion reflects the by then well-established conciliar movement, but it also explicitly admits that consensus is not a self-evident fact even within the 'orthodox' church.

The definitions of creeds and doctrines at the various councils and the increasing influence of juridical thinking in the church throughout the Middle Ages promoted the further formalisation of 'tradition'. For the Church Fathers 'tradition' referred to the whole *depositium fidei* [the deposit of faith] as handed on, lived, and protected by the church. For them, this 'canon of truth' included, of course, the Scriptures as the ultimate witness to the original Christian identity, but it also included the theological and practical, especially liturgical, developments in the church. Yet what gave rise to the Protestant challenge to the ecclesiastical *status quo* in the sixteenth century was the Reformers' rejection of some of the particular historical developments in the church and of their authoritative backing by Rome's special understanding of tradition. The public critique of the Roman Church's 'heterodox' development and of the legalist and triumphalist attitudes of its hierarchy opened a new debate on criteria of authenticity for Christian faith. The Protestant criterion which will be examined in more detail below consisted in a new appreciation of the biblical texts. The Roman Catholic response to the new challenge was formulated at the Council of Trent and at subsequent councils.

7.3.2 The Defence of Orthodoxy

7.3.2.1 Scripture and Tradition

The answer of the Council of Trent is presented in the *Decretum de libris sacris et traditionibus recipiendis* of 8 April 1546. The aim of this decree was to get rid of the (admitted) errors and to preserve the purity of the gospel in the church. This truth and order [*disciplina*] are contained *'in libris scriptis et sine scripto traditionibus, quae ab ipsius Christi ore ab Apostolis acceptae, aut ab ipsis Apostolis Spiritu Sancto dictante quasi per manus traditae ad nos usque pervenerunt'* [in written books or orally transmitted texts which the Apostles have received from Christ's mouth or which through the inspiration of the Holy Spirit have been passed on to us by the Apostles and since then until today.][34] Hence, both the Scriptures and an apostolic oral tradition are the vessels of salvific truth and authentic order in the Church.[35] As far as the authentic interpretation of the Scriptures is concerned, the Council declared in a further decree at the same date that in questions of faith and morality nobody should dare to interpret the Scriptures against the sense held by the Church *'cuius est iudicare de vero sensu et interpretatione Scripturarum sanctarum'* [whose task it is to determine the true sense and interpretation of the Holy Scriptures].[36] Both the Fathers of the church and now Trent refer to 'the church' as the criterion by which to determine authentic interpretation, yet at Trent the development towards an exclusively hierarchical understanding of 'church' became more manifest than before.

The emerging reduction of 'church' to a two-class system consisting of the hierachy on the one hand and the laity on the other, the former being the leading class who alone can determine officially what the authentic understanding of the Christian tradition is, has been maintained by the Vatican authorities until today.[37] The authority of the hierarchy reached its climax at the First Vatican Council (1869–70) when the dogma of papal infallibility was formulated and accepted. This Council repeated the Tridentine statements on the two sources of revelation, Scripture and tradition, and affirmed the role of ecclesiastical authority in terms of adjudicating authentic interpretation. Thus, it meant to sanction once and for all the already existing split between general Christian experience and life on the one hand and the doctrinal positivism of the Magisterium on the other hand.[38] From now on Pope and Magisterium are not only the sole authoritative interpreters of the Scriptures and of tradition, but they also represent in themselves the only legitimate criterion for the validity of their own interpretation.[39]

Recent interpreters of the Tridentine definitions have emphasised that the Council of Trent did not specify exactly either what these orally transmitted traditions actually are or how they relate to the Scriptures.[40] This lack of clarity made it possible to use the conciliar decree to support a number of future ecclesial definitions, such as the mariological dogmas. Critical questions from within the Roman Church and from outside could be dismissed with reference to the validity of the continuous tradition as administered by Pope and Magisterium. Thus, the authenticity of Christian tradition has now become a matter of adequate administration.

7.3.2.2 The Bible versus Tradition

Martin Luther, whose hermeneutical breakthrough we have already discussed above (cf. 2.2.5), challenged not only certain 'heterodox' practices in the church, but questioned some of the ecclesiastical criteria for authentic Christian discipleship. While his 95 Theses of 1517 were particularly aimed at rejecting the indulgence practices in the church, his major writings of 1520 attacked the authority of the Roman Church in a much more radical and systematic way. Luther challenged the three 'walls' of Rome: that the spiritual authority was above the worldly, that only the Pope had the right to interpret the Scriptures, and that only he had the right to call a council. Against this Roman reduction of authority in the church Luther claimed that every Christian was an equal member of the church and in principle enjoyed the same spiritual authority, the same right to interpret the Scriptures, and the same right to call a council if necessary.[41] For Luther, as for the other Reformers, the Scriptures provided the only legitimate criterion for the authenticity of Christian praxis. However, the *sola scriptura* principle received further precision through Luther's concentration on those biblical texts which are especially concerned with Christ (*Christum treiben*).[42] Thus, the wider biblical criterion was modified and redefined according to Luther's own spiritual understanding of the christological centre of the Bible.[43]

All the practices and claims to authority in the Roman Church were now judged in the light of this newly defined criterion. With reference to it all sacraments other than Baptism and Eucharist were rejected. Scriptural proofs for the other sacraments were dismissed as illegitimate uses of the Bible or simply rejected as misunderstandings of the texts. The success of Luther's appeal for reform was based to a large extent on his theological achievement in retrieving the material aspect of the Christian experience of God's love, grace and forgiveness, and by pointing out the failure of the Roman Church to proclaim these experiences adequately.

The new freedom of the Protestant Christian to interpret the biblical texts outside the control of Rome's legal influence was, however, soon limited by the Lutheran and Reformed confessions, 'which took on the character of inspired, inerrant documents – an ersatz teaching authority in Protestant dress. And of course the patristic dogmas were never questioned, nor was the authority of the Church Fathers, or the ecumenical creeds'.[44] Thus, the Protestant Reformation did not actually deny the existence of a tradition wider than the biblical texts, yet it submitted all dimensions of faith and church life at least in theory to the sovereign criterion of Scripture.[45]

While for Luther the authority of Scripture was determined theologically, Lutheran Orthodoxy, as we have seen (cf. above 2.2.6), developed it into a formalist principle. The backing for this new principle was provided by the dogma of the Scriptures' verbal inspiration.[46] Thus, over against the infallibility of the Pope on the other side of the ecclesial divide, we find here the infallibility of the Scriptures. The material, i.e. theological, centre of Christian praxis was once more reduced to a formal principle which provided the illusion of security at the cost of trivialising and desiccating the Christian praxis.

This security of later Protestantism was finally destroyed when the historical-critical exegesis rediscovered the diversity and tensions within the New Testament itself. Simplistic references to the pure and authentic tradition enshrined in these biblical texts could no longer function as the authoritative criterion for a determination of authentic Christian praxis.[47] The Enlightenment critique of all formal authority demanded ultimately from Christian theology that criteria for the determination of authentic Christian faith must be developed. This challenge brings us back to the overall question of this chapter. How can we meet the double crisis of the Christian movement today, namely the crisis of the Christian self-understanding in the modern world and the crisis of theological methodology itself.

7.4 CHRISTIAN TRADITION AND CRITICAL HERMENEUTICS

7.4.1 The Need for a Critical Theology

These very sketchy historical considerations have at least, I hope, shown that the official preservation of the Christian faith and the formal continuity of the church have always been in danger of becoming the ultimate concern in the church at the expense of the continuing experience of this faith in different times and cultural circumstances.[48] This concern for the intact preservation of Christian identity has often led to 'colonial' attitudes towards different models of Christian praxis, especially towards those which differed from the models advocated by the European centres of the church. This 'eurocentricity' of Christian identity is rejected nowadays by many non-Western Christians. Moreover, the often neurotic anxiety of losing Christian identity and the authoritarian measures adopted by church authorities to prevent this from happening have ironically accelerated this very loss.

In our contemporary intellectual context and in this radically pluralistic cultural environment no religious tradition (now in the larger sense of the term) can be saved from death through simplistic references to its old age (antiquity), its formal continuity with the original apostolic witnesses to the originating event (succession), or episcopal or synodal agreements on its values (consensus). In the eyes of contemporary men and women these criteria do not at all guarantee that a tradition merits further continuity. The possible and actual distortions and ideological features in Christian claims to tradition have burdened the renewed search for Christian identity even more.

Yet most challenging is the critique which comes from within the Christian tradition itself. This critique asks whether the strong concern for ecclesiastical continuity is not in itself a betrayal of the eschatological faith that the Kingdom of God is at hand.[49] In other words, is the existence of a formally and institutionally organised church not only not a valid criterion but in itself a possible obstacle to authentic Christian praxis.[50]

These observations of theological and ecclesiological challenges to the Christian tradition have drawn our attention once more to the necessity of a proper theological methodology which could help us to understand the Christian message today, but also to understand the multi-dimensional context in which we are trying to grasp the heart of this Christian project. A thorough theological job is necessary, since neither the mere repetition of Christian doctrines nor the pious evocation of biblical passages any longer convince most contemporary women and men (inside and outside the church) of the significance of Christian faith for their lives and for the future of this creation. If the Christian tradition is not to end soon altogether, a critical theology and a critical faith-praxis are urgently demanded. While it is the task of theologians to reflect upon the tradition and the present praxis and to develop proposals for a better praxis, it is this actual praxis, i.e. the life and thought of the Christian communities, which decides about the future of Christianity's role in this world. Only if Christian faith is lived today, only if the centre of this faith, that is the presence of God in Christ and in all of our lives, is experienced today, only if the universal call of God to all people is freed again from the legalistic deposits which have been distorting its proclamation, and only if the hope for the future fullness of the experience of God provokes us to change our lives and so the fate of this world, will authentic Christianity continue. That the formal dogmatic support structures of this faith are more and more losing their authority is not a disaster, rather this situation provides all Christians with the unique possibility of accepting their critical and constructive responsibilities for participating in God's creative project. The primary Christian concern cannot be the mere survival of an old tradition – the church as museum – but the actualisation of a challenging message in our generation according to our best abilities – the church as a community of responsive and responsible fellow builders.

7.4.2 The Need for Critical Hermeneutics

When we understand the Christian church not as a museum which displays once meaningful deposits, but as a living organism[51], then the practical tasks of each of its members will have to change accordingly. In such a living organism the theologian functions predominantly as an interpreter of the ambiguous tradition, of its experiences, insights, contributions and failures. All of these aspects of the tradition must be critically assessed by the theologian. But he or she must also be critical of his or her own possible distortions, biases and failures. The theologian must be careful not to become an 'intellectual tyrant'.[52] The best precaution against such a temptation may be the willingness to respect otherness and even radical otherness in his or her interpretative activity. That is to say that the theologian must not understand appropriation as the act in which every text is interpreted in such a way that it fits his or her preunderstanding. Rather by adopting a critical and self-critical method of text-interpretation theologians will always be prepared to challenge and transform their own preunderstandings and interpretative horizons.

David Tracy has developed such a critical methodology. He proposed that every theologian must be involved in the interpretation of both the Christian tradition and the present world as the context of such interpretation. The results of this twofold hermeneutical effort need to be assessed in a mutually critical correlation.[53] This method does not suggest either the dilution of Christian experiences into general human experiences or the 'Christianisation' of all human experiences. Rather Tracy's method acknowledges that both of these distinct though related sets of experiences are ambiguous and that both call for critical interpretation.[54] Only if the interpretation of the Christian tradition reveals the power of this tradition to be a continuously meaningful challenge to our understanding of being in this world, and only if this interpretation is a critical act of appropriation, i.e. an activity guided by a hermeneutics of retrieval and of suspicion as described above in Chapter 5, will the disclosure of Christian revelation have any possibility of succeeding to address contemporary women and men. Such a critical hermeneutics will allow us to come to terms with the ambiguity of all the classic texts of our tradition (Scriptures, creeds, confessions, doctrines, liturgies, prayers, songs etc.), and it will force us to renounce those traditionalist escapes into pseudo-authorities which we have already outlined in this chapter (cf. above 7.3).

Tracy's method is also helpful in terms of approaching the double pluralism with which theology is faced, the pluralism of its context and the pluralism of its interpretative results. As far as the contextual pluralism is concerned, theology cannot afford to ignore the pluralism of reading methods which we have discussed in Chapter 5, because it has too much to learn from it. The diversity of critical reading methods offers an opportunity to theologians to avail of the best and most critical insights into the process of text-interpretation. But as we have also seen, the hermeneutical insight into the plurality of adequate readings must not be confused with the dubious relativism according to which every reading is equally adequate (cf. above 5.3.3). Nor can Christian theology ignore the host of other world-views, religious or secular, with which it competes for the attention of contemporary human beings. The credibility of the Christian message and contribution to the transformation of this universe will be measured first of all by the Christian readiness to participate in the wider human conversation on the fundamental questions of humankind past and present.[55]

As far as the pluralism within the Christian tradition is concerned, it is important to see that this pluralism is at the very root of the Christian movement itself.[56] Different people have witnessed to the original Christ event in very different communities, times and linguistic and cultural contexts. Accepting this pluralism is a necessity for every Christian and not just an option reserved for critical theologians. The crucial question presented by biblical, doctrinal, liturgical and spiritual pluralism is whether we find a common central focus in all of the supposedly authentic ways of Christian witness past and present.

Stephen Sykes has argued in favour of a formal description of the basic Christian focus. '[F]ormally speaking, a Christian is defined as one who gives attention to Jesus whose achievement is contextualised by God'.[57] And he goes on to define the 'identity of Christianity' as a process of interaction between the 'inward element and the external forms of Christianity'.[58] Thus, Sykes has overcome the reduction of Christian identity to a purely inward element as Adolf von Harnack had defined it at the turn of the century.[59] This insistence that Christianity lives in a dialectical tension between individual experience and general expression is most helpful. However, Sykes' *formal* recognition of Christian identity does not yet answer our *material* question of what constitutes an authentic Christian praxis. The process of interaction between this 'inward element and the external forms of Christianity' may be ideologically, neurotically or otherwise distorted, as we have seen. Although Sykes has offered a formal description of the dynamic nature of Christian identity which is open to the plurality of Christian witnesses, he has not introduced a method by which we could examine critically whether or not the interactive process either of individual appropriation or of general expression of the Christian tradition does justice to God's creative challenge of traditional religious authorities in the original Christ event.

7.4.3 Plurality and Ambiguity at the Heart of the Christian Tradition

The originating event of the Christian tradition is accessible to us only through the Christian tradition itself; it is a constitutive part of this tradition. The Christian disciple of today encounters Jesus Christ and his particular theological initiatives through the various biblical witnesses and through the witness of the ongoing Christian movement. Yet both of these *loci* of encounters are pluralistic and ambiguous by nature. The pluralistic witness of the Christian tradition is, however, not without critical focus. It is precisely the function of adequate theology to strive to formulate this focus again and again. And it is the function of the entire community of disciples to validate or challenge the always limited interpretations of this focus.

Any interpreter of the Christian tradition ought to realise that already the earliest witnesses had warned the Christian disciple of the possibility of ideological appropriations of the significance of Jesus Christ. The portrayal of Christ's disciples in Mark's Gospel, for instance, is full of dramatic corrections of false interpretations and anticipations of Christ's identity.[60] The reader of the gospel is explicitly alerted to the temptation of reducing the gospel to his or her biased and limited perspective. And Mark demands instead a new seeing, a new perspective. Analogically, the Christian disciple of today must be willing to interpret the apostolic tradition through always fresh and critical perspectives. As Mark's Gospel emphasises, the apostolic tradition itself is full of inauthentic acts of discipleship. The self-critical dimension of Markan and other New Testament texts has added to their 'classic' character. They ultimately resist efforts of automatisation, domestication and manipulation by their readers.[61]

Thus warned by the originating expressions of the foundations of Christian tradition itself, we may wish to be particularly careful not to accept uncritically any biblical or even christological justification of past or present claims by any member or authority in the church. Rather we should test any such claim over against our best and most sincere appropriations of the salvific inititiatives of God in Jesus Christ as experienced and textualised by the different biblical communities. In this task of locating the primary material focus of Christian identity, our christological interpretation of the biblical canon functions as a critical tool for our interpretation of ecclesial models of authentic Christian praxis in the Christian tradition until today. Yet even this christological interpretation which Martin Luther had proposed as the critical aim of all biblical interpretation (cf. above 7.3.2.2) can only claim a preliminary authority, for it too will always need revision.[62]

7.4.4 Tradition in Spite of Tradition

The critique of the formalisation of the Christian tradition and the discussion of the need for a critical hermeneutics in theology have revealed the necessity of re-interpreting again and again the originating event of this tradition. In a sense all Christian tradition might be seen as the more or less adequate attempt to respond to the new theological initiatives manifested in the life, death and resurrection of Jesus of Nazareth.[63] When we consider the actual content of these initiatives we realise that they all had to do with a constructive critique of specific features of Jewish religious tradition. The objects of Jesus' religious critiques as recorded in the Christian Scriptures were the religious authority of the Temple, the Torah, the Land, the family, the City of Jerusalem, and also the ideology of certain messianic expectations. However, Jesus' critique of his own religious tradition did not attempt to destroy the experiential, prophetic and historical nature of Israel's faith in God. Rather it aimed at a thorough reformation of the particular faith-praxis and its most prominent sacred institutions. Most of all, Jesus rejected the absolutist claims of these monuments of tradition, namely to represent the essential *loci* of valid encounter with the God of Israel. Over against such a legalistic understanding of religious praxis Jesus proposed the immediate experience and worship of God in prayer, table-fellowship and in reaching out to all the outcasts of his society. Jesus insisted at the cost of his life that the true reign of God, i.e. the authentic experience of God's loving presence, is at hand for all those who care to see.

Jesus' own discipleship was total, though he was not totalitarian in his demands. He urged his friends to take their crosses and follow him – not to take his cross.[64] His critical retrieval of the love command from his tradition[65] and his suspicion of all totalitarian religious institutions are the two sides of the same initiative. However, his appropriation of his tradition brought him into conflict with those groups whose lives, hopes and professional careers were built on a different appropriation of tradition.

The experiences with the resurrected-crucified Jesus and the recognition of his Lordship, that is the recognition of the authenticity of his critical retrieval of their religious tradition, finally convinced his disciples and friends to change their religious praxis from within the pluralist context of Palestinian and Hellenistic Judaism.[66]

The Christian conflicts with Judaism are reflected in various New Testament texts and presented there as the conflict between an old tradition with a codified and formalised worship and religious life and an emerging new tradition. The competition between both traditions as to which of the two best represented God's true people deteriorated quickly into mutual vilification.[67]

In recent New Testament scholarship it has been shown to what extent the Pauline Churches remained thoroughly Jewish in their fundamental theology, while developing rather differently in terms of their social identity.[68] Thus, however we account theologically for the widening gulf between Christians and Jews in the first Christian centuries, the mutually offensive polemics between Christians and Jews were to a large extent of a social nature and were certainly promoted by the increasing Christian desire to establish a new religious tradition outside of Judaism.[69]

The critique of tradition as articulated by Jesus of Nazareth in his ministry, death and resurrection and his focus on the reform of human relationship with both God and fellow humans ironically became a victim of the Christians' effort to establish themselves as a legitimate religious movement over against Judaism. This is not to deny the actual difficulties which many Christian Jews encountered in their original community. Rather it is to suggest that in the process of the Christian creation of a new system of symbols, very similar organisational, legalistic and hierarchical attitudes and structures to those rejected by Jesus were suddenly introduced. The efforts to create valid religious structures and institutions in order to maintain an independent identity vis-à-vis the Jews led to the emergence of a new priesthood and eventually to a sharp distinction between clergy and laity.[70] The by now destroyed Jewish Temple found its symbolic parallel in the emerging High Christology: Jesus as the true Temple. The 'New Israel', i.e. the church, defined its boundaries in terms of those who were part of its salvific, institutional and sacramental realm and who is not. It interpreted the destruction of Jerusalem as the inevitable fate of the 'Old Israel', while at the same time establishing some of the institutions of 'Old Israel' again in Rome.

A critical reading of the development of the christological dogma would also need to assess to what extent anti-Jewish polemics and Christian institutional longings have influenced the christological discussion in addition to the already known factors.[71] Thus, even our most basic confessional formulas cannot be considered to be innocent texts. While they undoubtedly point forward to some disclosure of God's mystery in the life, death and resurrection of Jesus, they also reflect ideological efforts to demonstrate the exclusivism of the new tradition. That the proclaimer of God's Kingdom became the centre of all proclamation at the expense of an important aspect of his own original proclamation, i.e. his critique of ideologies in religious tradition, would need to be re-examined much more critically by Christian theologians.

Although I can refer here only to some studies of the relationship between Christians and Jews during the first Christian centuries, the results of these investigations should help us to recognise the ideological distortions right at the heart of the Christian tradition. This is not to claim that a critical interpretation of the tradition is impossible. Rather I would like to emphasise that the success of any such interpretation depends on our willingness to recognise not only our own hermeneutical situation but also the hermeneutical situation of all former generations of Christians whose norms, creeds and understandings of tradition we interpret today.

In spite of all its cultural and ideological overlay the Christian tradition continues to reflect the challenging experience of the disciples of Jesus Christ, of his ministry, death, and of God's confirmation of the crucified one in his resurrection. However, those reflections can only be brought to their full light through the active response of people in history. By 'response' I mean that faith-praxis which acts in analogy to the experiences of Christ which have been mediated through the Christian tradition and critically retrieved by the community of interpreters. This communal response represents the only possible criterion for verification of any claim to authenticity of Christian faith.[72]

The *communal character* of such response follows both from the experience of Jesus' vision of a redeemed humanity and from the need to transcend the hermeneutical limitations of each individual interpreter. The experiences of Christians as part of God's people have disclosed anew God's Spirit and the dynamics of the community which is united in that Spirit.[73] This Spirit, however, cannot be evoked in order to protect anybody from the conditions of human life or from coming to terms with the pluralism of appropriations of the Christian tradition. Thus, this Spirit cannot be appealed to in order to establish criteria for the superiority of a particular praxis or dogmatic expression. Rather, this Spirit has been experienced in the human condition by all those who strive towards a critical communal response to God's self-disclosure in human history.

In view of these reflections on the pluralistic and ambiguous nature of tradition it seems to me that the Christian community, i.e. the church, requires a continuous assessment of all its manifestations and doctrinal symbols. This assessment may well lead to a thorough rethinking of all the present criteria of ecclesial authenticity and to an always renewed search for the most adequate understanding of and response to Jesus Christ's call on us to participate in God's creative and redemptive project.

7.5 CONCLUSION: THE SIGNIFICANCE OF HERMENEUTICS FOR THEOLOGY

Our brief discussion of the problems involved in the interpretation of the Christian tradition has stressed the significance of hermeneutical thinking for Christian theology. Thus, hermeneutics has proven to be not an optional occupation for sophisticated theologians, but a vital necessity for any theologian who understands his or her task as a critical service to the church, the world and to the pursuit of truth.

As we have seen in Chapter 2, Christian theologians throughout the early church, the Middle Ages and the Reformation have been involved in the discussion of hermeneutical models. Only since the dawn of modernity do we observe a theological refusal to participate in this discussion. The various forms of Christian 'orthodoxies' which emerged in reaction to the challenge of modern science and culture denied that they were involved in the application of any methodological instruments. Rather, they claimed, they were simply approaching the truth of the Gospel. But as we have seen throughout this book, there is no such simple and innocent approach to anything in this world, be it a written text, an ontological statement, or an entire tradition. And most of all, no hermeneutical model can claim to be innocent either. A critical interpretation of interpretation theory itself is of particular importance for any branch of the human sciences which wishes to make a claim to intellectual integrity. Nor does religious faith in God's presence absolve Christian thinkers from the hermeneutical task. As we have seen, even the most sacred human insights can become distorted or corrupted.

The question whether theology requires its own particular methodology or ought to particiapte in the development of a general hermeneutics seems to me to have been answered by Schleiermacher, even though there are still theologians who would wish to see theology isolated from other human pursuits of knowledge. The very different focus of theological thinking, i.e. God's revelation in this universe, from that of other disciplines of human knowledge does not only not justify a different interpretation theory, rather it demands the application of a general hermeneutics both in order to point out this different focus and precisely because of the fact that we have been able to proclaim in our human language God's presence in our human world and history.

Hermeneutics, however, must not be overrated either. It cannot be a replacement for Christian thinking and praxis in this universe. Rather it should help to clarify our human condition and our mode of approaching the living tradition of faith in God. Thus, it may help to sharpen human awareness for the challenge of God's presence and for the context in which this challenge is recognised and responded to.

Finally, hermeneutical thinking may be able to make the theologian more sensitive towards the need to engage in a world-wide conversation on all aspects of the human search for meaning in this universe.[74] All interpreters who have become aware of the linguistic nature of their thinking and the social and historical conditioning of their language will already have experienced the need to challenge and transcend their own narrow horizon. Thus, a proper hermeneutical training may very well be an appropriate starting-point for any journey towards a more adequate understanding of God, the human self and the mystery of our being in this world.

Notes

The abbreviation 'ET' stands for English translation

CHAPTER 1: THE PURPOSE OF HERMENEUTICS

1. See also my book *Text and Interpretation as Categories of Theological Thinking*, trans. Thomas J. Wilson (Dublin: Gill and Macmillan, and New York: Crossroad, 1988), esp. 68f. where I have introduced and defended this terminology in greater detail.
2. Cf. Paul Ricœur, *Essays on Biblical Interpretation*, ed. Lewis S. Mudge (Philadelphia: Fortress, 1980), 106.
3. Hans-Georg Gadamer, *Truth and Method*, trans. from the 2nd German edn by William Glen-Doepel and ed. by John Cumming and Garrett Barden. 2nd edn (London: Sheed and Ward, 1979), 333ff.; and David Tracy, *The Analogical Imagination: Christian Theology and the Culture of Pluralism* (New York: Crossroad, 1981), 102.
4. Cf. here David Jasper, *The Study of Literature and Religion: An Introduction*. Studies in Literature and Religion (London: Macmillan, 1989), esp. 83–96.
5. Cf. Gadamer, *Truth and Method*, 5–10.
6. Cf. Paul Ricœur, *Hermeneutics and the Human Sciences: Essays on Language, Action and Interpretation*, ed. and trans. John B. Thompson (Cambridge: Cambridge University Press, 1981), 63ff.
7. I borrow this terminology from David Tracy, *Blessed Rage for Order: The New Pluralism in Theology* (New York: Seabury, 1975), 45f.

CHAPTER 2: THE DEVELOPMENT OF THEOLOGICAL HERMENEUTICS (I): FROM THE BEGINNINGS TO THE ENLIGHTENMENT

1. Cf. H. D. F. Kitto, *The Greeks* (Harmondsworth: Penguin, 1957), 55.
2. Cf. Gerhard Ebeling, 'Hermeneutik', in *Die Religion in Geschichte und Gegenwart* (= RGG), vol. 3, 3rd edn (Tübingen: J.C.B. Mohr [Paul Siebeck], 1959), 242–62, here 245; and J. C. Joosen and J. H. Waszink, 'Allegorese', in *Reallexikon für Antike und Christentum*, vol. 1 (Stuttgart: Anton Hiersemann, 1950), 283.
3. Cf. Richard N. Longenecker, *Biblical Exegesis in the Apostolic Period* (Grand Rapids, Michigan: Eerdmans, 1975), 19.
4. Cf. Gershom Scholem, *Über einge Grundbegriffe des Judentums* (Frankfurt/M.: Suhrkamp, 1970), esp. 'Offenbarung und Tradition als religiöse Kategorien im Judentum', 90–120.
5. For the following cf. Longenecker, op. cit., 28ff.
6. Cf. Martin Hengel, *Judaism and Hellenism: Studies in their Encounter*

in Palestine during the Early Hellenistic Period, vol. 1 trans. John Bowden (London: SCM, 1974), 99f.; and Geza Vermes, *Post-Biblical Jewish Studies* (Leiden: Brill, 1975), esp. 'The Qumran Interpretation of Scripture in its Historical Setting', 37–49.

7. Longenecker, op. cit., 46.
8. Cf. Thomas H. Tobin, *The Creation of Man: Philo and the History of Interpretation*, The Catholic Biblical Quarterly Monograph Series 14 (Washington, DC: The Catholic Biblical Association of America, 1983), 36ff.
9. Cf. Ebeling, 'Hermeneutik', 246.
10. Cf. James Barr, *Old and New in Interpretation: A Study of the Two Testaments* (London: SCM, 1966), 103–48, esp. 139f. See also Leonhard Goppelt, *Typos: Die typologische Deutung des Alten Testaments im Neuen*. Reprint (Darmstadt: Wissenschaftliche Buchgesellschaft, 1990).
11. Robert M. Grant with David Tracy, *A Short History of the Interpretation of the Bible*, 2nd edn (Philadelphia: Fortress, 1984), 37.
12. Ibid., 36.
13. Irenaeus of Lyons, *Adversus Haereses*. Sources Chrétiennes (Paris, Cerf), I (=SC 263–4) 1979; II (293–4) 1982; III (34) 1974; IV (100) 1965; and V (152–3) 1969. Cf. Norbert Brox, *Offenbarung, Gnosis und gnostischer Mythos bei Irenäus von Lyon* (Salzburg and Munich: Pustet, 1966), 206.
14. Cf. Tertullian, *De Praescriptione Haereticorum*, 37. English excerpt 'Heretics Have No Right to the Scriptures' in J. Stevenson, ed., *A New Eusebius: Documents illustrative of the history of the Church to A.D. 337* (London: SPCK, 1983), 181.
15. Cf. R. M. Grant, op. cit., 55.
16. Origenes, *Peri Archon/De Principiis/Von den Prinzipien*, ed. and trans. Herwig Görgemanns and Heinrich Karpp (Darmstadt: Wissenschaftliche Buchgesellschaft, 1976).
17. *Peri Archon* IV 2,4 and IV 3,5.
18. Ibid., IV 2,6.
19. Ibid., IV 3,14.
20. R. M. Grant, op. cit., 66. However, the Antiochene system of reading was occasionally open to engage in allegorical interpretation as well. Cf. J. C. Joosen and J. H. Waszink, 'Allegorese', op. cit., 294f.
21. Aurelius Augustinus, *De Doctrina Christiana*. Corpus Christianorum: Series Latina XXXII (Tournhout: Brepols, 1962), 1–167. The translations in the text are my own. For an English translation of the text see Saint Augustine, *On Christian Doctrine*, trans. D. W. Robertson, Jr. The Library of Liberal Arts (New York: Macmillan, 1958).
22. *De Doctrina Christiana*, I, 40 and 41.
23. Ibid., I, 44: 'Quapropter, cum quisque cognouerit finem praecepti esse caritatem, de corde puro et conscientia bona et fide non ficta, omnem intellectum diuinarum scripturarum ad ista tria relaturus ad tractationem illorum librorum securus accedat.'
24. Ibid., I, 43.
25. Ibid., III, 23.

26. Ibid., III, 32.
27. Ibid., III, 38.
28. Ibid., II, 63.: In Book III Augustine also discusses Tyconius' *Book of Rules* which has had a significant influence on hermeneutical considerations at the time. A new bilingual edition of that work has just appeared and will make future studies of Tyconius' impact on the development of hermeneutics much easier. *Tyconius: The Book of Rules*, trans. William S. Babcock. Texts and Translations 31. Early Christian Literature Series 7 (Atlanta: Scholars Press, 1989).
29. Vincent of Lérins, 'The Commonitory', in *A Select Library of Nicene and Post-Nicene Fathers of the Christian Church*. Second Series. Vol. XI (Oxford: James Parker, and New York: The Christian Literature Company, 1894), 127–59, here 132. Cf. also the excerpt in J. Stevenson, ed., *Creeds, Councils and Controversies: Documents illustrative of the history of the Church A.D. 337–461* (London: SPCK, 1983), 298–300.
30. *The Didascalicon of Hugh of St. Victor: A Medieval Guide to the Arts*, trans. Jerome Taylor (New York and London: Columbia University Press, 1961).
31. Cf. Hennig Brinkmann, *Mittelalterliche Hermeneutik* (Darmstadt: Wissenschaftliche Buchgesellschaft, 1980), 225.
32. Ibid., 238.
33. Cf. ibid., 243, and R. M. Grant, op. cit., 85. The English translation given here is taken from Grant.
34. Thomas Aquinas, *Summa Theologiae*, Ia. 1,10. (Trans. by Grant, op. cit., 88f.) Latin text ed. Thomas Gilby, O.P., *St Thomas Aquinas SUMMA THEOLOGIAE*, vol. 1: Christian Theology (Ia.I) (Cambridge: Blackfriars [in conjunction with London: Eyre & Spottiswoode, and New York: McGraw-Hill], 1964), 36ff.
35. Cf. Per Erik Persson, *Sacra Doctrina: Reason and Revelation in Aquinas*, trans. Ross Mackenzie (Oxford: Blackwell, 1970), 89:

> Theology is not to be regarded here as an addition to scripture, nor a study which may be pursued independently of scripture: in Thomas's view it is rather the extension of scriptural teaching through the ages, the *traditio* of imparting doctrine which must always be found within the church. Since it is the content of scripture which is being transmitted, *sacra doctrina* and *sacra scriptura* may be used interchangeably as synonyms. This means for Thomas that the subject of theology is preeminently *biblical theology*, and *sacra doctrina* may be regarded, to use an apt expression of Etienne Gilson, as 'holy scripture received in a human intellect'.

Cf. Henri de Lubac, S. J., *Exégèse Médiévale: Les Quatre Sens de l'Écriture*, Part II, vol. 2 (Paris: Aubier, 1964), 301.
36. Cf. Helmut Feld, *Die Anfänge der modernen biblischen Hermeneutik in der spätmittelalterlichen Theologie* (Wiesbaden: Franz Steiner, 1977).
37. Again, these individualist tendencies in biblical hermeneutics had already been prepared for both by Italian Rennaissance thinking and by some late medieval theologians. Cf. Feld, op. cit., esp. 7–22. Here

Feld emphasises also the individualist religious self-understanding of St Francis of Assisi.

38. Cf. esp. Gerhard Ebeling's contributions to the discussion of Luther's theological hermeneutics in *Evangelische Evangelienauslegung: Eine Untersuchung zu Luthers Hermeneutik* (Darmstadt: Wissenschaftliche Buchgesellschaft, 1962 [Reprint of the original edition of 1942]), and 'Die Anfänge von Luthers Hermeneutik', in *Lutherstudien*, vol. 1 (Tübingen: J. C. B. Mohr [Paul Siebeck], 1971), 1–68.
39. Cf. Ebeling, 'Die Anfänge', op. cit., 4.
40. Ibid., 36.
41. Ibid., 51.
42. Ibid., 55.
43. Cf. ibid., 58ff.
44. Cf. Josef Blank, 'Was Christum Treibet – Martin Luther und die Bibel', in *Martin Luther, 1483–1983: Ringvorlesung der Philosophischen Fakultät, Sommersemester 1983* (Saarbrücken: Universität des Saarlandes, 1983), 63.
45. Cf. ibid., 64.
46 Cf. William J. Bouwsma, *John Calvin: A Sixteenth-Century Portrait* (Oxford and New York: Oxford University Press, 1988), 120, note 71.
47. Cf. Paul L. Lehmann, 'The Reformers' Use of the Bible', in *Theology Today* 3 (1946), 328–344. Lehmann emphasises Calvin's interest in a wider humanistic education not only for civil but also for ecclesiastical leadership. Ibid., 336. See also Thomas F. Torrance, *The Hermeneutics of John Calvin* (Edinburgh: Scottish Academic Press, 1988), 62: Torrance shows Calvin's ambition to help the ordinary Christian believer to approach the Bible afresh, and how Calvin hoped to provide a tool for such a new approach with his *Institutes*.
48. The relevant decrees of the Tridentine Council may be found in Henricus Denzinger and Adolfus Schönmetzer, eds, *Enchiridion Symbolorum: definitionum et declarationum de rebus fidei et morum* (Barcelona, Freiburg i.B., and Rome: Herder, 1965), 364–366 (nrs. 1501–1507). We shall return to these decrees below (cf. 7.3.2.1).
49. Cf. Gottfried Hornig, *Die Anfänge der historisch-kritischen Theologie: Johann Salomo Semlers Schriftverständnis und seine Stellung zu Luther* (Göttingen: Vandenhoeck & Ruprecht, 1961), 51.
50. Cf. Klaus Scholder, *Ursprünge und Probleme der Bibelkritik im 17. Jahrhundert: Ein Beitrag zur Entstehung der historisch-kritischen Theologie* (Munich: Kaiser, 1966), 137 and 145.
51. Hornig, op. cit., 52 (my translation).
52. Cf. Scholder, op. cit., 148f.
53. Ibid., 154.
54. Ibid., 159.
55. Pietism is, of course, not a unitary phenomenon, but includes various trends and schools. From our hermeneutical point of view, the thought of Nikolaus Ludwig Graf von Zinzendorf (1700–1760) is of particular interest. He favoured a doctrine of inspiration which com-

bined the reading of the Scriptures with a charismatic experience by the reader, and thus, in this particular mode, overcame a purely literalistic reading of the biblical texts. For further information see Peter Stuhlmacher, *Vom Verstehen des Neuen Testaments: Eine Hermeneutik*. Grundrisse zum Neuen Testament. NTD Ergänzungsreihe 6. 2nd edn (Göttingen: Vandenhoeck & Ruprecht, 1986), 132–40.

56. Emanuel Hirsch, *Geschichte der neuern evangelischen Theologie*, vol. 4 (Gütersloh: Bertelsmann, 1954), 59f.
57. Hornig, op. cit., 79.
58. Ibid., 80f.
59. Ibid., 82.
60. Ibid., 89f.
61. Ibid., 141.
62. Ibid., 182ff.
63. Ibid., 211ff.
64. Cf. Scholder, op. cit., 150, note 67.
65. Johann Salomo Semler, *Vorbereitung zur theologischen Hermenevtik*, 4 vols (Halle: Carl Hermann Hemmerde, 1760–1769).
66. For some pointers to the study of these cross-religious hermeneutical encounters see my forthcoming article 'Biblical Interpretation, History and Principles' in the *Anchor Bible Dictionary* (New York: Doubleday, 1992).

CHAPTER 3: THE DEVELOPMENT OF PHILOSOPHICAL HERMENEUTICS: FROM SCHLEIERMACHER TO RICŒUR

1. For a detailed discussion of Schleiermacher's hermeneutics and of the state of publication of the more important texts cf. my article 'The Impact of Schleiermacher's Hermeneutics on Contemporary Interpretation Theory', in David Jasper, ed., *The Interpretation of Belief: Coleridge, Schleiermacher and Romanticism* (London: Macmillan, 1986), 81–96. Here I shall follow mainly Fr. D. E. Schleiermacher, *Hermeneutik*, ed. Heinz Kimmerle, 2nd edn (Heidelberg: Carl Winter, 1974), and, wherever possible, refer to the section of this work in English as given by Kurt Mueller-Vollmer, *The Hermeneutics Reader: Texts of the German Tradition from the Enlightenment to the Present* (London: Blackwell, 1986), 73–97. From now on this collection by Mueller-Vollmer will be referred to by the abbreviation *MV*. Mueller-Vollmer gives part of the English Translation of Schleiermacher's *Hermeneutik*, ed. Kimmerle: Friedrich D. E. Schleiermacher, *Hermeneutics: The Handwritten Manuscripts by F. D. Schleiermacher*. Ed. Heinz Kimmerle. Trans. James Duke and Jack Forstman (Missoula: Scholars Press, 1977). See also Hans Frei's detailed study of Schleiermacher's hermeneutics in his *The Eclipse of Biblical Narrative: A Study in Eighteenth and Nienteenth Century Hermeneutics* (New Haven and London: Yale University Press, 1974), 287–306.
2. *Hermeneutik*, ed. Kimmerle, 57 (my translation).

3. MV, 94.
4. MV, 75.
5. *Hermeneutik*, ed. Kimmerle, 44ff.
6. MV, 95.
7. MV, 83.
8. Ibid.
9. *Hermeneutik*, ed. Kimmerle, 83 (my translation); cf. MV, 83.
10. Cf. MV, 84.
11. Cf. MV, 96.
12. Friedrich Schleiermacher, *Hermeneutik und Kritik. Mit einem Anhang sprachphilosophischer Texte Schleiermachers*, ed. Manfred Frank (Frankfurt/M.: Suhrkamp, 1977), 344 (my translation). For a recent English edition of Schleiermacher's Academy Addresses see David E. Klemm, *Hermeneutical Inquiry*, vol. 1: *The Interpretation of Texts* (Atlanta: Scholars Press, 1986), 86. By suggesting that the interpreter ought to consult similar texts in order to better understand the text in question, Schleiermacher already anticipated aspects of the current discussion of 'intertextuality' in interpretation theory (cf. below 5.2.3)
13. MV, 74.
14. *Hermeneutik und Kritik*, 346. Cf. *Hermeneutical Inquiry* I, 88.
15. Cf. especially Manfred Frank, *Das individuelle Allgemeine: Textstrukturierung und –interpretation nach Schleiermacher* (Frankfurt/M.: Suhrkamp, 1977); and Paul Ricœur, 'Schleiermacher's Hermeneutics', *The Monist* 60 (1977), 181–97.
16. *Hermeneutik*, ed. Kimmerle, 81 (my italics and my translation).; cf. MV, 80.
17. *Hermeneutik*, ed. Kimmerle, 55.
18. Ibid. See also Joachim Wach, *Das Verstehen: Grundzüge einer Geschichte der hermeneutischen Theorie im 19. Jahrhundert*, 3 vols (Tübingen: J. C. B. Mohr (Paul Siebeck), 1926–33), esp. vol. 2: *Die theologische Hermeneutik von Schleiermacher bis Hofmann* (1929), 56ff., where he discusses the question whether or not to submit biblical interpretation to general hermeneutics. (Wach's masterly study of the development of hermeneutics in the nineteenth century continues to deserve close attention today.)
19. Cf. *Hermeneutik*, ed. Kimmerle, 89ff. (not given in MV).
20. Cf. *Hermeneutik*, ed. Kimmerle, 162.
21. Friedrich Schleiermacher, *Brief Outline on the Study of Theology*, trans. Terrence N. Tice (Atlanta: John Knox Press, 1966). I refer to the appropriate paragraphs in the text of the present chapter.
22. Cf. especially section 6.2 below which deals with the Barth-Bultmann debate on theological hermeneutics.
23. Wilhelm Dilthey, *Gesammelte Schriften*, vol. 5. 4th edn (Stuttgart: B. G. Teubner, and Göttingen: Vandenhoeck & Ruprecht, 1964), 172 (my translation). Cf. Richard E. Palmer, *Hermeneutics: Interpretation Theory in Schleiermacher, Dilthey, Heidegger, and Gadamer* (Evanston: Northwestern University Press, 1969), 115. (My translation repeats Palmer's translation of the initial sentence of the present quotation.)

24. Cf. Dilthey's essay 'The Development of Hermeneutics' (1900) reprinted in Klemm, *Hermeneutical Inquiry* I, 93–105, here 95. In 'The Understanding of Other Persons and Their Life-Expression', printed in Mueller-Vollmer, op. cit., 152–64, Dilthey defines 'hermeneutics' in the following way: 'As the life of the mind only finds its complete, exhaustive and therefore, objectively comprehensible expression in language, explication culminates in the interpretation of the written records of human existence. This art is the basis of philology. The science of this art is hermeneutics.' MV, 161.
25. *Gesammelte Schriften*, vol. 5, 143f.
26. MV, 153.
27. *Hermeneutical Inquiry* I, 104.
28. Cf. Palmer, op. cit., 100ff.
29. *Hermeneutical Inquiry* I, 93.
30. MV, 153 (translation altered).
31. Ibid.
32. Ibid.
33. MV, 154.
34. Ibid. – Cf. David Tracy's definition of 'the classic text' in his *Plurality and Ambiguity: Hermeneutics, Religion, Hope* (San Francisco: Harper & Row, 1987), 12: '[C]lassics are those texts that bear an excess and permanence of meaning, yet always resist definitive interpretation.' Tracy continues by describing the classic in terms of representing 'an example of both radical stability become permanence and radical instability become excess of meaning through ever-changing receptions.' Ibid, 14. The radical instability of these texts escaped Dilthey's attention.
35. MV, 155.
36. MV, 157.
37. MV, 163.
38. Palmer, op. cit., 106.
39. Edmund Husserl, *Logische Untersuchungen*, 3 vols. Reprint of 2nd edn (Tübingen: Niemeyer, 1980). Also in *Husserliana*, vols XVIII and XIX (cf. note 44 below).
40. Edmund Husserl, *Ideen zu einer reinen Phänomenologie und phänomenologischen Philosophie*. Erstes Buch. Allgemeine Einführung in die reine Phänomenologie. In: *Jahrbuch für Philosophie und phänomenologische Forschung*, vol. 1. Reprint (Tübingen: Niemeyer, 1980).
41. Edmund Husserl, 'Phenomenology' (1927). Article for the *Encyclopaedia Britannica*. Revised Translation by Richard E. Palmer, in David E. Klemm, *Hermeneutical Inquiry*, vol. II: *The Interpretation of Existence* (Atlanta: Scholars Press, 1986), 63–82, here 65.
42. Ibid., 64.
43. Ibid., 82 (square brackets in the original).
44. Edmund Husserl, *Logische Untersuchungen*, vol. 2, Part I, ed. Ursula Panzer. Husserliana XIX/1 (The Hague: Martinus Nijhoff, 1984), 23 (my translation). Cf. here also Wolfgang Künne, 'Edmund Husserl: Intentionalität', in Josef Speck, ed., *Grundprobleme der großen*

Philosophen: Philosophie der Neuzeit IV (Göttingen: Vandenhoeck & Ruprecht, 1986), 165–215, here 176ff.

45. Klemm, *Hermeneutical Inquiry* II, 69.
46. Cf. Hans-Georg Gadamer, 'Die phänomenologische Bewegung' (1963), *Gesammelte Werke*, vol. 3: *Neuere Philosophie I: Hegel-Husserl-Heidegger* (Tübingen: J.C.B. Mohr [Paul Siebeck], 1987),105–46, here 109.
47. For a discussion of the relationship between Husserl's and Heidegger's approaches to philosophy see Hans-Georg Gadamer, 'Die phänomenologische Bewegung', op. cit., esp. 113f.
48. Martin Heidegger, *Sein und Zeit*. 13th edn (Tübingen: Niemeyer, 1976), 43. ET: *Being and Time*, trans. John Macquarrie and Edward Robinson (Oxford: Blackwell, 1973), 67.
49. *Sein und Zeit* is dedicated to Edmund Husserl. The dedication of 8 April 1926 reads: '*EDMUND HUSSERL in Verehrung und Freundschaft zugeeignet*' [ET: Dedicated to EDMUND HUSSERL in friendship and admiration].
50. *Being and Time*, 65.
51. MV, 216.
52. MV, 216 [*Sein und Zeit*, 191].
53. MV, 218.
54. *Sein und Zeit*, 200 (my translation). Cf. MV, 223.
55. MV, 223.
56. *Sein und Zeit*, 201 (my translation).
57. Ibid., 201 (my translation).
58. MV, 225.
59. MV 226 (translation altered) [*Sein und Zeit*, 203].
60. Martin Heidegger, *Unterwegs zur Sprache*. 4th edn (Pfullingen: Neske, 1971), 15 and 19.
61. Ibid., 19, (my translation).
62. Ibid., 26ff.
63. Ibid., 31.
64. Ibid., 33, (my translation).
65. MV., 226.
66. Hans-Georg Gadamer, *Wahrheit und Methode: Grundzüge einer philosophischen Hermeneutik*. 4th edn (Tübingen: J.C.B. Mohr [Paul Siebeck], 1975). ET: *Truth and Method*, trans. from the 2nd German edn by William Glen-Doepel and ed. by John Cumming and Garrett Barden. 2nd edn (London: Sheed and Ward, 1979).

    See also Hans-Georg Gadamer, *Kleine Schriften*, 4 vols (Tübingen: J.C.B. Mohr [Paul Siebeck], 1967–77). Some of Gadamer's articles on hermeneutics have been published in ET: Hans-Georg Gadamer, *Philosophical Hermeneutics*, trans. and ed. David E. Linge (Berkeley, Los Angeles, and London: University of California Press, 1976). I have discussed Gadamer's hermeneutics in my book *Text and Interpretation as Categories of Theological Thinking*, trans. Thomas J. Wilson (Dublin: Gill and Macmillan, and New York: Crossroad, 1988), 8–37.
67. Hans-Georg Gadamer, *Reason in the Age of Science*, trans. Frederick

G. Lawrence (Cambridge, Mass., and London: MIT Press, 1981), 112.
68. *Truth and Method*, 258f.
69. Ibid., 105.
70. Ibid., 273–4.
71. Ibid., 345–6.
72. Ibid., 350.
73. Ibid., 415 and 432. Here Gadamer's close connection to Heidegger's later approach to language is evident. Cf. above section 3.3.3 on Heidegger's theory of language.
74. Ibid., 433.
75. For a more detailed critique of Gadamer's philosophical hermeneutics and for further literature on this topic cf. my *Text and Interpretation*, 22–37.
76. Jürgen Habermas, 'On Hermeneutics' Claim to Universality' (1970), now in MV, 294–319, here 302.
77. MV, 302.
78. See Jürgen Habermas, *Theorie des kommunikativen Handelns*, 2 vols (Frankfurt/M.: Suhrkamp, 1981).
79. MV, 313.
80. Cf. Gadamer's reply to Habermas which is reprinted in MV, 274–92, esp. 283.
81. Paul Ricœur, 'Hermeneutics and the Critique of Ideology', in his *Hermeneutics and the Human Sciences: Essays on Language, Action and Interpretation*, ed. and trans. John B. Thompson (Cambridge: Cambridge University Press, 1981), 63–100.
82. Paul Ricœur, *The Conflict of Interpretations: Essays in Hermeneutics*, ed. Don Ihde (Evanston: Northwestern University Press, 1974).
83. Paul Ricœur, *Freud and Philosophy: An Essay on Interpretation*, trans. Denis Savage (New Haven: Yale University Press, 1970), 43.
84. Cf. *The Conflict of Interpretations*, 44–54. See my discussion of structuralism in Chapter 5 (5.2.3).
85. For a more detailed study of Schleiermacher's contribution to the development of textuality see my article 'The Impact of Schleiermacher's Hermeneutics on Contemporary Interpretation Theory' [see above note 1], 90f.
86. Paul Ricœur, *Interpretation Theory: Discourse and the Surplus of Meaning* (Fort Worth: Texas Christian University Press, 1976), 87f.
87. Ibid., 94.
88. Ricœur, *Hermeneutics and the Human Sciences*, 95f.
89. Ibid., 100.
90. Cf. *Freud and Philosophy*, 28–36.
91. The original French term is *'ontologie brisée'*. Cf. Paul Ricœur, *Le Conflit des Interprétations: Essais d'Herméneutique* (Paris: Seuil, 1969), 23. The term used in Kathleen McLaughlin's translation is 'truncated ontology'. Cf. *The Conflict of Interpretations*, 19.
92. *Interpretation Theory*, 87f. – More recently, Ricœur has opted for a change in terminology. He now prefers to speak about 'refiguration' instead of 'reference'. This change would suggest

that the refiguration of the text by the reader is that act which leads to a grasp of what I have called the 'sense' of the text. Cf. Ricœur, *Time and Narrative*, vol. 3, trans. Kathleen [McLaughlin] Blamey and David Pellauer (Chicago: University of Chicago Press, 1988), 100.

93. Cf. my *Text and Interpretation*, esp. 56–61.
94. *Freud and Philosophy*, 46.
95. Cf. Paul Ricœur, *Essays on Biblical Interpretation*. Ed. Lewis S. Mudge (Philadelphia: Fortress Press, 1980).

CHAPTER 4: THE WRITTEN TEXT

1. Cf. Paul Ricœur, *Interpretation Theory*, 43ff.
2. Quoted by Joachim Kaiser in his preface to the trilingual Suhrkamp edition of Samuel Beckett, *Warten auf Godot/En attendant Godot/Waiting for Godot* (Frankfurt/M.: Suhrkamp, 1971), 12.
3. For a recent argument against a purely historical reading of the Gospels see Seán Freyne, *Galilee, Jesus and the Gospels: Literary Approaches and Historical Investigations* (Dublin: Gill and Macmillan, 1988), 25–30.
4. For a more detailed discussion of text-linguistics and its significance for theological thinking see my article 'The Theological Understanding of Texts and Linguistic Explication', *Modern Theology* 1 (1984), 55–66; and the relevant sections in my *Text and Interpretation*, 75–103.
5. Cf. Hans-Werner Eroms, *Funktionale Satzperspektive*. Germanistische Arbeitshefte 31 (Tübingen: Niemeyer, 1986), 90–7.
6. Ricœur, *Interpretation Theory*, 87.
7. See Norbert Brox, *Falsche Verfasserangaben: Zur Erklärung der frühchristlichen Pseudepigraphie*. Stuttgarter Bibelstudien 79 (Stuttgart: Katholisches Bibelwerk, 1975).
8. For a treatment of 'style' as a linguistic phenomenon cf. Hans-Werner Eroms, 'Stilistik' in Magareta Gorschenek and Annamaria Rucktäschel, eds, *Kritische Stichwörter zur Sprachdidaktik* (Munich: Fink, 1983), 235–46; and Barbara Sandig, *Stilistik: Sprachpragmatische Grundlegung der Stilbeschreibung* (Berlin and New York: de Gruyter, 1978).
9. Cf. Eroms, 'Stilistik', 240.
10. Cf. Daniel W. Hardy and David F. Ford, *Jubilate: Theology in Praise* (London: Darton, Longman & Todd, 1984), 132–4.
11. Cf. Eroms, 'Stilistik', 237.

CHAPTER 5: THE TRANSFORMATIVE POWER OF READING

1. E. D. Hirsch, *Validity in Interpretation* (New Haven and London: Yale University Press, 1967), 46.

2. Cf. E. D. Hirsch, *The Aims of Interpretation* (Chicago: University of Chicago Press, 1976), 17–35 and 88–92.
3. *Validity in Interpretation*, 180.
4. Ibid., 9, and *The Aims of Interpretation*, 89.
5. Cf. 'Old and New in Hermeneutics', in *The Aims of Interpretation*, 17–35.
6. Roland Barthes, *The Pleasure of the Text*, trans. Richard Miller (New York: Hill and Wang, 1975), 52.
7. Ibid., 51f.
8. Roland Barthes, *Leçon/Lektion*. Bilingual edition (Frankfurt/M.: Suhrkamp, 1980), 18: 'Mais la langue, comme performance de tout langage, n'est ni réactionnaire, ni progressiste; elle est tout simplement: fasciste; car le fascisme, ce n'est pas d'empêcher de dire, c'est d'obliger à dire.'
9. Ibid. (my translation).
10. Stanley Fish, *Is There a Text in This Class? The Authority of Interpretive Communities* (Cambridge, Mass., and London: Harvard University Press, 1980), 171ff., attributes differences in interpretation to the influence of respective communities of interpreters. Cf. my comments on Fish's proposals in my *Text and Interpretation*, 110–13.
11. Barthes, *The Pleasure of the Text*, 4.
12. Wolfgang Iser, *The Act of Reading: A Theory of Aesthetic Response* (Baltimore: Johns Hopkins University Press, 1978), 10. The subtitle of this book in German is *'Theorie ästhetischer Wirkung'*. It appears that in the English speaking world there is no real distinction made between the two related movements of reader-response criticism and theories of aesthetic effect. – For a more comprehensive treatment of Iser's theory see my *Text and Interpretation*, 106–10.
13. Wolfgang Iser, *The Implied Reader: Patterns of Communication in Prose Fiction from Bunyan to Beckett* (Baltimore: Johns Hopkins University Press, 1974).
14. For further information on reader-response criticism see Susan R. Suleiman and Inge Crosman, eds, *The Reader in the Text: Essays on Audience and Interpretation* (Princeton: Princeton University Press, 1980); and Jane P. Tompkins, ed., *Reader-Response Criticism: From Formalism to Post-Structuralism* (Baltimore and London: Johns Hopkins University Press, 1980).
15. For further information on theories of aesthetic effect see Rainer Warning, *Rezeptionsästhetik: Theorie und Praxis*. 2nd edn (Munich: Fink, 1979).
16. Cf. Susan R. Suleiman's comments in her introduction to *The Reader in the Text*, 22.
17. Cf. Ricœur, *Hermeneutics and the Human Sciences*, 152–7.
18. For instance John Sturrock, *Structuralism* (London: Paladin Grafton Books, 1986). See also John Sturrock, ed., *Structuralism and Since: From Lévi-Strauss to Derrida* (Oxford: Oxford University Press, 1979); and Richard Macksey and Eugenio Donato, eds, *The Structuralist Controversy: The Languages of Criticism and the Sciences of Man* (Baltimore and London: Johns Hopkins University Press, 1972).

19. Ferdinand de Saussure, *Course in General Linguistics*, trans. Roy Harris (London: Duckworth, 1983). Cf. *Structuralism*, 4.
20. Manfred Frank has discussed the affinity between contemporary structuralist theories and Schleiermacher's approach to language and text-interpretation in *Das individuelle Allgemeine: Textstrukturierung und -interpretation nach Schleiermacher* (Frankfurt/M.: Suhrkamp, 1977).
21. Cf. *Structuralism*, 14–20.
22. De Saussure, *Course in General Linguistics*, 118 (original italics). – See *Structuralism*, 20.
23. Cf. *Structuralism*, 78f.
24. *Structuralism*, 103.
25. Jan Mukařovský, *Kapitel aus der Ästhetik*, trans. Walter Schamschula. 3rd edn (Frankfurt/M.: Suhrkamp, 1978), 11–34.
26. Ibid., 19.
27. Jacques Derrida, *Of Grammatology*, trans. Gayatri Chakravorty Spivak (Baltimore: Johns Hopkins University Press, 1976), 158. For further information on Post-structuralism see Jonathan Culler, *On Deconstruction: Theory and Criticism after Structuralism* (Ithaca, N.Y.: Cornell University Press, 1982); Frank Lentricchia, *After the New Criticism* (London: Methuen, 1983), esp. 156–210; and Josué V. Harari, ed., *Textual Strategies: Perspectives in Post-Structuralist Criticism* (Ithaca, N.Y.: Cornell University Press, 1979).
28. Jaques Derrida, *Writing and Difference*, trans. Alan Bass (Chicago: University of Chicago Press, 1978), 280.
29. Ibid., 281.
30. Cf. Rodolphe Gasché, *The Tain of the Mirror: Derrida and the Philosophy of Reflection* (Cambridge, Mass., and London: Harvard University Press, 1986), 278–93.
31. Mark C. Taylor, 'Deconstruction: What's the Difference?', *Soundings* 66 (1983), 400. Cf. also Stephen D. Moore's excellent analysis of Derrida's programme of deconstruction in *Literary Criticism and the Gospels: The Theoretical Challenge* (New Haven and London: Yale University Press, 1989), 131ff. (Moore provides also an extensive bibliography on the post-structuralist movement.)
32. Derrida, *Writing and Difference*, 26.
33. Cf. *Structuralism*, 148.
34. Cf. Gasché, *The Tain of the Mirror*, 285f. Gasché emphasises the need to consider Derrida's understanding of 'text' in the context of his discussion of Heidegger's notion of 'being'.
35. Charles Taylor, *Sources of the Self: The Making of Modern Identity* (Cambridge, Mass.: Harvard University Press, 1989), 489.
36. Cf. David Tracy, *Plurality and Ambiguity: Hermeneutics, Religion, Hope* (San Francisco: Harper & Row, 1987), 60f.
37. Michel Foucault, *Von der Subversion des Wissens*, ed. and trans. Walter Seitter (Frankfurt/M.: Ullstein, 1978), 13. See also Michel Foucault, *The Order of Things: An Archaeology of the Human Sciences* (New York: Vintage Books, 1973).
38. Ibid.

39. Cf. *Structuralism*, 50. Lévi-Strauss did admit to some of the limitations of his structuralist anthropology by pointing to the vasteness of its subject-matter. See Claude Lévi-Strauss, *Mythos und Bedeutung: Fünf Radiovorträge*, ed. Adelbert Reif (Frankfurt/M.: Suhrkamp, 1980), 76f. But in conversation with Paul Ricœur he insisted once more that it was not a matter of choice when he decided in favour of syntax and against semantics. See ibid., 85f.:

> Es gibt keine Wahl insofern, als jene phonologische Revolution, die Sie [i.e. Ricœur] mehrfach erwähnen, in der Entdeckung besteht, daß der Sinn stets aus der Kombination von Elementen resultiert, die selber nicht sinnvoll sind. Was Sie also suchen . . . das ist der Sinn des Sinnes, ein Sinn hinter dem Sinn; in meiner Perspektive ist der Sinn dagegen nie ein ursprüngliches Phänomen: Der Sinn ist immer auf etwas zurückzuführen.

40. Salman Rushdie, *The Satanic Verses* (London: Viking, 1988); Hans Küng, *Infallible? An Enquiry*, trans. Eric Mosbacher (London: Collins, 1971). A comprehensive documentation of the 'case' of Hans Küng is now available: Leonard Swidler, ed., *Küng in Conflict* (Garden City, N.Y.: Doubleday, 1981).
41. Jürgen Habermas, *Knowledge and Human Interests*, trans. Jeremy J. Shapiro. 2nd edn (London: Heinemann, 1978); and Habermas, *Theorie des kommunikativen Handelns*, 2 vols (Frankfurt/M.: Suhrkamp, 1981).
42. Michel Foucault, 'Nietzsche, Genealogy, History', in Paul Rabinow, ed., *The Foucault Reader* (New York: Pantheon Books, 1984), 76–100, here 89.
43. Ibid., 97.
44. 'Wie einst bei Bergson, Dilthey und Simmel "Leben" zum transzendentalen Grundbegriff einer Philosophie erhoben worden ist, die noch den Hintergrund für Heideggers Daseinsanalytik bildete, so erhebt nun Foucault "Macht" zum transzendental-historistischen Grundbegriff einer vernunftkritischen Geschichtsschreibung.' Jürgen Habermas, *Der philosophische Diskurs der Moderne: Zwölf Vorlesungen* (Frankfurt/M.: Suhrkamp, 1988), 298.
45. Cf. Anne Carr, *Transforming Grace: Christian Tradition and Women's Experience* (San Francisco: Harper & Row, 1988), 101:

> The Christian feminist critique of ideology, developed in the study of the theological tradition in its historical, social, and ecclesiastical contexts, is not merely negation of the past. As theology, both systematic and practical, it explicitly claims to be rooted in an eschatological and emancipatory interest in the future.

For further studies of feminist readings of the Scriptures see Letty M. Russell, ed., *Feminist Interpretation of the Bible* (Oxford: Blackwell,

1985); and Elisabeth Schüssler Fiorenza, *In Memory of Her: A Feminist Theological Reconstruction of Christian Origins* (New York: Crossroad, and London: SCM, 1983).

46. Cf. Julia Kristeva, 'Women's Time', in Toril Moi, ed., *The Kristeva Reader* (New York: Columbia University Press, 1986), 190ff.
47. Toril Moi in the Introduction to *The Kristeva Reader*, 17.
48. Terry Eagleton, *Literary Theory: An Introduction* (Oxford: Blackwell, 1983), 60.
49. Ibid., 65f.
50. Ibid., 195.
51. Ibid., 209.
52. Ibid., 211.
53. Ibid.
54. From a historical perspective, it would also be interesting to examine to what extent critical thinking, such as promoted by the Frankfurt School, has itself been inspired precisely by the development of theological and philosophical hermeneutics.
55. Cf. Ricœur, *Freud and Philosophy*; and 'The Question of Proof in Freud's Psychoanalytic Writings', in *Hermeneutics and the Human Sciences*, 247–73.
56. Ricœur, *Hermeneutics and the Human Sciences*, 94.
57. Cf. my *Text and Interpretation*, 64–72.
58. Ricœur, *Hermeneutics and the Human Sciences*, 94.
59. *Text and Interpretation*, 68–71.
60. Klaus Berger, *Hermeneutik des Neuen Testaments* (Gütersloh: Gütersloher Verlagshaus Gerd Mohn, 1988), 25.
61. David Tracy has coined this term and defended it recently again in *Plurality and Ambiguity*, 44: 'Interpretation is never exact but, at its best, relatively adequate.'
62. Mueller-Vollmer, op. cit., 74 [F.D.E. Schleiermacher, *Hermeneutik*, ed. Kimmerle, 76].

CHAPTER 6: THE DEVELOPMENT OF THEOLOGICAL HERMENEUTICS (II): BARTH, BULTMANN, AND THE NEW HERMENEUTIC

1. For a more detailed discussion of the rise of historicism see Robert Morgan with John Barton, *Biblical Interpretation*. The Oxford Bible Series (Oxford: Oxford University Press, 1988), 44–92.
2. Cf. Albert Schweitzer's discussion of these problems in *Geschichte der Leben-Jesu-Forschung*, 2 vols, 3rd paperback edn (Gütersloh: Gerd Mohn, 1977), vol. 1, 45–55.
3. G. E. Lessing, 'Über den Beweis des Geistes und der Kraft', in *Lessings Werke*, vol. 3, ed. Kurt Wölfel. *Schriften II* (Frankurt/M.: Insel, 1967), 307–312, here 309. See also Lessing's later work 'Die Erziehung des Menschengeschlechts', ibid., 544–563.
4. Friedrich Schleiermacher, *On Religion: Speeches to Its Cultured Despisers*, trans. John Oman (San Francisco: Harper & Row, 1958), 29f.

5. On Hegel's influence on theological interpretations of the Bible cf. *Biblical Interpretation*, 63f.
6. Morgan with Barton, *Biblical Interpretation, op. cit.*; Hans-Joachim Kraus, *Geschichte der historisch-kritischen Erforschung des Alten Testaments*, 3rd edn (Neukirchen-Vluyn: Neukirchener Verlag, 1982); and Peter Stuhlmacher, *Vom Verstehen des Neuen Testaments: Eine Hermeneutik*, op. cit. [cf. above Chapter 2, note 55].
7. *Geschichte der Leben-Jesu-Forschung*, Vol. 1, 48.
8. Karl Barth, *The Epistle to the Romans*, trans. Edwyn C. Hoskyns (Oxford: Oxford University Press, 1968), 8: 'The critical historian needs to be more critical.' – Rudolf Bultmann, 'Existentialist Interpretation', in Roger Johnson, ed., *Rudolf Bultmann: Interpreting Faith for the Modern Era* [abreviated from now on as *Interpreting Faith*] (London: Collins, 1987), 129–57, here 131: 'Historical and psychological exegesis establish primarily that this or that has been thought, said, or done at a particular time and under such and such historical circumstances and psychological conditions, without reflecting on the meaning and demands of what is said.' See also Bultmann's review of Barth's *Romans*, in *Rudolf Bultmann: Interpreting Faith*, 54–65, esp. 65.
9. Cf. Klaus Scholder, *Die Kirchen und das Dritte Reich*, vol. 1 (Frankfurt/M.: Ullstein, 1986), 46–64.
10. Cf. Eberhard Jüngel, *Barth-Studien*. Ökumenische Theologie 9 (Zürich and Köln: Benziger, and Gütersloh: Gerd Mohn, 1982), 40.
11. 'The Strange New World Within the Bible', in Karl Barth, *The Word of God and the Word of Man*, trans. Douglas Horton (London: Hodder and Staughton, 1928), 28–50.
12. Karl Barth, *Der Römerbrief*. 1st edn (Bern: Bäschlin, 1919); 2nd rev. edn (Munich: Kaiser, 1922), now 12th edn (Zürich: Theologischer Verlag, 1978). ET: *The Epistle to the Romans*, (see note 8 above), abbreviated *Romans*.
13. Karl Barth, *Church Dogmatics*, 8 vols. ET ed. by G. W. Bromiley and T. F. Torrance (Edinburgh: T.& T. Clark, 1956–75). References to *Church Dogmatics* in the text are abreviated *CD*. Here we are especially concerned with CD I/1: The Doctrine of the Word of God. Part 1. 2nd edn. Trans. G. W. Bromiley (1975); and CD I/2: The Doctrine of the Word of God. Part 2. Trans. G. T. Thompson and Harold Knight (1956).
14. Karl Barth, *Evangelical Theology: An Introduction*, trans. Grover Foley (London: Weidenfeld and Nicolson, 1963), 5.
15. CD I/1 and I/2.
16. Barth, *Romans*, 1–26.
17. Karl Barth-Rudolf Bultmann, *Briefwechsel 1922–1966*. Ed. Bernd Jaspert. Karl Barth Gesamtausgabe V: Briefe, vol. 1 (Zürich: Theologischer Verlag, 1971). ET: Karl Barth-Rudolf Bultmann, *Letters 1922–1966*, ed. Bernd Jaspert. Trans. and ed. Geoffrey W. Bromiley (Edinburgh: T.&.T. Clark, 1982). This translation does not include all the letters printed in the original German edition.
18. For Bultmann's development of hermeneutics see esp. Rudolf

Bultmann, *Glauben und Verstehen: Gesammelte Aufsätze*, 4 vols (Tübingen: J. C. B. Mohr [Paul Siebeck], 1933–65); 'New Testament and Mythology', in Hans-Werner Bartsch, ed., *Kerygma and Myth: A Theological Debate*, trans. Reginald H. Fuller (London: SPCK, 1953), 1–44; and *Jesus Christ and Mythology* (New York: Scribner's, 1958).

19. Cf. *Glauben und Verstehen*, vol. 3, 3rd edn (1965), 147.
20. Barth-Bultmann, *Letters*, 89f.
21. Cf. Bultmann, 'Liberal Theology and the Latest Theological Movement', in *Interpreting Faith*, 65–79.
22. Karl Barth, 'Rudolf Bultmann – An Attempt to Understand Him', in Hans-Werner Bartsch, ed., *Kerygma and Myth: A Theological Debate*, vol. 2 (London: SPCK, 1962), 83–132, here esp. 112ff.
23. CD I/1: 295f. – See Peter Eicher, *Offenbarung: Prinzip neuzeitlicher Theologie* (Munich: Kösel, 1977), 189ff.
24. Barth, *Der Römerbrief*, xxi. The term *Treueverhältnis* is lost in the English translation, cf. *Romans*, 18.
25. *Romans*, 19.
26. *Der Römerbrief*, xii. Here the English translation is not precise enough. Cf. *Romans*, 8.
27. *Der Römerbrief*, x.
28. Ibid., xiii (my translation – italics according to the German original); cf. *Romans*, 10.
29. Cf. Bultmann, 'New Testament and Mythology', 3f., and Bultmann's reply to Barth in *Letters 1922–1966*, 87f.
30. *Kirchliche Dogmatik* I/2, 7th edn (Zürich: Theologischer Verlag, 1983), 805 (my translation).
31. Eberhard Jüngel, *Barth-Studien*, 94 (my translation).
32. Dietrich Bonhoeffer, *Widerstand und Ergebung: Briefe und Aufzeichnungen aus der Haft*. Ed. Eberhard Bethge. 11th pbk. edn (Gütersloh: Gerd Mohn, 1980), 137. Cf. Peter Eicher, *Offenbarung*, 234–42.
33. Karl Barth, *The Theology of Schleiermacher*. Ed. Dietrich Ritschl, trans. Geoffrey W. Bromiley (Edinburgh: T. &. T. Clark, 1982), 178–83.
34. Cf. ibid., 183.
35. Eberhard Jüngel, *Gottes Sein ist im Werden: Verantwortliche Rede vom Sein Gottes bei Karl Barth*. 3rd edn (Tübingen: J. C. B. Mohr [Paul Siebeck], 1976), 27.
36. Cf. S. W. Sykes, 'Barth on the Centre of Theology', in S. W. Sykes, ed., *Karl Barth: Studies of His Theological Method* (Oxford: Clarendon Press, 1979), 381–401, here 393f.
37. Cf. R. D. Williams, 'Barth on the Triune God', in Sykes, ed., *Karl Barth: Studies of His Theological Method*, 147–93. Williams examines some major problems of Barth's doctrine of the Spirit.
38. Karl Barth, *The Humanity of God*, trans. John Newton Thomas and Thomas Wieser (London: Collins, 1961).
39. See Eberhard Jüngel's assessment of Barth's Theantropologie and its implications in 'Theologische Existenz: Erinnerung an Karl Barth, *Evangelische Kommentare* 19 (1986), 258–60.
40. Karl Barth, 'Rudolf Bultmann – An Attempt to Understand Him' (see

above note 22), and Rudolf Bultmann's reply in *Letters 1922–1966*, 87–104.

41. Karl Barth, *Fides Quaerens Intellectum: Anselms Beweis der Existenz Gottes im Zusammenhang seines theologischen Programms*. Ed. Eberhard Jüngel and Ingolf U. Dalferth. Karl Barth Gesamtausgabe II: Akademische Werke (Zürich: Theologischer Verlag, 1981).

42. The same question has to be addressed to some of Barth's disciples. See for instance Georg Eicholz, *Tradition und Interpretation: Studien zum Neuen Testament* (Munich: Kösel, 1965), 190–209: 'Der Ansatz Karl Barths in der Hermeneutik'.

43. Cf. my entry 'Neo-Orthodoxy' in J. A. Komonchak, M. Collins, D. A. Lane, eds, *The New Dictionary of Theology* (Dublin: Gill and Macmillan, 1987), 713.

44. Cf. Eugen Biser, 'Hermeneutische Integration: Zur Frage der Herkunft von Rudolf Bultmanns hermeneutischer Interpretation', in Bernd Jaspert, ed., *Rudolf Bultmanns Werk und Wirkung* (Darmstadt: Wissenschaftliche Buchgesellschaft, 1984), 211–33.

45. Cf. the four volumes of *Glauben und Verstehen* (see above note 18).

46. Bultmann, 'The Problem of a Theological Exegesis of the New Testament' (1925), *Interpreting Faith*, 132.

47. Bultmann, 'The Problem of Hermeneutics', *Interpreting Faith*, 137–57.

48. Ibid., 143.

49. Bultmann, 'Is Exegesis Without Presuppositions Possible?' (1957), MV [cf. Chapter 3, note 1], 242–8, here 242 (original italics).

50. 'The Problem of Hermeneutics', *Interpreting Faith*, 151.

51. 'Is Exegesis Without Presuppositions Possible?', MV, 245f.

52. 'The Problem of Hermeneutics', *Interpreting Faith*, 153.

53. Ibid., 154.

54. Ibid., 156.

55. 'Is Exegesis Without Presuppositions Possible?', MV, 246f.

56. 'The Problem of a Theological Exegesis of the New Testament', *Interpreting Faith*, 137.

57. Cf. David E. Klemm's introduction to Bultmann's 'The Problem of Hermeneutics', *Hermeneutical Inquiry* I, 110.

58. Bultmann, 'Neues Testament und Mythologie: Das Problem der Entmythologisierung der neutestamentlichen Verkündigung', in Hans-Werner Bartsch, *Kerygma und Mythos: Ein theologisches Gespräch*. 3rd edn (Hamburg: Herbert Reich – Evangelischer Verlag, 1954), 15–48 (see here also the discussion of Bultmann's proposal by other theologians). ET: Rudolf Bultmann, *New Testament and Mythology and other Basic Writings*, ed. and trans. Schubert M. Ogden (London: SCM, 1985), 1–43.

59. Bultmann, *Jesus Christ and Mythology* (New York: Charles Scribner's Sons, 1958), 18 [= *Interpreting Faith*, 293] (original italics).

60. Ibid., 36 [= *Interpreting Faith*, 300].

61. Ibid., 83 [= *Interpreting Faith*, 327]: '. . . and it has become evident that faith itself demands to be freed from any world-view produced by man's thought, whether mythological or scientific.'

62. Ibid., 33f. [= *Interpreting Faith*, 299f.].
63. Ibid., 55 [= *Interpreting Faith*, 311].
64. Ibid., 57f. [= *Interpreting Faith*, 312].
65. Paul Ricœur, 'Preface to Bultmann', in *Essays on Biblical Interpretation*. Ed. Lewis S. Mudge (Philadelphia: Fortress, 1980), 49–72.
66. Ibid., 66.
67. Ibid.
68. Ibid., 69.
69. Ibid., 72: 'I do not say that theology *must* go by way of Heidegger. I say that, *if* it goes by way of Heidegger, then it is by this path and to this point that it must follow him. This path is longer. It is the path of patience and not of haste and precipitation.' (Original italics.)
70. James M. Robinson and John B. Cobb, Jr., eds, *The New Hermeneutic*. New Frontiers in Theology II (New York: Harper & Row, 1964). Note that many English publications in the context of the New Hermeneutic speak of hermeneutic. I shall use this spelling only in quotations or in order to highlight connections with this specific movement in modern theological hermeneutics.
71. Ernst Fuchs, *Hermeneutik*. 2nd edn (Bad Cannstadt: Müllerschön, 1958). Cf. also his *Marburger Hermeneutik* (Tübingen: J. C. B. Mohr [Paul Siebeck], 1968).
72. James Robinson, 'Hermeneutic Since Barth', *The New Hermeneutic*, 1–77.
73. Ibid., 49.
74. Fuchs, *Hermeneutik*, 142.
75. *Hermeneutik*, 63. I follow the translation given by Robinson in 'Hermeneutic Since Barth', 49f. (original italics).
76. Fuchs, 'The New Testament and the Hermeneutical Problem', in *The New Hermeneutic*, 111–145, here 144. (See also Fuchs, *Hermeneutik*, 57.)
77. Ibid., 139.
78. Ibid., 141.
79. Ibid., 141f.
80. *Hermeneutik*, 101.
81. Ibid., 10f.
82. Ernst Fuchs, *Glaube und Erfahrung: Zum christologischen Problem im Neuen Testament* (Tübingen: J. C. B. Mohr [Paul Siebeck], 1965), 131f.
83. Ibid., 135: 'Die Hermeneutik wird von mir eine "Sprachlehre des Glaubens" genannt, weil ich gelernt zu haben meine, daß die Evidenz unseres theologischen Denkens aus der Evidenz des Hörens, aus der Evidenz der Stimme der Liebe Christi stammt.' Cf. also Fuchs, *Hermeneutik*, iii.
84. Cf. *Glaube und Erfahrung*, 186.
85. Fuchs treats of theological problems already under the heading of *Allgemeine Hermeneutik* [General Hermeneutics] in his *Hermeneutik*, 103–58. Thus, in spite of his distinction in the organisation of *Hermeneutik*, there is no real distinction between general and applied hermeneutics for him as there is in Schleiermacher's hermeneutics.
86. Gerhard Ebeling, *Evangelische Evangelienauslegung: Eine Untersuchung*

zu Luthers Hermeneutik [1942] (Darmstadt: Wissenschaftliche Buchgesellschaft, 1962 [reprint]).

87. Cf. the bibliography of Ebeling's work until 1981 given by Mikka Ruokanen, *Hermeneutic as an Ecumenical Method in the Theology of Gerhard Ebeling*. Publications of the Luther-Agricola Society B 13 (Helsinki: Luther-Agricola Society, 1982), 316–323.
88. Ebeling, 'Hermeneutik', in *Religion in Geschichte und Gegenwart*, vol. 3, 3rd edn (Tübingen: J. C. B. Mohr [Paul Siebeck], 1959, 242–62.
89. Ebeling, 'The Significance of the Critical Historical Method for Church and Theology in Protestantism', in Ebeling, *Word and Faith*, trans. James W. Leitch (London: SCM, 1963), 17–61.
90. Ebeling, 'Word of God and Hermeneutics', in *Word and Faith*, 305–32.
91. Ebeling, 'God and Word', in Klemm, *Hermeneutical Inquiry* I, 195–224.
92. Ebeling, 'The Meaning of Biblical Theology', in *Word and Faith*, 79–97, here 82f.; and 'The Significance of the Critical Historical Method', 40: '[I]t is a simple fact that the Reformation was not sufficiently aware of its own distance from early Christianity.'
93. Cf. 'Word of God and Hermeneutics', 331f.
94. 'The Significance of the Critical Historical Method', 56.
95. 'God and Word', 205.
96. 'Word of God and Hermeneutics', 318.
97. 'God and Word', 212.
98. Ibid., 217 (translation altered).
99. Ibid., 218.
100. Ibid., 219.
101. Ebeling, 'Hermeneutische Theologie?', in *Wort und Glaube*, vol. 2: *Beiträge zur Fundamentaltheologie und zur Lehre von Gott* (Tübingen: J.C.B. Mohr [Paul Siebeck], 1969), 99–120, here 106 (my translation).
102. 'God and Word', 223f.
103. Thus, the title of his three books which contain his hermeneutical writings: *Wort und Glaube*, 3 vols (Tübingen: J. C. B. Mohr [Paul Siebeck], 1960–75).
104. 'Word of God and Hermeneutics', 323.
105. Cf. Ebeling, *Einführung in Theologische Sprachlehre* (Tübingen: J.C.B. Mohr [Paul Siebeck], 1971).
106. 'Hermeneutische Theologie?', 120.
107. Among the more recent Roman Catholic contributions to the study of theological hermeneutics which we have not discussed in this book see Kurt Frör, *Biblische Hermeneutik: Zur Schriftauslegung in Predigt und Unterricht*. 2nd edn (Munich: Kaiser, 1964); Eugen Biser, *Theologische Sprachtheorie und Hermeneutik* (Munich: Kösel, 1970); and Anton Grabner-Haider, *Semiotik und Theologie: Religiöse Rede zwischen analytischer und hermeneutischer Philosophie* (Munich: Kösel, 1973).
108. Ebeling, 'Hermeneutische Theologie?', 106.

CHAPTER 7: THE DEVELOPMENT OF THEOLOGICAL HERMENEUTICS (III): HERMENEUTICS AND CHRISTIAN IDENTITY

1. Peter Stuhlmacher, *Vom Verstehen des Neuen Testaments: Eine Hermeneutik*. Grundrisse zum Neuen Testament. NTD Ergänzungsreihe, vol. 6, 2nd edn (Göttingen: Vandenhoeck & Ruprecht, 1986); Duncan S. Ferguson, *Biblical Hermeneutics: An Introduction* (Atlanta: John Knox Press, 1986); Robert Morgan with John Barton, *Biblical Interpretation*. Oxford Bible Series (Oxford: Oxford University Press, 1988).
2. Stuhlmacher, op. cit., 222.
3. Ibid., 223.
4. Ibid., 214 and 223f. (my translation).
5. Cf. his revealing comments on Schleiermacher's hermeneutics: 'Die allgemeine Hermeneutik saugt bei Schleiermacher das spezifische Problem des Verständnisses des Evangeliums auf.' Ibid., 148.
6. Ferguson, op. cit., 191.
7. Morgan with Barton, op. cit., 286.
8. George A. Lindbeck, *The Nature of Doctrine: Religion and Theology in a Postliberal Age* (Philadelphia: Westminster Press, 1984).
9. Ibid., 117.
10. Ibid., 119–24.
11. Ibid., 128ff.
12. David Tracy, *Plurality and Ambiguity: Hermeneutics, Religion, Hope* (San Francisco: Harper & Row, 1987), 8.
13. Klaus Berger, *Hermeneutik des Neuen Testaments* (Gütersloh: Gütersloher Verlagshaus Gerd Mohn, 1988), 14.
14. Klaus Berger, *Exegese und Philosophie*. Stuttgarter Bibelstudien 123/124 (Stuttgart: Katholisches Bibelwerk, 1986), esp. 178–94.
15. David Tracy, 'The Uneasy Alliance Reconceived: Catholic Theological Method, Modernity, and Postmodernity', *Theological Studies* 50 (1989), 548–70; Hans Küng, *Theologie im Aufbruch: Eine Ökumenische Grundlegung* (Munich and Zürich: Piper, 1987), esp. 67–85.
16. See Hans Frei, *The Eclipse of Biblical Narative: A Study in Eighteenth and Nineteenth Century Hermeneutics* (New Haven and London: Yale University Press, 1974); and Frei, *The Identity of Jesus Christ: The Hermeneutical Bases of Dogmatic Theology* (Philadelphia: Fortress, 1975).
17. Lindbeck, op. cit., 48ff.
18. Cf. David Tracy, 'The Uneasy Alliance', 555f.
19. See Tracy's discussion of the three publics of theology, *The Analogical Imagination* [cf. Chapter 1, note 3], 3–31.
20. Cf. above 3.4.2 and 3.5.
21. Here I analyse the phenomenon of tradition only from a theological perspective. However, 'tradition' is a general human phenomenon and has implications for all dimensions of culture and society. Cf. Hans-Georg Gadamer, 'Tradition: Phänomenologisch', *Religion in Geschichte und Gegenwart*. Vol. 6, 3rd edn (Tübingen: J. C. B. Mohr

[Paul Siebeck], 1962), 966f; J. P. Mackey, *Tradition and Change in the Church* (Dublin and Sidney: Gill, 1968), 150–191; Carl J. Friedrich, *Tradition and Authority*. Key Concepts in Political Science (London: Macmillan, 1972), esp. 13–22; and James M. Byrne, *Tradition and Deconstruction: The Theological Implications of the Postmodern Crisis of Continuity*. Ph.D. Diss. University of Dublin 1989.

22. For a detailed study of the narrower meaning of 'tradition' in Christian theology see Yves Congar, *Tradition and Traditions: An historical and a theological essay*, trans. Michael Naseby and Thomas Rainborough (London: Burns & Oates, 1966), esp. 296–307. For a critical appraisal of Congar's work, cf. Byrne, *Tradition and Deconstruction*, 85ff.
23. Cf. Peter L. Berger, *The Heretical Imperative: Contemporary Possibilities of Religious Affirmation* (Garden City, N.Y.: Anchor Press/Doubleday, 1979), esp. 46–54.
24. For a balanced view of the problems implied in any use of the term 'heresy' see Norbert Brox, *Kirchengeschichte des Altertums*. 2nd edn (Düsseldorf: Patmos, 1986), 137–45; and Brox, 'Häresie', *Reallexikon für Antike und Christentum*, vol. XIII (Stuttgart: Anton Hiersemann, 1984), 248–97.
25. *Adversus Haereses*, I 22.1 passim. Cf. Brox, *Offenbarung* [cf. Chapter 2, note 13], 109: The rule of faith 'wird von Irenäus nicht undbedingt und wesentlich, sondern nur gelegentlich in festen Formeln gedacht, denn sie ist immer mehr als die Formeln, wie sie auch mehr ist als die Schrift. . . . Sie ist das, was die Kirche glaubt, die ganze einsichtige und geoffenbarte Wahrheit.' Cf. also R. P. C. Hanson, *Tradition in the Early Church* (London: SCM, 1962), 127ff. Hanson defines the general significance of the rule of faith as 'a graph of the interpretation of the Bible by the Church in the second and third centuries'.
26. *Adv. Haer.*, II 30.9.
27. *Adv. Haer.*, III 3. Cf. Brox, *Offenbarung*, 140ff., and Hanson, *Tradition*, 144–57.
28. Cf. Brox, *Offenbarung*, 159.
29. *Adv. Haer.*, III 3.4. Cf. Brox, *Offenbarung*, 144–50.
30. *Adv. Haer.*, III 24.1. Tr. according to Henry Bettenson, *The Early Christian Fathers* (Oxford: Oxford University Press, 1969), 83.
31. Cf. *Adv. Haer.*, III 18.1.
32. *Adv. Haer.*, V 20.2.
33. Unlike Robert M. Grant, *A Short History of the Interpretation of the Bible* [cf. above Chapter 2, note 11], 81, I think that Vincent's theory of tradition differs from that of his predecessors in so far as he introduced the new principle of *consensus*.
34. Henricus Denzinger and Adolfus Schönmetzer, eds, *Enchiridion Symbolorum* (= *DS*). 36th edn (Freiburg i. B.: Herder, 1976), 1501 (my translation).
35. Cf. Congar, *Tradition*, 156–76.
36. *DS*, 1507 (my translation).
37. For a more detailed assessment of the fate of the laity in the Roman Catholic Church see my essay 'One Church: Two Classes? The

Lessons of History', in Seán MacRéamoinn, ed., *Pobal: the laity in Ireland* (Dublin: Columba Press, 1986), 22–34.

38. Cf. Joseph Ratzinger, 'Tradition Systematisch', *Lexikon für Theologie und Kirche*, vol. X (Freiburg i.B.: Herder, 1965), 296f.
39. Cf. Edward Farley, *Ecclesial Reflection: An Anatomy of Theological Method* (Philadelphia: Fortess, 1982), 118f.; and the detailed study by August Bernhard Hassler, *How the Pope Became Infallible: Pius IX and the Politics of Persuasion* (Garden City, N.Y.: Doubleday, 1981); see also Hans Küng, *Infallible? An Enquiry*, trans. Eric Mosbacher (London: Collins, 1971).
40. Congar, *Tradition*, 182; and Ratzinger, 'Tradition: Systematisch', 297.
41. Cf. Kurt Aland, *Die Reformatoren* (Gütersloh: Gerd Mohn, 1976), 26f.
42. Martin Luther, Weimarer Ausgabe DB, 384, 22–32. Cf. Inge Lønning, 'Kein anderes Evangelium', in Peter Manns and Harding Meyer, eds, *Ökumenische Erschließung Martin Luthers* (Paderborn: Bonifatius, 1983), 274–92.
43. Cf. Grant, *A Short History*, 94ff.
44. Edmund Farley and Peter C. Hodgson, 'Scripture and Tradition', in Peter C. Hodgson and Robert H. King, eds, *Christian Theology: An Introduction to Its Traditions and Tasks* (Philadelphia: Fortress, 1982), 46.
45. Cf. Congar, *Tradition*, 145.
46. Cf. Bernhard Lohse, *Epochen der Dogmengeschichte*. 3rd edn (Stuttgart: Kreuz, 1974), 220f.
47. Cf. Farley, *Ecclesial Reflection*, 139.
48 Cf. Gerhard Ebeling, 'Tradition: Dogmatisch', in *Religion in Geschichte und Gegenwart*, vol. VI [cf. note 8 above], 982; and Gotthold Hasenhüttl, *Kritische Dogmatik* (Graz: Styria, 1979), 38f.
49. Cf. Karl Barth's warning: 'Christentum, das nicht ganz und gar und restlos Eschatologie ist, hat mit Christus ganz und gar und restlos nichts zu tun.' *Der Römerbrief*. 2nd edn (1922) (Zürich: Theologischer Verlag, 1978), 298 [ET: *Romans*, 314].
50. Gotthold Hasenhüttl, *Herrschaftsfreie Kirche: Sozio-theologische Grundlegung* (Düsseldorf: Patmos, 1974), 147–50, suggests an understanding of church as 'institutionalised anarchy'.
51. While the Second Vatican Council in its decree on the church, *Lumen Gentium*, initially suggested this understanding, it qualified it immediately in the same document by reaffirming the particular hierarchical constitution of the Roman Catholic Church.
52. See Stephen Sykes, *The Identity of Christianity: Theologians and the Essence of Christianity from Schleiermacher to Barth* (London: SCPK, 1984), 7.
53. David Tracy, *Blessed Rage for Order: The New Pluralism in Theology* (New York: Seabury, 1975), 32ff.
54. Cf. Tracy, *The Analogical Imagination: Christian Theology and the Culture of Pluralism* (New York: Crossroad, 1981), 99–153; and his *Plurality and Ambiguity*, 28–46.
55. Tracy's *Plurality and Ambiguity* may well be read as a manifesto

for such a critical and self-critical human conversation. For a more detailed appraisal of Tracy's manifesto see my review in *Religious Studies Review* 15 (1989), 218–21.

56. Cf. Sykes, *The Identity*, 240.
57. Ibid., 255.
58. Ibid., 261.
59. Cf. Adolf von Harnack, *What is Christianity*, trans. Thomas Bailey Saunders (New York: Harper and Row, 1957).
60. See esp. Mk 8 and 14:50. Cf. Werner H. Kelber, *Mark's Story of Jesus* (Philadelphia: Fortress, 1979), esp. 93; also Seán Freyne, 'The Disciples in Mark and the Maskilim in Daniel: A Comparison', *Journal for the Study of the New Testament* 16 (1982), 7–23, and his 'At Cross Purposes: Jesus and the Disciples in Mark', *The Furrow* 33 (1982), 331–9.
61. For a discussion of what constitutes a 'classic' text see Tracy, *Plurality and Ambiguity*, 12f.; and my *Text and Interpretation*, 140–2.
62. Cf. also Edward Schillebeeckx, *The Church with a Human Face: A New and Expanded Theology of Ministry*, trans. John Bowden (London: SCM, 1985), 14.: '. . . the whole history of Christianity consists of a constant ongoing process of interpretation.'
63. Thus, the crucial question may not be who Jesus was in himself, but what is his significance for our understanding of God's project with this creation. Schillebeeckx, *The Church with a Human Face*, 30f. makes a similar distinction.
64. Cf. Mk 8:34; Mt 16:24; Lk9:23.
65. Cf. Dt 6:44ff.; Lev 19:18; Mt 22:37 etc.
66. See Seán Freyne, *The World of the New Testament* (Dublin: Veritas, 1980), 99–128.
67. Cf. Seán Freyne, 'Vilifying the Other and Defending the Self: Matthew's and John's Anti-Jewish Polemics in Focus', in Jakob Neusner and Ernest S. Frerichs, eds, *'To See Ourselves as Others See Us': Christians, Jews, 'Others' in Late Antiquity* (Chico: California: Scholars Press, 1985), 117–43.
68. Cf. Wayne A. Meeks, 'Breaking Away: Three New Testament Pictures of Christianty's Separation from the Jewish Communities', in *'To See Ourselves as Others See Us'*, 93–115, esp. 104–8.
69. See Seán Freyne, *Christians in a Jewish World*. Unpublished Lecture (1986). 19 pages, esp. 19: 'In attempting to understand the mutual vilifications of the past we need to be aware that the rhetoric is a rhetoric of fear, based on deep-seated anxieties about ourselves which cannot tolerate diversity, especially when the other that is different is very close to us.'
70. For an illustration of these tendencies see *The First Epsitle of Clement to the Corinthians*. English Text in Maxwell Stainforth, ed., *Early Christian Writings: The Apostolic Fathers* (Harmondsworth: Penguin, 1968), 23–59, esp. chapters 40ff. of the Epistle.
71. Cf. Freyne, *Christians in a Jewish World*, 16.
72. Cf. Claude Geffré, *Le Christianisme au Risque de l'Interprétation* (Paris: Cerf, 1983), 103.

73. Cf. Schillebeeckx, *The Church with a Human Face*, 34f.
74. Cf. Tracy, *Plurality and Ambiguity*, 20: 'Conversation in its primary form is an exploration of possibilities in the search for truth.'

Bibliography

This bibliography lists only the major sources used in this book. The abbreviation *ET* stands for 'English Translation'

1. Readers and Collections of Essays on Hermeneutical Issues

Hans-Georg Gadamer and Gottfried Boehm, eds, *Seminar: Philosophische Hermeneutik*. 2nd edn. Frankfurt/M.: Suhrkamp, 1979.

Hans-Georg Gadamer and Gottfried Boehm, eds, *Seminar: Die Hermeneutik und die Wissenschaften*. Frankfurt/M.: Suhrkamp, 1978.

Josué V. Harari, ed., *Textual Strategies: Perspectives in Post-Structuralist Criticism*. Ithaca, N.Y.: Cornell University Press, 1979.

Roger Johnson, ed., *Rudolf Bultmann: Interpreting Faith for the Modern Era*. London: Collins, 1987.

David Klemm, ed., *Hermeneutical Inquiry*, 2 vols. American Academy of Religion Studies in Relgion 43/44. Vol. 1: *The Interpretation of Texts*. Vol. 2: *The Interpretation of Existence*. Atlanta: Scholars Press, 1986.

Richard Macksey and Eugenio Donato, eds, *The Structuralist Controversy: The Languages of Criticism and the Sciences of Man*. Baltimore and London: Johns Hopkins University Press, 1972.

Toril Moi, ed., *The Kristeva Reader*. New York: Columbia University Press, 1986.

Kurt Mueller-Vollmer, ed., *The Hermeneutics Reader: Texts of the German Tradition from the Enlightenment to the Present*. Oxford: Blackwell, 1986.

Gayle L. Ormiston and Alan D. Schrift, eds, *The Hermeneutic Tradition: From Ast to Ricœur*. Albany: State University of New York Press, 1990.

Paul Rabinow, ed., *The Foucault Reader*. New York: Pantheon Books, 1984.

Letty M. Russell, ed., *Feminist Interpretation of the Bible*. Oxford: Blackwell, 1985.

John Sturrock, ed., *Structuralism and Since: From Lévi-Strauss to Derrida*. Oxford: Oxford University Press, 1979.

Susan R. Suleiman and Inge Crosman, eds, *The Reader in The Text: Essays on Audience and Interpretation*. Princeton: Princeton University Press, 1980.

Jane P. Tompkins, ed., *Reader-Response Criticism: From Formalism to Post-Structuralism*. Baltimore and London: Johns Hopkins University Press, 1980.

Rainer Warning, ed., *Rezeptionsästhetik: Theorie und Praxis*. 2nd edn Munich: Fink, 1979.

2. Other Writings

Aurelius Augustinus, *De Doctrina Christiana*. Corpus Christianorum: Series Latina XXXII. Tornhout: Brepols, 1962, 1–167. ET: *On Christian Doctrine*, trans. D. W. Robertson, Jr. The Library of Christian Art. New York: Macmillan, 1958.

James Barr, *Old and New in Interpretation: A Study of the Two Testaments*. London: SCM, 1966.

Karl Barth, *The Epistle to the Romans*, trans. Edwyn C. Hoskyns. Oxford: Oxford University Press, 1968.

——, *Church Dogmatics*, 8 vols. ET ed. by G. W. Bromiley and T. F. Torrance. Edinburgh: T. & T. Clark, 1956–75.

——, *Evangelical Theology: An Introduction*, trans. Grover Foley. London: Weidenfeld and Nicolson, 1963.

Roland Barthes, *The Pleasure of the Text*, trans. Richard Miller. New York: Hill and Wang, 1975.

Klaus Berger, *Exegese und Philosophie*. Stuttgarter Bibelstudien 123/124. Stuttgart: Katholisches Bibelwerk, 1986.

——, *Hermeneutik des Neuen Testaments*. Gütersloh: Gütersloher Verlagshaus Gerd Mohn, 1988.

Peter L. Berger, *The Heretical Imperative: Contemporary Possibilities of Religious Affirmation*. Garden City, N.Y.: Anchor Press/Doubleday, 1979.

William J. Bouwsma, *John Calvin: A Sixteenth-Century Portrait*. Oxford and New York: Oxford University Press, 1988.

Hennig Brinkmann, *Mittelalterliche Hermeneutik*. Darmstadt: Wissenschaftliche Buchgesellschaft, 1980.

Norbert Brox, *Falsche Verfasserangaben: Zur Erklärung der frühchristlichen Pseudepigraphie*. Stuttgarter Bibelstudien 79. Stuttgart: Katholisches Bibelwerk, 1975.

——, *Kirchengeschichte des Altertums*. 2nd edn. Düsseldorf: Patmos, 1986.

Rudolf Bultmann, *Glauben und Verstehen: Gesammelte Aufsätze*, 4 vols. Tübingen: J. C. B. Mohr (Paul Siebeck), 1933–65.

——, *Jesus Christ and Mythology*. New York: Scribner's, 1958.

——, *New Testament and Mythology and other Basic Writings*, ed. and trans. Schubert M. Ogden. London: SCM, 1985.

Anne Carr, *Transforming Grace: Christian Tradition and Women's Experience*. San Francisco: Harper & Row, 1988.

Yves Congar, *Tradition and Traditions: An historical and a theological essay*, trans. Michael Naseby and Thomas Rainborough. London: Burns & Oates, 1966.

Jonathan Culler, *On Deconstruction: Theory and Criticism after Structuralism*. Ithaca, N.Y.: Cornell University Press, 1982.

Jacques Derrida, *Of Grammatology*, trans. Gayatri Chakravorty Spivak. Baltimore: Johns Hopkins University Press, 1976.

——, *Writing and Difference*, trans. Alan Bass. Chicago: University of Chicago Press, 1978.

Terry Eagleton, *Literary Theory: An Introduction*. Oxford: Blackwell, 1983.

Gerhard Ebeling, *Evangelische Evangelienauslegung: Eine Untersuchung zu Luthers Hermeneutik* [1942]. Darmstadt: Wissenschaftliche Buchgesell-

schaft, 1962.
——, *Wort und Glaube*, 3 vols. Tübingen: J. C. B. Mohr (Paul Siebeck), 1960–75.
——, *Word and Faith*, trans. James W. Leitch. London: SCM, 1963.
——, 'Hermeneutik', in *Die Religion in Geschichte und Gegenwart*, vol. 3, 3rd edn. Tübingen: J. C. B. Mohr (Paul Siebeck), 1959, 242–62.
——, *Lutherstudien*, vol. 1. Tübingen: J. C. B. Mohr (Paul Siebeck), 1971.
Hans-Werner Eroms, *Funktionale Satzperspektive*. Germanistische Arbeitshefte 31. Tübingen: Niemeyer, 1986.
Edward Farley, *Ecclesial Reflection: An Anatomy of Theological Method*. Philadelphia: Fortress, 1982.
Helmut Feld, *Die Anfänge der modernen biblischen Hermeneutik in der spätmittelalterlichen Theologie*. Wiesbaden: Franz Steiner, 1977.
Duncan S. Ferguson, *Biblical Hermeneutics: An Introduction*. Atlanta: John Knox Press, 1986.
Stanley Fish, *Is There a Text in This Class? The Authority of Interpretive Communities*. Cambridge, Mass., and London: Harvard University Press, 1980.
Michel Foucault, *The Order of Things: An Archaeology of the Human Sciences*. New York: Vintage Books, 1973.
Hans Frei, *The Eclipse of Biblical Narrative: A Study in Eighteenth and Nineteenth Century Hermeneutics*. New Haven and London: Yale University Press, 1974.
Seán Freyne, *Galilee, Jesus and the Gospels: Literary Approaches and Historical Investigations*. Dublin: Gill and Macmillan, 1988.
Ernst Fuchs, *Hermeneutik*. 2nd edn. Bad Cannstadt: Müllerschön, 1958.
——, *Glaube und Erfahrung: Zum christologischen Problem im Neuen Testament*. Tübingen: J. C. B. Mohr (Paul Siebeck), 1965.
——, *Marburger Hermeneutik*. Tübingen: J. C. B. Mohr (Paul Siebeck), 1968.
Hans-Georg Gadamer, *Truth and Method*, trans. William Glen-Doepel. Ed. John Cumming and Garrett Barden. 2nd edn. London: Sheed and Ward, 1979.
——, *Philosophical Hermeneutics*, trans. and ed. David E. Linge. Berkeley, Los Angeles, and London: University of California Press, 1976.
——, *Reason in the Age of Science*, trans. Frederick G. Lawrence. Cambridge, Mass., and London: MIT Press, 1981.
Rodolphe Gasché, *The Tain of the Mirror: Derrida and the Philosophy of Reflection*. Cambridge, Mass., and London: Harvard University Press, 1986.
Claude Geffré, *Le Christianisme au Risque de l'Interprétation*. Paris: Cerf, 1983.
Leonhard Goppelt, *Typos: Die typologische Deutung des Alten Testaments im Neuen*. Reprint. Darmstadt: Wissenschaftliche Buchgesellschaft, 1990.
Robert M. Grant with David Tracy, *A Short History of the Interpretation of the Bible*. 2nd edn. Philadelphia: Fortress, 1984.
Jürgen Habermas, *Knowledge and Human Interest*, trans. Jeremy J. Shapiro. 2nd edn. London: Heinemann, 1978.
——, *Der philosophische Diskurs der Moderne: Zwölf Vorlesungen*. Frankfurt/M.: Suhrkamp, 1988.
R. P. C. Hanson, *Tradition in the Early Church*. London: SCM, 1962.

Gotthold Hasenhüttl, *Herrschaftsfreie Kirche: Sozio-theologische Grundlegung*. Düsseldorf: Patmos, 1974.

Martin Heidegger, *Being and Time*, trans. John Macquarrie and Edward Robinson. Oxford: Blackwell, 1973.

——, *Unterwegs zur Sprache*. 4th edn. Tübingen: Neske, 1971.

E. D. Hirsch, *Validity in Interpretation*. New Haven and London: Yale University Press, 1967.

——, *The Aims of Interpretation*. Chicago: University of Chicago Press, 1976.

Gottfried Hornig, *Die Anfänge der historisch-kritischen Theologie: Johann Salomo Semlers Schriftverständnis und seine Stellung zu Luther*. Göttingen: Vandenhoeck & Ruprecht, 1961.

Hugh of St Victor: *The Didascalicon of Hugh of St Victor: A Medieval Guide to the Arts*, trans. Jerome Taylor. New York and London: Columbia University Press, 1961.

Bernahrd Lohse, *Epochen der Dogmengeschichte*. 3rd edn. Stuttgart: Kreuz, 1974.

Irenaeus of Lyons, *Adversus Haereses*, 5 vols. Sources Chrétiennes. Paris: Cerf, 1965–82.

Wolfgang Iser. *The Act of Reading: A Theory of Aesthetic Response*. Baltimore: Johns Hopkins University Press, 1978.

David Jasper, *The Study of Literature and Religion: An Introduction*. Studies in Literature and Religion. London: Macmillan, 1989.

Bernd Jaspert, ed., *Rudolf Bultmanns Werk und Wirkung*. Darmstadt: Wissenschaftliche Buchgesellschft, 1984.

Werner G. Jeanrond, *Text and Interpretation as Categories of Theological Thinking*, trans. Thomas J. Wilson. Dublin: Gill and Macmillan, and New York: Crossroad, 1988.

——, 'The Theological Understanding of Texts and Linguistic Explication', *Modern Theology* 1 (1984), 55–66.

——, 'The Impact of Schleiermacher's Hermeneutics on Contemporary Interpretation Theory', in David Jasper, ed., *The Interpretation of Belief: Coleridge, Schleiermacher and Romanticism*. London: Macmillan, 1986, 81–96.

Eberhard Jüngel, *Barth-Studien*. Ökumenische Theologie 9. Zürich and Köln: Benziger, and Gütersloh: Gerd Mohn, 1982.

Hans-Joachim Kraus, *Geschichte der historisch-kritischen Erforschung des Alten Testaments*. 3rd edn. Neukirchen-Vluyn: Neukirchener Verlag, 1982.

Hans Küng and David Tracy, eds, *Paradigm Change in Theology: A Symposium for the Future*, trans. Margaret Kohl. New York: Crossroad, 1989.

Paul L. Lehmann, 'The Reformers' Use of the Bible', in *Theology Today* 3 (1946), 328–44.

Frank Lentricchia, *After the New Criticism*. London: Methuen, 1983.

Claude Lévi-Strauss, *Mythos und Bedeutung: Fünf Radiovorträge*, ed. Adalbert Reif. Frankfurt/M.: Suhrkamp, 1980.

George A. Lindbeck, *The Nature of Doctrine: Religion and Theology in a Postliberal Age*. Philadelphia: Westminster Press, 1984.

Richard N. Longenecker, *Biblical Exegesis in the Apostolic Period*. Grand Rapids, Michigan: Eerdmans, 1975.

J. P. Mackey, *Tradition and Change in the Church*. Dublin and Sidney: Gill, 1968.

Stephen D. Moore, *Literary Criticism and the Gospels: The Theoretical Challenge*. New Haven and London: Yale University Press, 1989.

Robert Morgan with John Barton. *Biblical Interpretation*. The Oxford Bible Series. Oxford: Oxford University Press, 1988.

Jan Mukařovský, *Kapitel aus der Ästhetik*, trans. Walter Schamschula. 3rd edn. Frankfurt/M.: Suhrkamp, 1978.

Jakob Neusner and Ernest S. Frerichs, eds, *'To See Ourselves as Others See Us': Christians, Jews, 'Others' in Late Antiquity*. Chico, California: Scholars Press, 1985.

Origenes, *Peri Archon/De Principiis/Von den Prinzipien*, ed. and trans. Herwig Görgemanns and Heinrich Karpp. Darmstadt: Wissenschaftliche Buchgesellschaft, 1976.

Richard E. Palmer, *Hermeneutics: Interpretation Theory in Schleiermacher, Dilthey, Heidegger, and Gadamer*. Evanston: Northwestern University Press, 1969.

Per Erik Persson, *Sacra Doctrina: Reason and Revelation in Aquinas*, trans. Ross Mackenzie. Oxford: Blackwell, 1970.

Paul Ricœur, *Freud and Philosophy: An Essay on Interpretation*, trans. Denis Savage. New Haven: Yale University Press, 1970.

——, *The Conflict of Interpretations: Essays in Hermeneutics*, ed. Don Ihde. Evanston: Northwestern University Press, 1974.

——, *Interpretation Theory: Discourse and the Surplus of Meaning*. Fort Worth: Texas Christian University Press, 1976.

——, *Essays on Biblical Interpretation*, ed. Lewis S. Mudge. Philadelphia: Fortress, 1980.

——, *Hermeneutics and the Human Sciences: Essays on Language, Action and Interpretation*, ed., trans. and introd. by John B. Thompson. Cambridge: Cambridge University Press, and Paris: Editions de la Maison des Sciences de l'Homme, 1981.

——, *Time and Narrative*, 3 vols, trans. Kathleen McLaughlin and David Pellauer. Chicago and London: University of Chicago Press, 1984–88.

James M. Robinson and John Cobb, Jr., eds, *The New Hermeneutic*. New Frontiers in Theology II. New York: Harper & Row, 1964.

Mikka Ruokanen, *Hermeneutics as an Ecumenical Method in the Theology of Gerhard Ebeling*. Publications of the Luther-Agricola Society B 13. Helsinki: Luther-Agricola Society, 1982.

Barbara Sandig, *Stilistik: Sprachpragmatische Grundlegung der Stilbeschreibung*. Berlin and New York: de Gruyter, 1978.

Ferdinand de Saussure, *Course in General Linguistics*, trans. Roy Harris. London: Duckworth, 1983.

Edward Schillebeeckx, *The Church with a Human Face: A New and Expanded Theology of Ministry*, trans. John Bowden. London: SCM, 1985.

Friedrich D. E. Schleiermacher, *Hermeneutics: The Handwritten Mansucripts*. Ed. Heinz Kimmerle. Trans. James Duke and Jack Forstman. Missoula: Scholars Press, 1977.

——, *Hermeneutik und Kritik. Mit einem Anhang sprachphilosophischer Texte Schleiermachers*. Ed. Manfred Frank. Frankfurt/M.: Suhrkamp, 1977.

——, *Brief Outline on the Study of Theology*, trans. Terence N. Tice. Atlanta: John Knox Press, 1966.

Klaus Scholder, *Ursprünge und Probleme der Bibelkritik im 17. Jahrhundert: Ein Beitrag zur Entstehung der historisch-kritischen Theologie*. Munich: Kaiser, 1966.

Elisabeth Schüssler Fiorenza, *In Memory of Her: A Feminist Theological Reconstruction of Christian Origins*. New York: Crossroad, and London: SCM, 1983.

Johann Salomo Semler, *Vorbereitung zur theologischen Hermeneutik*, 4 vols. Halle: Carl Hermann Hemmerde, 1760–69.

John Sturrock, *Structuralism*. London: Paladin Grafton Books, 1986.

Peter Stuhlmacher, *Vom Verstehen des Neuen Testaments: Eine Hermeneutik*. Grundrisse zum Neuen Testament. NTD Ergänzungsreihe 6. 2nd edn. Göttingen: Vandenhoeck & Ruprecht, 1986.

Stephen W. Sykes, ed., *Karl Barth: Studies of His Theological Method*. Oxford: Clarendon Press, 1979.

——, *The Identity of Christianity: Theologians and the Essence of Christianity from Schleiermacher to Barth*. London: SPCK, 1984.

Charles Taylor, *Sources of the Self: The Making of Modern Identity*. Cambridge, Mass.: Harvard University Press, 1989.

Thomas H. Tobin, *The Creation of Man: Philo and the History of Interpretation*. The Catholic Biblical Quarterly Monograph Series 14. Washington, DC: The Catholic Biblical Association of America, 1983.

Thomas F. Torrance, *The Hermeneutics of John Calvin*. Edinburgh: Scottish Academic Press, 1988.

David Tracy, *Blessed Rage for Order: The New Pluralism in Theology*. New York: Seabury, 1975.

——, *The Analogical Imagination: Christian Theology and the Culture of Pluralism*. New York: Crossroad, 1981.

——, *Plurality and Ambiguity: Hermeneutics, Religion, Hope*. San Francisco: Harper & Row, 1987.

——, 'The Uneasy Alliance Reconceived: Catholic Theological Method, Modernity, and Postmodernity', *Theological Studies* 50 (1989), 548–70.

Geza Vermes, *Post-Biblical Jewish Studies*. Leiden: Brill, 1975.

Vincent of Lérins, 'The Commonitory'. in *A Select Library of Nicene and Post-Nicene Fathers of the Christian Church*. Second Series, vol. IX. Oxford: James Parker, and New York: The Christian Literature Company, 1894, 127–59.

Joachim Wach, *Das Verstehen: Grundzüge einer Geschichte der hermeneutischen Theorie im 19. Jahrhundert*, 3 vols. Tübingen: J. C. B. Mohr (Paul Siebeck), 1926–33.

Name Index

Subject Index